Parliaments, nations
and identities in

Long Loan

This book is due for return on or before the last date shown below.

MANCHESTER
UNIVERSITY PRESS

UCL/NEALE SERIES ON BRITISH HISTORY

editors
Catherine Hall
Julian Hoppit

Parliaments, nations and identities in Britain and Ireland, 1660–1850

edited by
Julian Hoppit

Manchester University Press
Manchester and New York
distributed exclusively in the USA by Palgrave

Published by Manchester University Press
Oxford Road, Manchester M13 9NR, UK
and Room 400, 175 Fifth Avenue, New York, NY 10010, USA
www.manchesteruniversitypress.co.uk

Distributed exclusively in the USA by
Palgrave, 175 Fifth Avenue, New York,
NY 10010, USA

Distributed exclusively in Canada by
UBC Press, University of British Columbia, 2029 West Mall,
Vancouver, BC, Canada V6T 1Z2

British Library Cataloguing-in-Publication Data
A catalogue record for this book is available from the British Library

Library of Congress Cataloging-in-Publication Data applied for

ISBN 0 7190 6246 2 *hardback*
0 7190 6247 0 *paperback*

First published 2003

11 10 09 08 07 06 05 04 03   10 9 8 7 6 5 4 3 2 1

Typeset in 10/12pt Minion
by Graphicraft Limited, Hong Kong
Printed in Great Britain
by Bookcraft (Bath) Ltd, Midsomer Norton

Contents

CONTENTS

Figures

Tables

Contributors

David Armitage is Associate Professor of History at Columbia University. He is the author of *The ideological origins of the British empire* (2000), editor of *Bolingbroke: political writings* (1997) and *Theories of empire* (1998) and co-editor of *The British Atlantic world, 1500–1800* (forthcoming). He is currently working on a study of the foundations of modern international thought 1688–1848, a global history of the American Declaration of Independence and an edition of John Locke's colonial writings.

Joshua Civin is concurrently pursuing a JD at Yale Law School and a D.Phil. in modern history at Merton College, Oxford, supported by a Rhodes scholarship, entitled: 'Civic Experiments: Community-Building in Liverpool and Baltimore, 1785–1835'. Firsthand experience in legislative arenas comes from his three years on the New Haven Board of Aldermen.

G. M. Ditchfield is Reader in Eighteenth-Century History at the University of Kent at Canterbury. He is co-editor of *British parliamentary lists, 1660–1800. A register* (1995) and author of *The Evangelical revival* (1998) and many articles and essays on eighteenth-century British history.

Bob Harris is a Senior Lecturer in History at the University of Dundee. His *Politics and the nation: Britain in the mid eighteenth century* was published in 2002. He is also the author of *Politics and the rise of the press: Britain and France 1620–1800* (1996). He is currently working on a volume of essays on Scotland in the age of the French Revolution and a cultural and social history of gambling in eighteenth-century Britain and Ireland.

David Hayton is Reader in Modern History at the Queen's University of Belfast. He is one of the editors of the 1690–1715 volumes of the *History of Parliament* (2002) and for which he has written the introductory survey. His other publications have concentrated on British and Irish political history in the late seventeenth and early eighteenth centuries, including editing *The parliamentary diary of Sir Richard Cocks, 1698–1702* and a collection of essays on *The Irish parliament in the eighteenth century* (2001). He is now preparing a new edition of Defoe's *History of the Union*.

Julian Hoppit is Professor of British History at University College London. He is the author of *A land of liberty? England 1689–1727* (2000) and editor of *Failed legislation, 1660–1800: extracted from the Commons and Lords Journals* (1997). He is interested in the early industrial revolution in Britain, particularly its institutional and legislative context.

Joanna Innes has been a Fellow of Somerville College Oxford since 1982. She has published extensively on social problems and social policy in eighteenth-century England, often in a comparative perspective. She plans shortly to compile two volumes of her essays, under the titles *Inferior politics* and *English poverty in law and practice*. For ten years she was an editor of *Past and Present*.

Peter Jupp is Professor of History at The Queen's University of Belfast. Among his many publications on British and Irish history are *British politics on the eve of reform: the duke of Wellington's administration, 1828–30* (1998) and *Lord Grenville, 1754–1834* (1985). He is currently working on the growth of government in Hanoverian Britain.

Rosemary Sweet is Lecturer in Economic and Social History at the University of Leicester and Deputy Director of the Centre for Urban History. Her publications include *The writing of urban histories in eighteenth century England* (Oxford, 1997) and *The English town 1680–1840* (1999). She is currently working on a book on antiquarian culture in the eighteenth century.

Miles Taylor is Professor of History at the University of Southampton. He is the author of *The decline of British radicalism, 1847–1860* (1995) and editor of *Party, state and society: electoral behaviour in Britain since 1820* (1997) and Walter Bagehot's *The English constitution* (2001).

Acknowledgements

This volume pivots around Joanna Innes' Neale lecture in British history, given at University College London in March 2001. Most of the remaining papers were discussed at a colloquium which immediately followed, much inspired by the comments of Mike Braddick, Peter Mandler, Peter Marshall, Jennifer Ridden and Chris Smout. All the contributors to this volume are grateful to those who offered so many ideas and suggestions at the colloquium.

For continuing to support the Neale lecture UCL is most grateful to Random House – successor to Sir John Neale's publisher, Jonathan Cape. Manchester University Press also helped to meet the costs of the lecture. Speakers at the colloquium came from far and wide and the British Academy generously met their travel and accommodation costs. The Royal Historical Society also kindly provided financial aid for graduate students attending.

Much of the success of the Neale lecture and colloquium was due to the tireless organisation of Nazneen Razwi in the UCL History Department. Finally, thanks should go to Vanessa Graham and Alison Whittle at Manchester University Press who have been so supportive of this project.

Abbreviations

CJ	*Journals of the House of Commons*
Cobbett, *Parliamentary History*	W. Cobbett (ed.), *The parliamentary history of England*, 36 vols (1806–20)
LJ	*Journals of the House of Lords*
PP	Parliamentary Papers, House of Commons

Place of publication is London unless stated otherwise.

1

Introduction[1]

Julian Hoppit

In 1660 the four nations of the British Isles were governed by one imperial crown but by three parliaments.[2] In 1707 the Edinburgh parliament was abolished and the Scots given some representation at Westminster. In 1801 something similar happened to the Dublin parliament. At the same time (though somewhat independently) what Westminster did in terms of legislation, legal appeals, debate and inquiry developed significantly and in 1832 the nature of its representation was overhauled. Consequently, the nineteenth century marked the heyday of the idea of an imperial parliament and an imperial crown. But what did the making of that monolith mean for the four nations? Did conceptions of English, Irish, Scottish and Welsh identities flourish, mutate or wither as a consequence of the growth of the imperial parliament and to what extent did that parliament help or hinder a developing sense of Britishness as a new nationality? These are the questions at the heart of this volume of essays and the answers to them are strikingly multi-faceted. Though it might be expected that the unification of the parliaments of Britain and Ireland was integral to the development of Britishness, the essays here suggest that at those parliaments both distinctions and similarities were drawn between nations. Moreover, parliaments contributed to non-national as well as national identities within Britain and Ireland, with the former sometimes cutting across the latter. Though Westminster was frequently celebrated as the fount of absolute power and a guardian of liberty and property within the British imperial polity, it was used and seen in very different ways by highly distinctive communities, some national, some not.

In recent years much has been written from very different intellectual perspectives about the relationship between state formation and national identity, both for the distant past and the immediate present. In Britain and Ireland this is a very current concern because of developments within the European Union and the creation of devolved representative institutions at Cardiff, Edinburgh and Stormont in the late 1990s. More broadly, the traumas caused by numerous states pursuing nationalist agendas across the twentieth century have prompted considerable and often multi-disciplinary studies of the nature of geo-political identities. Initially,

1

much weight was given here to the interaction between 'modernisation' and emerging nationalism. Famously, Gellner and Hobsbawm saw nationalism as consequent upon the French and the industrial revolutions of the late eighteenth century.[3] Increasingly, however, doubt has been cast upon the emphasis they accorded to secular rationalism and economic growth as the stimulus of developing nationalism.[4] The role of religion, ethnicity, law, myths and culture have all been emphasised. It is now recognised that nationalism is a particular expression of national identity and that the latter, as an imagined community, can be traced back well before 1800.[5] Indeed, medieval historians have particularly stressed that national identities can often be found in Europe after about 1000.[6]

If it is helpful to distinguish between nationalism and national identities, then it is also important to note that geo-political identities exist at both the more specific and the more general levels than the national. Sub-national identities include, for example, local or regional affiliations and supra-national identities include, for example, those based on religious beliefs. Consequently, to understand the development of a national identity often requires these narrower and broader identities to be assessed and assimilated. Moreover, to focus upon national identity as the most important form of geo-political identity risks a descent into inappropriate anachronism and teleology: the importance of national identity today should not be assumed to be the importance that it had in earlier periods. The situation is complicated further because states and nations are two distinct entities, the former 'a legal and political organisation' the latter 'a community of people'.[7] The boundaries of states can, therefore, coincide with, fall within or extend beyond the boundaries of nations.

Historians of Britain and Ireland have done much to develop this complex understanding, and not only for the period covered by this volume.[8] On the one hand much profit has been gained by considering the attractions and perils of a so-called 'new British history'. Arguably initiated by J. G. A. Pocock, that history abandons Anglo-centrism in favour of a truly British or even British and Irish perspective. This has been especially significant for scholars of the early modern period, more particularly for those of the civil wars and revolutions of the mid-seventeenth century.[9] A second closely related historiographical stream explicitly addresses the 'making' of Great Britain or the United Kingdom of Britain and Ireland, both in terms of the state and of national identities.[10] Particular attention has been directed at the Anglo-Scottish Union of 1707 and of developing ideas of Britishness within the context of existing national identities, especially in relation to political thought, the waging of war and 'culture'.[11] Thirdly, and often independently, considerable advances have been made in understanding the development of the state, mainly in England, including the imperial dimension, but also in Scotland and Ireland (hardly at all in Wales). This has emphasised the growth of state power and, at least by implication, one aspect of 'British' unification, the loss of America aside.[12]

This volume takes state formation as its starting point, unquestionably a vital aspect of the development of nations and national identities. As Smith has noted

' "national" identity involves some sense of political community . . . [which] in turn implies at least some common institutions and a single code of rights and duties for all members of the community.'[13] This makes it singularly appropriate to assess the role of parliaments in Britain and Ireland between the Restoration and the mid-nineteenth century, for the four nations lacked 'a common British history, ethnic identity or confessional commitment' but came to be governedly a highly active common parliament.[14] Indeed, given the proliferation of the 'new British history' and the associated literature on Britishness it is surprising that the role of parliament has so often been overlooked. In some measure that is because of the legacy of a 'Namierite' approach to parliamentary history and the complexity of writing a history of three parliaments becoming one which does more than tell the tale of the unions (which has been done effectively).[15] Recently, however, new and more structural approaches to the history of the Westminster parliament have been developed which, by emphasising the importance of ideology and showing patterns of activity, hold out the prospect for integrating the legislatures into a long-term story.[16] New approaches to the Dublin and Edinburgh parliaments are also being developed.[17]

To provide some background for this volume it is helpful to consider the similarities and differences between the parliaments of Dublin, Edinburgh and Westminster. This can best be examined by considering the issues of their constitution, size, representation, frequency of meeting and business conducted. As to the first, Dublin and Westminster were bicameral, both with a House of Lords and a House of Commons, whereas Edinburgh was unicameral. In the eighteenth century the Dublin parliament comprised 300 MPs (64 county, 234 borough and 2 Trinity College Dublin), 22 spiritual peers and a variable number of lay peers – some 88 in 1700 and 169 in 1800.[18] The Edinburgh parliament was made up of unelected nobles, higher clergy (before 1689) and officers of state and those elected to 33 county and 67 burgh two-member constituencies. In practice, however, Scottish constituencies often returned only one member and there was significant absenteeism among the other groups. Only in the parliaments of 1703 and 1705 were there more than 200 Scottish parliamentarians.[19] At Westminster in 1700 the House of Commons had 514 MPs, as detailed in Table 1.1.

The House of Lords had a variable number of lay peers (173 in 1700) and 26 spiritual peers.[20] Put very baldly, in the early eighteenth century total membership of the parliament at Dublin numbered around 410, at Edinburgh perhaps 200 and at Westminster about 712. But because England and Wales had a significantly larger population they had one elected member for about every 10,000 people, whereas for Ireland the ratio was one per 6,600 and for Scotland one per 5,200.[21]

Union in 1707 and 1801 radically diminished the amount of parliamentary representation for Scotland and Ireland – Scotland was given 45 MPs and 16 representative peers at Westminster, Ireland 100 MPs, 28 representative peers and 4 bishops – thereby significantly enhancing the relative position of England

Table 1.1   Composition of the Westminster House of Commons in 1700

	England	Wales
Two-member counties	40	–
One-member counties	–	12
Four-member boroughs	2	–
Two-member boroughs	196	–
One-member boroughs	5	5
One-member borough groupings	–	7
Two-member universities	2	–
Total MPs	489	24

Source: C. Cook and J. Stevenson, *The Longman handbook of modern British history, 1714–1980* (Harlow, 1983), 56–7.

and Wales.[22] In 1801, consequently, the ratio of MPs to population was now one to 17,800 in England and Wales, one to 50,000 in Ireland and one to 36,000 in Scotland. Between 1700 and 1801 representation was strikingly diluted for Ireland, markedly diluted for Scotland and somewhat diluted for England and Wales. This was not significantly changed by parliamentary reform in 1832, as Table 1.2 shows.

Table 1.2   Composition of the Westminster House of Commons in 1833

	England	Ireland	Scotland	Wales
Six-member counties	1	–	–	–
Four-member counties	26	–	–	–
Three-member counties	7	–	–	–
Two-member counties	6	32	–	3
One-member counties	1	–	27	9
Single-member county groupings	–	–	3	–
Four-member boroughs	1	–	–	–
Two-member boroughs	133	6	2	–
One-member boroughs	54	27	5	–
One-member borough groupings	–	–	14	13
Two-member universities	2	1	–	–
Total MPs	472	105	53	28
Population (millions)	13.1	7.8	2.4	0.8
Ratio of MPs to population	1:27,754	1:74,286	1:45,283	1:28,571

Note: England's four member counties were each divided into two constituencies. The Isle of Wight has been classed as a single member county. Scottish urban constituencies have been classed for convenience as boroughs.
Source: M. Brock, *The Great Reform Act* (1973), 310–11; B. Mitchell, *British historical statistics* (Cambridge, 1988), 9–10, 31.

Table 1.3 Size of the electorates in the British Isles, 1831–33

	England and Wales	Ireland	Scotland
Electors in 1831	435,000	49,000	4,500
MPs	513	100	45
Ratio of MPs to voters	1:848	1:490	1:100
Ratio of voters to population	1:31	1:159	1:533
Electors in 1833	653,000	90,000	65,000
MPs	500	105	53
Ratio of MPs to voters	1:1,306	1:857	1:1,226
Ratio of voters to population	1:21	1:86	1:37

Note: J. Cannon, *Parliamentary reform, 1640–1832* (Cambridge, 1973), puts the number of electors in England and Wales in 1831 at 366,000. That makes for a ratio of MPs to voters of 1:713 and of voters to population of 1:38.
Source: Brock, *Great Reform Act*, 312; Mitchell, *British historical statistics*, 9–10.

Certainly the reform acts of 1832 were more concerned with representation in intra rather than 'inter' national terms and, as Table 1.3 shows, national variations were also apparent in terms of numbers of voters. Most adults could not vote at any point in this period, notably women, but in national terms it is usually the exclusion of Irish Catholics which is commented upon. However, as Table 1.3 makes plain, the restricted nature of the franchise in Scotland was much more marked before 1832, with parliamentary reform bringing it much closer to parity with England and Wales than was the case with Ireland. As Ferguson has noted, 'A case can be made for the assertion that the Scottish Reform Act, like the Irish, was more revolutionary than its English counterpart.'[23]

The place of parliament in national life was only partly consequent upon the nature of representation, partly upon what parliaments did. Parliamentary activity can be thought of in terms of the frequency of meeting, the nature of debate and of inquiry, the passage of legislation and the determination of legal appeals. As to the first, in the period between 1660 and 1706 the Dublin parliament held 11 sessions, the Edinburgh parliament 24 and the Westminster parliament 42. After the Glorious Revolution the Dublin parliament usually met biannually until 1782, when it became annual, whereas the Westminster parliament usually met annually – so Westminster had about twice as many sessions as Dublin between 1689 and Union.[24] Sessions were not of course of fixed length, but that the Westminster parliament met more frequently and for longer is clear. For example, between 1690 and 1800 the Commons in Dublin sat for a total of 5,293 days, whereas its counterpart at Westminster sat for 12,016 days.[25] These differences reflected the differing degrees of 'self-determination' enjoyed by parliaments in the British Isles over when they met. As is well known, from 1689

Westminster, exploiting its absolute authority in matters of public finance, established frequent sessions by providing the crown with revenue to cover no more than a year's expenditure. By keeping the crown on a tight financial rein it assured that it would need to be recalled reasonably often. Similarly, in Edinburgh the Glorious Revolution led to the abolition of the Lords of the Articles who had done so much to control their business. But at Dublin, a high degree of self-determination over meetings was not formally established until 1782. Painting with a very broad brush, Westminster developed considerable autonomy first, Edinburgh second and Dublin third. In turn this influenced what those parliaments could do, in terms of scrutiny, debate (especially of the work of the executive) and of legislation. So, for example, when Princess Anne's only surviving child died in 1700 the succession question was a vital matter for Edinburgh and Westminster but caused hardly a ripple of concern at Dublin.

The degree of self-determination enjoyed by the three parliaments was directly related to their capacity to debate issues or inquire into them. A major feature of the development of Westminster in this period was the increasing resort it made to collecting information, often from government departments, which was fed into the deliberations of its committees. For example, between the 1716 and 1799–1800 sessions the number of accounts and papers ordered by the Commons rose from 36 to 231.[26] This was an important way in which it gained some sense of the state of the nation, even if the concerns were overwhelmingly of a military-fiscal nature. The Dublin parliament developed in similar ways, its Commons producing some 1,751 'subject' interest reports between 1692 and 1800, representing 'an important contemporary account of the changing Irish society during the eighteenth century'.[27] At Edinburgh, by contrast, the parliament had no long tradition of scrutiny to draw upon and only in the last fifteen years or so of its life did it begin to develop such powers, and when that happened it was negotiated out of existence.

One of the striking features of the history of the parliaments of the British Isles in this period is that each became highly (though distinctively) productive in legislative terms. The picture before the Union of 1707 is set out in Table 1.4.

Table 1.4   Number of acts passed by the Dublin, Edinburgh and Westminster parliaments, 1660–1706

	Dublin	Edinburgh	Westminster
1660–88	58	1,388	564
1689–1706	134	829	1,298

Sources: *The statutes at large, passed in the parliaments held in Ireland,* 21 vols (Dublin, 1786–1804), i–iv; *Acts of the parliaments of Scotland*; O. Ruffhead (ed.), *Statutes at large,* 18 vols (1769–1800), iii–iv.

The fecundity of the Edinburgh parliament in the Restoration era is especially notable, 75 per cent of whose acts were technically classed as 'private' and some 77 per cent subjectively as specific rather than general in scope.[28] The abolition of the Lords of the Articles may not have led to a dramatic surge in legislative action, quite the contrary, but it provided the context in which only 59 per cent of legislation was now private and 61 per cent specific. The comparison here with Dublin and Westminster is striking. For them the Glorious Revolution was followed by much more legislation, for Edinburgh it was not.

Differences between Dublin and Westminster as legislatures have long been appreciated by historians, especially because of the operation of Poynings' law upon the former. Theoretically that law disallowed the Dublin parliament from initiating legislation or amending bills presented to it; it was meant only to respond in simple yes or no terms to the bills passed to it via the privy councils in Dublin and London. In practice, however, the Dublin parliament had devised ways round Poynings' law by the early eighteenth century, framing not bills but 'heads' of bills. That said, the constitutional superiority of the Westminster parliament over its Dublin counterpart was loudly asserted in the 1720 Declaratory act. Not until 1782 was that act repealed and Poynings' law formally modified, allowing the Dublin parliament much greater theoretical and actual freedom. Certainly, 1782 led to many more acts being passed at Dublin – from 1,215 for 1689–1782 to 1,054 for 1782–1800 – though still much less than at Westminster which passed 4,157 acts during the era of Grattan's parliament.

The Dublin parliament did not produce numbers of acts to match Edinburgh or Westminster. Between 1689 and 1800 it passed 2,269 acts compared to 13,652 at Westminster. Put another way, from 1660 to 1706 the Edinburgh parliament passed 69 per cent of all legislation within the British Isles, but from 1689 to 1800 the Dublin parliament accounted for only 14 per cent (20 per cent for 1782–1800). One important point about the Dublin parliament was the very high proportion of its legislation which was formally classed as public and which might be subjectively classed as 'general', a point detailed in Table 1.5.

Table 1.5 Nature of legislation at Dublin and Westminster, 1689–1800

	Dublin		Westminster	
	% public	% general	% public	% general
1689–1714	70	65	39	33
1714–60	81	64	54	26
1760–82	85	62	50	20
1782–1800	93	75	65	31

Sources: *The statutes at large, passed in the parliaments held in Ireland*, i–xxi; Ruffhead (ed.), *Statutes*, iii–xviii.

Edinburgh and Westminster passed large numbers of acts dealing with very specific issues, often to do with estates, titles, market rights and, in England at least, turnpike roads. By contrast, the majority of legislation enacted at Dublin concerned public questions of general import. Ireland's legislative independence from 1782 was not seized upon by private interests in the ways that had been true at Edinburgh and was still very much the case at Westminster. In that way the role of the Dublin parliament as a point of negotiation between centre and localities and between national and sectional interests was rather different from at Westminster.

Legal appeals are another area of expertise to be considered and again there were distinctive national experiences, though this has attracted very little attention from historians. With the developing institutionalisation of the Dublin parliament after the Glorious Revolution the role of its House of Lords as a court of appeal began to loom larger. In this it was following the example of its counterpart at Westminster. However, in 1720 the appellate jurisdiction of the Irish parliament was circumscribed by Westminster who asserted the supremacy of its Lords in such matters, though this was changed in 1782.[29] At Edinburgh, by contrast, the parliament did not act as an appeal court but, rather, allowed the supremacy of the Court of Sessions and Court of Justiciary in legal matters and the General Assembly in ecclesiastical ones – though many acts passed at Edinburgh between 1660 and 1707 appear to be resolutions of disputes over land and/or titles. However, though the Union of 1707 left Scottish law intact and discrete, appeals to the House of Lords began to assume some significance, to the extent that it has even been claimed that 'During the eighteenth century the bulk of appellate work was Scottish.'[30] If that is something of an exaggeration, it is clear that Scottish cases at Westminster increased significantly, from 8 per cent of appeals in 1708–9, to 22 per cent in 1740–41, 35 per cent in 1772–73 and 38 per cent in 1795–96, though the growth was not quite as steady as these figures suggest.

It is clear that the parliaments of Dublin, Edinburgh and Westminster developed in different and distinct ways, though they certainly shared some common ground. They varied in terms of their composition, electoral element and nature and volume of debate, inquiry, legislation and legal appeals undertaken. Consequently, the place of those parliaments in national life varied. For example, Terry believed that 'The Scottish Parliament before the Union was never precisely what the English Parliament was to Englishmen, the pulse of the nation's being, popular as the guardian of national interests, an institution whose membership was prized both by the constituencies and their representatives. Even ... when it acquired powers and developed a procedure which enabled it to act in that character, the hearts of the people beat rather with the General Assembly of the Kirk than with the Meeting of the Estates.'[31] Similarly, the Dublin parliament after the Glorious Revolution could not match the position of Westminster because of its religious antipathy towards the majority Roman Catholic and minority Presbyterian populations. And, of course, the Westminster parliament conceived of itself as superior. The parliaments at Dublin and Edinburgh were never more than national bodies, but Westminster claimed a much wider juris-diction and the unions were less mergers than assimilations by Westminster.

As an influence upon geo-political identities the nature of parliaments at Dublin, Edinburgh and Westminster, both before and after the unions, was obviously profoundly important. But the foregoing discussion does no more than provide a somewhat mechanical general context in which to understand the crucial issues of how parliaments were perceived and utilised by individuals and communit-ies. It is those issues which the essays in this volume tackle. This is done by the authors adopting a variety of perspectives, not merely the national, which for convenience can be divided into three. Firstly, Sweet, Ditchfield and Hoppit are concerned with examining how non-national issues related to the national dimension. Secondly, Innes, Hayton, Harris and Jupp explicitly adopt a national approach. And finally, Armitage, Civin and Taylor consider how some interna-tional questions were framed and addressed at Westminster. All the time the authors have parliament at the heart of their concerns – usually the Westminster parliament but on occasions Dublin and Edinburgh also. It is hoped that this variety of approaches does justice to the complexity of the interactions between parliaments, nations and identities in the emergence of the imperial parliament at Westminster. Certainly a complex picture emerges from the essays.

Very much at the heart of this book is Joanna Innes' Neale lecture, in which she explores legislation at Westminster in unambiguously national terms, consider-ing the acts that were framed for the four nations, individually or in combinations. She shows how there was both integrative and disintegrative legislation, that if Westminster was the source of some centrifugal forces, it was also the site for some centripetal ones. Moreover, she shows how in legislative terms Union in 1707 had different consequences than Union in 1801. If those unions shared strikingly similar causes and took very similar forms the consequences for Scotland and Ireland were rather different. Her essay provides a focal point for the others in this volume, but their direction also owes something to the desire to ensure that identities in the parliamentary context are considered in much more than merely national terms.

A number of important points emerge from this volume, but three are dealt with by almost all authors. The first and most obvious point is that the unions were limited in scope and were palpably not incorporating – as Kidd has put it, 'It would be a teleological error to view Britishness in terms of the *union achieved* to the exclusion of the *union denied*.'[32] Most obviously, citizenship continued to be exclusive, something felt most sorely by Irish Roman Catholics but which, as Taylor shows, was also of growing concern in a colonial and imperial context, not least because of the idea of virtual representation was badly battered by American independence. Also important was the fact that many national dis-tinctions remained intact, especially in terms of law, institutions and culture. Ditchfield, for example, powerfully demonstrates how the relationship between the Anglican Church and parliament set England apart from Scotland and conformist from non-conformist within England. One crucial point that emerges is that not only did the three kingdoms have very different legal traditions, but each had available different alternatives to the use of parliament. From the modern perspective it is easy to assume that statute is at the heart of parliament. But the supremacy of parliament should not be read to mean that other institutions could not provide an alternative means for the redress of grievances. In Scotland, for example, Harris shows how the General Assembly and the Convention of the Royal Burghs were both used in some of the ways that parliament was in England and Wales. Even in England many disputes might be settled by a judicial decision in a central court rather than by passing a statute.

The second point developed in this volume is that, depending upon the issue, parliament required or encouraged not only different arguments but different voices. It was a site of national deliberation, but much of what it considered or did originated from local or what might loosely be called 'sectional' initiatives. Those initiatives, however, often resulted in outcomes which applied nationally but were more appropriate to some sections or areas than to others. Crucially, parliament was concerned not with identities but with interests. And if the importance of the national interest was always allowed and always pre-eminent, many issues concerned quite different interests. Sweet brings this point out well in her essay, showing how local interests struggled to define themselves clearly and to make themselves entirely complementary to the national interest. There was, moreover, nothing certain about interests either, for they might be constructed for tactical reasons, brought into use for a specific occasion and just as quickly put aside. So, it suited landowners in England and Scotland to invent themselves as a landed interest from time to time, but this lacked conviction and their counterparts in Ireland felt no need to indulge in the same imaginings. Identities and interests might be easily invented and to that extent might be chosen, but to work they had to be plausible, both to the anticipated 'insiders' and 'outsiders'. Those which were implausible, either because they were unintentionally fragile or intentionally ephemeral, might subject their more robust counterparts to cynical and unreasonable doubt from onlookers.

As the first two points suggest, the final general conclusion to emerge from these essays is that utility of 'national identity' as a way of understanding how people in the period conceived of themselves and their relationship to the state is not as clear and certain as might be first thought. National identity was one amongst a number of geo-political communities people might belong to, albeit a very important one. David Armitage is particularly at pains to show its limitations when considering the role of parliament in international terms in the eighteenth century. Just as with religion, certain legal discourses did not frame themselves in national terms. Some identities fell within ideas of nationhood, but others cut across them. Indeed, contemporaries were often happier employing a language of interests than a language of identities. Moreover, in the period covered by this book it is clear that not only was there a tension between English,

Irish, Scottish and Welsh identities and Britishness, but that the older national identities were themselves contested. Famously, Defoe satirised the polymorphous, even polyglot, nature of Englishness in the early eighteenth century. But what it meant to be Irish, Scottish and, to a lesser extent, Welsh were similarly uncertain, something parliament played a part in because it was a site of so much sectionalism.[33]

Superficially, the parliamentary unification of the British Isles in this period created a unitary state. What this volume shows is how conditional and uncertain that unity was. Unification produced a highly complex state which was difficult to use and hard to imagine as a whole. So if there were, as Colley and others have shown, major points of common concern which bound together people of different backgrounds and interests, the most important unitary institution, the Westminster parliament, was not unambiguously one of these. It remained an institution predicated upon exclusion and difference. It united, but fundamentally it also divided and as such was a major break on the development of national identities. Even at the ideological level, the idea of Westminster as the defender of liberty and the fount of authority attracted some but repulsed others.

Notes

1 I am grateful to Joanna Innes for comments on a draft of this introduction.

2 Throughout, 'British Isles' is used only as a geographical expression.

3 E. Gellner, *Nations and nationalism* (Oxford, 1983); E. J. Hobsbawm, *Nations and nationalism since 1780: programme, myth, reality* (Cambridge, 1990).

4 Notably by A. D. Smith in *National identity* (1991) and *Myths and memories of the nation* (Oxford, 1999).

5 H. Seton-Watson, *Nations and states: an enquiry into the origins of nations and the politics of nationalism* (1977); B. Anderson, *Imagined communities: reflections on the origin and spread of nationalism* (1983).

6 For an introduction to which see A. Hastings, *The construction of nationhood: ethnicity, religion and nationalism* (Cambridge, 1997).

7 Seton-Watson, *Nations and states*, 1.

8 For a recent heavily referenced overview see J. C. D. Clark, 'Protestantism, nationalism, and national identity, 1660–1832', *Historical Journal*, xliii (2000), 249–76.

9 J. G. A. Pocock, 'The limits and divisions of British history: in search of the unknown subject', *American Historical Review*, lxxxvii (1982), 311–36; a recent survey is provided in G. Burgess (ed.), *The new British history: founding a modern state 1603–1715* (1999). As has been noted, particular historical questions require setting different geo-political or national boundaries; what matters is the nature of the question. There is nothing inherently superior about a British and Irish perspective over, say, English, European, Atlantic or imperial perspectives. Given appropriate questions all are valid.

10 See L. Colley, *Britons: forging the nation 1707–1837* (1991) – a pivotal study; R. G. Asch (ed.), *Three nations – a common history? England, Scotland, Ireland and British history, c. 1600–1920* (Bochum, 1993); S. G. Ellis and S. Barber (eds), *Conquest and union: fashioning a British state, 1485–1725* (Harlow, 1995); A. Grant and K. J. Stringer (eds), *Uniting the kingdom? The making of British history* (1995); L. Brockliss and D. Eastwood

(eds), *A union of multiple identities: the British Isles,* c. *1750–c. 1850* (Manchester, 1997); B. Bradshaw and P. Roberts (eds), *British consciousness and identity: the making of Britain, 1533–1707* (Cambridge, 1998); J. Smyth, *The making of the United Kingdom, 1660–1800* (2001).

11 B. P. Levack, *The formation of the British state: England, Scotland, and the Union, 1603–1707* (Oxford, 1987); G. Newman, *The rise of English nationalism: a cultural history, 1740–1830* (1987); J. Robertson (ed.), *A union for empire: political thought and the British Union of 1707* (Cambridge, 1995); M. G. H. Pittock, *Inventing and resisting Britain: cultural identities in Britain and Ireland, 1685–1789* (Basingstoke, 1997); J. E. Cookson, *The British armed nation, 1793–1815* (Oxford, 1997); A. Murdoch, *British history 1660–1832: national identity and local culture* (Basingstoke, 1998); C. Kidd, *British identities before nationalism: ethnicity and nationhood in the Atlantic world, 1600–1800* (Cambridge, 1999); S. Conway, *The British Isles and the War of American Independence* (Oxford, 2000); P. Langford, *Englishness identified: manners and character, 1650–1850* (Oxford, 2000).

12 M. Braddick, *State formation in early modern England,* c. *1550–1700* (Cambridge, 2000) and T. Ertman, *Birth of the Leviathan: building states and regimes in medieval and early modern Europe* (Cambridge, 1997) provide excellent points of departure. For the period covered by this volume see: P. G. M. Dickson, *The financial revolution in England: a study in the development of public credit, 1688–1756* (1967); J. P. Greene, *Peripheries and center: constitutional development in the extended polities of the British empire and the United States, 1607–1788* (Athens, Georgia, 1986); P. K. O'Brien, 'The political economy of British taxation, 1660–1815', *Economic History Review,* xli (1988), 1–32; J. Brewer, *Sinews of power: war, money and the English state, 1688–1783* (1989); L. Stone (ed.), *An imperial state at war: Britain from 1689 to 1815* (1994); P. Harling, *The waning of 'old corruption': the politics of economical reform in Britain, 1779–1846* (Oxford, 1996); J. Brewer and E. Hellmuth (eds), *Rethinking Leviathan: the eighteenth-century state in Britain and Germany* (Oxford, 1999).

13 Smith, *National identity,* 9.

14 C. Kidd, 'Protestantism, constitutionalism and British identity under the later Stuarts', in Bradshaw and Roberts (eds), *British consciousness,* 322.

15 On the 1707 Union see W. Ferguson, *Scotland's relations with England: a survey to 1707* (Edinburgh, 1977); P. W. J. Riley, *The Union of England and Scotland. A study in Anglo-Scottish politics of the eighteenth century* (1978). On the 1801 Union see G. C. Bolton, *The passing of the Irish act of Union* (1966); J. Kelly, 'The origins of the act of Union: an examination of unionist opinion in Britain and Ireland, 1650–1800', *Irish Historical Studies,* xxv (1987), 236–63; P. M. Geoghegan, *The Irish act of Union: a study in high politics, 1798–1801* (Dublin, 1999); and a series of essays in *Transactions of the Royal Historical Society,* 6th series, x (2000).

16 For a recent assessment of Namier's legacy for parliamentary history J. Hoppit, 'An embarrassment of riches', *Parliamentary History,* xviii (1999), 189–205. One positive aspect of this is that the History of Parliament Trust's volumes on the House of Commons now completely cover the period 1660 to 1820 with the publication in 2002 of the 1690–1715 section (that for 1820–32 is also in progress). For developing alternative approaches J. Brewer, *Party ideology and popular politics at the accession of George III* (Cambridge, 1976); P. Langford, 'Property and "virtual representation" in eighteenth-century England', *Historical Journal,* xxxi (1988), 83–115; J. Innes, 'Parliament and the shaping of eighteenth-century English social policy', *Transactions of the*

Royal Historical Society, 5th series, xxxix (1990), 63–92; P. Langford, *Public life and the propertied Englishman, 1689–1798* (Oxford, 1991); J. Hoppit, 'Patterns of parliamentary legislation, 1660–1800', *Historical Journal*, xxxix (1996), 109–31; J. Hoppit and J. Innes, 'Introduction' to Hoppit (ed.), *Failed legislation, 1660–1800: extracted from the Commons and Lords Journals* (1997), 1–40.

17 At present more has been done with regard to Ireland. For an introduction see the special issue of *Parliamentary History*, xx (2001), 1–156 edited by D. W. Hayton. At length see M. Johnston-Liik (ed.), *History of the Irish parliament, 1692–1800*, 5 vols (Belfast, 2002). For Scotland, work by the Scottish parliament project at the University of St Andrews, which is producing a modern edition of Scottish legislation, should be a major advance that can also stimulate further developments.

18 J. L. McCracken, *The Irish parliament in the eighteenth century* (Dundalk, 1971), 5–7. J. Cannon, *Aristocratic century: the peerage of eighteenth-century England* (Cambridge, 1984), 32.

19 C. S. Terry, *The Scottish parliament: its constitution and procedure, 1603–1707* (Glasgow, 1905), 1–2, 19, 47.

20 Cannon, *Aristocratic century*, 15.

21 Population estimates for this and the succeeding discussion are from B. Mitchell, *British historical statistics* (Cambridge, 1988), 7–10.

22 It should also be noted that Westminster had some MPs who can be called 'Scottish' before 1707 and some who can be called 'Irish' before 1801.

23 W. Ferguson, 'The Reform Act (Scotland) of 1832: intention and effect', *Scottish Historical Review*, xlv (1966), 106.

24 *Acts of the parliaments of Scotland*, 12 vols (1820–75) provides dates of meetings of the Edinburgh parliament, but is amended at one point by M. D. Young (ed.), *The parliaments of Scotland: burgh and shire commissioners*, 2 vols (Edinburgh, 1992–3), ii, 759, note 104. For the Dublin parliament see D. J. Englefield, *The printed records of the parliament of Ireland, 1613–1800* (1978), 34–8. For the Westminster parliament see Hoppit (ed.), *Failed legislation*, 27–9.

25 D. W. Hayton, 'Introduction: the long apprenticeship', *Parliamentary History*, xx (2001), 9.

26 S. Lambert (ed.), *House of Commons sessional papers of the eighteenth century*, 147 vols (Wilmington, Delaware, 1975–6), i, 7–8, ii, 358–67.

27 Englefield, *Printed records*, 11.

28 An assessment usually based only on the full or short title of acts. The contemporary technical distinction between public and private legislation inconsistently represents their scope, hence the resort here to the categories general and specific.

29 From the *Journals* I have collected information about petitions for legal appeals to the Westminster House of Lords for nine sessions between 1660 and 1800. Interestingly, for four sessions prior to 1720 only two Irish cases were appealed to Westminster, but in 1724–25 forty-two were and in the remaining four sample sessions a total of just thirteen.

30 R. Stevens, *Law and politics: the House of Lords as a judicial body, 1800–1976* (1979), 7. On this question see A. J. MacLean, 'The House of Lords and appeals from the High Court of Justiciary, 1707–1887', *Juridical Review* (1985), 192–226; A. J. MacLean, 'The 1707 Union: Scots law and the House of Lords', *Journal of Legal History*, iv (1983), 50–75. I know of no wider study of the appellate business of the House of Lords in the eighteenth century. For the seventeenth century see J. Hart, *Justice upon petition: the House of Lords and the reformation of justice 1621–1675* (1991).

31 Terry, *The Scottish parliament*, 105–6. Furthermore, in the eighteenth century 'a positive verdict on Scottish parliamentary history was out of the question'. C. Kidd, *Subverting Scotland's past: Scottish whig historians and the creation of an Anglo-British identity, 1689–c. 1830* (Cambridge, 1993), 144.
32 Kidd, 'Protestantism', 334.
33 On Ireland see D. W. Hayton, 'Anglo-Irish attitudes: changing perceptions of national identity among the Protestant Ascendancy in Ireland, ca. 1690–1750', *Studies in eighteenth-century culture*, xvii (1987), 145–57.

2

Legislating for three kingdoms: how the Westminster parliament legislated for England, Scotland and Ireland, 1707–1830[1]

THE 2001 NEALE LECTURE

Joanna Innes

In 1707, the Edinburgh parliament was dissolved; the Westminster parliament gained forty-five Scottish MPs in the Commons, and sixteen representative peers in the Lords, and was renamed the Parliament of Great Britain. In 1801, following the abolition of the Dublin parliament, Westminster gained 100 Irish MPs, twenty-eight representative peers and four Church of Ireland bishops, and was renamed the Parliament of the United Kingdom or the Imperial Parliament.

Clearly these changes did not leave Westminster unaffected. Not only did the parliament gain on each occasion a new name and new members – some of whose ways grated on English legislators[2] – but also the range of its responsibilities grew. In 1801, change was marked also by the inauguration of a new series of parliamentary publications.

Yet continuities were also apparent – and these favoured the English. Parliament continued to meet at Westminster, in the same building as before; parliamentary procedures were carried over from one Westminster parliament to the next: newcomers had to adapt. Whereas Scots and Irish were newly elected to union parliaments, sitting Westminster members simply returned from one session to the next to a nominally different body. Suggestively, moreover, former statutes of English parliaments continued routinely to be cited by regnal year and chapter only – whereas statutes of Scottish and Irish parliaments were explicitly labelled 'Scottish' or 'Irish'. English practice was the norm, it seemed; the rest was local variation, and arguably more of historic than current concern.

Nor did the composition of the legislature give reason to suppose that this order of things would soon change. For English members dominated numerically, more even than the greater size of the English population would have justified. In 1801, the English population was about twice as great as the Irish, five times as great as the Scottish. Yet English MPs outnumbered Irish by about five to one, Scottish by over ten to one. Attempts to change the balance via the First Reform Bill were resisted.[3]

That all this represented unjust dealing was the cry of Scottish and Irish nationalists at the time, and has been ever since. Yet much about the impact of the unions remains understudied and insufficiently understood. Among such understudied topics is the precise impact of successive unions on patterns of legislation in the decades immediately following. The broad picture is not hard to establish, and appears to confirm pessimistic assessments. In both Scottish and Irish cases, quantities of legislation passed fell in the aftermath of union. The fall-off remains marked even when allowance is made for the fact that some matters – military, fiscal and such like – were henceforth, in whole or in part, the subjects of British or Imperial legislation.

Yet, as we shall see, in the Irish case, from an initial low base there was soon a marked pattern of recovery. Moreover, recent students of Scottish history have argued that the meaning of Scottish patterns is not as evident as might be supposed. Though relatively little British legislation may have dealt with Scotland, that in part reflected a Scottish choice. Scotland retained certain forms of self-governance, and the Scottish people – at least in the form of Scotland's ruling classes – were to a significant extent able to determine the terms on which Westminster dealt with them.[4]

In this essay, I draw upon databases of legislation passed at Westminster 1660–1830, and in the Edinburgh and Dublin parliaments, for as long as these existed, in an attempt to enhance our understanding of the legislative impact of the two unions.[5] These databases have important limitations as analytical tools; notably, they treat all acts as equal, though some were trivial and some of great significance. Useful interpretation of the data must therefore always depend on careful study of the underlying material. But with that caveat, I think that they provide a useful basis for inquiry.

Assessments of the impact of union are commonly framed in terms of final outcomes: in terms of the ultimate impact of post-union policies. Such assessments have their place. But legislators could not always anticipate these outcomes. Moreover, in a sense prior to choices about how to tackle particular issues were choices about how decisions should be made. We might distinguish two issues here: issues of 'process' and issues of 'approach'. Issues of process included such matters as: how was appropriate legislation to be generated; how should its fitness be established – should special attention be paid to the views of local representatives, or should efforts be made to consult local opinion; and how, if at all, might it be decided to vary something specified in foundational acts? Issues of approach related, ultimately, to the question of what union was for. Was it essentially a military and fiscal matter, necessary for the effective administration of the King's domains – but little more: might each, once separate kingdom otherwise go its own way? Or was it to entail a more extensive process of institutional and cultural convergence? If the latter, what were the kingdoms to converge on? Were Scotland and Ireland to be assimilated to an English model? Or might there be scope for more complex interaction? I will not suggest that legislators were entirely consistent in the way they dealt with these matters; on the contrary, their conduct often varied pragmatically or opportunistically, according to their perceptions of what was at stake. Nonetheless, it is possible to identify certain broad patterns informing their behaviour. It is with these broad patterns of process and approach, and their impact on the scale and character of legislation, that this essay is chiefly concerned.

In systems based on written constitutions, and perhaps particularly in federal systems, some of the issues of 'process' and 'approach' that I have identified may be explicitly addressed from the start. In the cases considered here, this was not so. The acts of union which prepared the way for first Scots', then Irish members' entry into Westminster each specified various elements of the new governmental order. Thus, the 1707 acts specified that the Scots would retain their own courts, church and universities, and that their burghs and heritable jurisdictions would be left intact. Scotland would accept a new fiscal regime. The Irish acts stated that Irish courts and law would remain as they were for the time being, subject to a right of appeal to the Lords being introduced. In contrast to the Scottish model, English and Irish established churches were to be united, and their unity was to be 'deemed and taken to be a fundamental and essential part of the union'. Conversely, British and Irish fiscal regimes were *not* to be immediately amalgamated: twenty years and more of adjustment might ensue. The acts specified what members would be sent to parliament from the newly incorporated country, and how they should be selected. But the acts did not prescribe positively how the new, hybrid parliament was to go about the task of legislating for the once separately administered territories now in its care.[6]

To the extent that it occurred to them to think about such matters at the outset, Westminster MPs at least may have been reassured by their experience in dealing with partly analogous matters: that is, the making of laws applying to particular subregions of the country – such as towns or counties. At the time of the Scottish union, parliament already dealt with several such local bills every year; they multiplied rapidly thereafter. By the end of the century, a hundred or so local bills were considered each session. Special weight was commonly attached to opinions in the area affected, though proposals were also vetted to ensure that they conformed to generally accepted standards. Ways of ascertaining and assessing local opinion were devised.[7]

This was not a matter of laying down strict rules about which MPs' views counted. That would not have been thought right, when any of a variety of considerations might be operating to shape MPs' concerns. Some had formal responsibilities, as representatives of affected regions; others owned land there, or had relatives, constituents or political associates with local interests. Peers, though not formally representing particular neighbourhoods, nonetheless had a similar range of local ties. In this context, though special weight was attached to local views, ways of ascertaining these varied pragmatically from case to case.

The business of legislating for Scotland or Ireland, countries formally represented by a minority of MPs, was to some extent analogous. In these cases too, there were reasons not to give peculiar weight to the views of local MPs, as not having a monopoly of knowledge or interest. Even before the Irish union, there were always MPs of Irish origin at Westminster. Some Scots sat as government nominees for English seats in the early eighteenth century; as more distinguished themselves in British service, and intermarried with English political dynasties, this became more common. Between 1790 and 1820, 130 Scotsmen and over 100 Irishmen sat for constituencies outside their own countries. By this time, the reverse phenomenon – carpetbaggers sitting for Scottish or Irish seats – was also beginning to emerge.[8]

Yet the analogy had its limits. Legislating for Scotland or Ireland was not the same as legislating for an English region. One difference was that Scotland especially, and to a lesser extent Ireland, had their own distinctive institutions and bodies of law: their own local government institutions; their own inheritance of statute; Scotland had its own common law. Equally significantly, Scotland and Ireland were conceived as nations, and as such were potentially the focus of peculiarly intense loyalties, not equalled by English localist attachments. This is a complicated matter: both these societies were internally fractured; no one enthusiastically identified with all their compatriots; in Ireland especially, even in the early nineteenth century by no means all the native-born elite regarded themselves as Irish. Furthermore, national loyalties were not necessarily – usually not – exclusive: one could be self-consciously Scottish or Irish and yet a loyal British subject. But it does not matter, to this argument, that different people differently conceived both the nation they felt loyal to, and the implications of that loyalty. What does matter is that the idea of the nation had special imaginative power. The charge that the English were presuming to determine what was good for the Scots or the Irish was always potentially an inflammatory charge.

So, for the Westminster parliament to legislate for three kingdoms was a distinctively difficult business. Not having grappled with the issues of process and approach that I have identified in advance, legislators did have to grapple with them in practice.[9] By exploring how they did so, we can add to our understanding of what union meant to contemporaries. Parliament provided an arena in which members of ruling elites had the opportunity to act out their ideas as to how union *should* work – in terms of how they went about the business of legislating, as well as in terms of the concrete policies they promoted. The nature and effects of their interactions in turn had consequences for how union was perceived by others.

Figures 2.1–2.3 set the scene for the inquiry. They describe in broad summary terms the geographical orientation of Westminster's legislative output between 1688, the era of the 'Glorious Revolution', and 1830, and the coming to power of the 'Reform ministry'. The graphs relate only to public and local acts: parliament also passed many private acts, including enclosure acts, acts relating to entailed property, and so forth, not represented here.[10] The first of the graphs lumps public and local acts together; the second and third focus on each of these subcategories in turn. The data is grouped into time periods not exactly equal, but mostly between eighteen and twenty years long, demarcation dates being chosen for their constitutional significance. The final two time periods are shorter, and to aid comparability, totals for these years have been adjusted as if the same

18

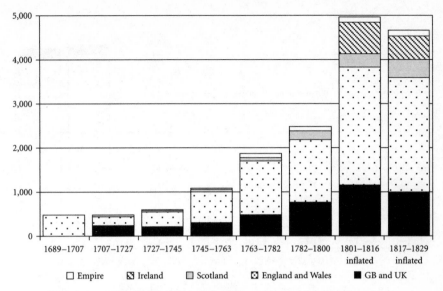

Figure 2.1 Geographical focus of public acts passed by the Westminster parliament, 1689–1829

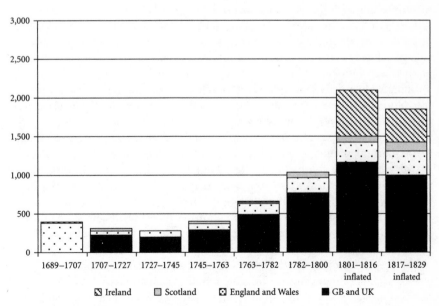

Figure 2.2 Geographical focus of public general acts passed by the Westminster parliament, 1689–1829

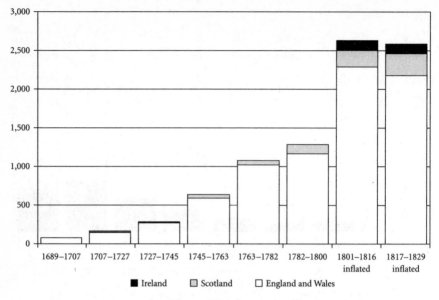

Figure 2.3 Geographical focus of local acts passed by the Westminster parliament, 1689–1829

rate of legislation had been continued over eighteen years in each case – to bring them into line with the immediately preceding period.

Two features of the patterns displayed will be immediately familiar to specialists. First, total legislation increased markedly from the mid-eighteenth century – falling back only in the last time frame, and then chiefly as a result of a programme of post-war rationalisation. Second, much of the long-sustained increase is attributable to a rise in the volume of local legislation – though it is evident that the volume of general legislation also increased in most periods: the local did not expand at the expense of the general.

These initial graphs also illustrate a number of points more strictly pertinent to the current inquiry. Thus, they illustrate one contrast that I have already drawn: between the volumes of Scottish and Irish legislation. It is clear that there was relatively little distinctly Scottish legislation – though it picked up a little towards the end of the eighteenth century. Irish legislation, by contrast, came in with a bang, and made a significant showing thereafter. Figures 2.2 and 2.3 qualify this broad picture, inasmuch as they show that in the subcategory of local legislation, Scotland made the better showing.

The graphs also illuminate changes in the balance of legislation. By 1830, it was considerably more diverse in geographical orientation than it had initially been. Alongside UK and British legislation were significant bodies of legislation relating to England, Scotland, Ireland, and other territories of the empire – this despite the fact that the later period also saw a growth in what I shall term

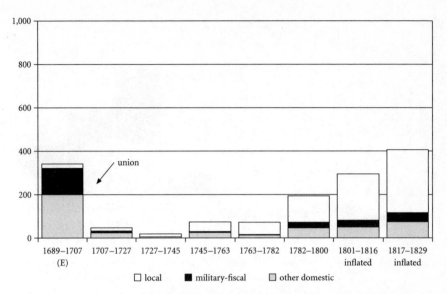

Figure 2.4 Subject breakdown of Scottish legislation passed by either Edinburgh or Westminster parliaments, 1689–1829

'integrative' legislation: legislation designed to unify domestic policies pursued in different parts of the British Isles. The name 'imperial parliament', adopted in 1801, emphasised Westminster's sovereignty, but also appropriately suggested something of the heterogeneity of this parliament's jurisdiction and concerns.

Figures 2.4 and 2.5 attempt to shed more light on the context for and character of Scotland and Ireland's contrasting experiences. These graphs incorporate data relating to Edinburgh and Dublin as well as Westminster parliaments.[11] They also break down 'general legislation' into two topical categories: 'military-fiscal' legislation and 'other domestic'.[12] 'Military-fiscal' legislation was, in this period, almost always initiated by ministers. Insofar as the two unions involved not merely parliamentary union but also the forging of a new relationship between executive government apparatuses in the several kingdoms, one would expect it to be directly affected by union, though precisely how would depend on the nature of post-union arrangements. The implications of union for 'other domestic' legislation were less foreseeable, and were less straightforwardly determined.[13]

In both Scottish and Irish cases, the graphs make plain the sharp fall-off in legislation in the aftermath of union. They further demonstrate that the fall in Scottish legislation was significantly greater: both proportionately greater, and also *to* a much lower level, indeed, almost to vanishing point. The shrinkage was differently distributed in the two cases. Total Irish legislation shrank by about 25 per cent. But – against the background of the prior policy decision not immediately to assimilate executive apparatuses in the two countries – military-fiscal

21

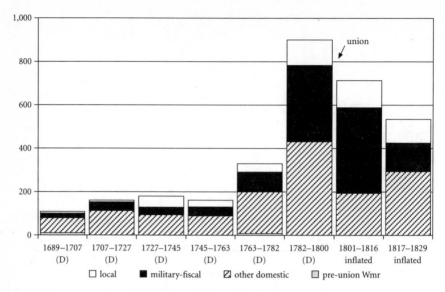

Figure 2.5 Subject breakdown of Irish legislation passed by either Dublin or Westminster parliaments, 1689–1829

legislation rose. Shrinkage was entirely concentrated in the 'other domestic' category, which shrank by some 55 per cent. With the end of the war, fiscal amalgamation began; military-fiscal legislation shrank, and 'other domestic' legislation showed some recovery: comparing the last period of the independent Irish parliament with the post-war timeslot, we see a fall in this category of only about 33 per cent. Irish other domestic legislation emerged as a significant element in the Westminster parliament's legislative output.

In the Scottish case, by contrast, total legislation shrank by about 85 per cent. Military-fiscal legislation almost disappeared; within a few decades, 'other domestic' legislation appeared to be headed that way as well. Interestingly, local legislation – legislation relating to particular towns or districts – was much less affected, declining by only 30 per cent, and remaining, as already noted, relatively buoyant thereafter. This suggests that decline was not solely the consequence of Scots' access to the Westminster parliament or of their ability to claim a share of parliamentary time, but instead also a matter of how they used their opportunities.[14]

How can contrasting Scottish and Irish patterns be explained? Figure 2.6 provides still more context. It removes military-fiscal legislation from the picture and focuses on what remains: on legislation I have termed 'other domestic' legislation – legislation concerned with elections, religion, civil and criminal law, local government, the relief of poverty, economic activity, transport and the like. It brings together information about the activities of the Westminster, Edinburgh and Dublin parliaments to give an overview of patterns in the issuing

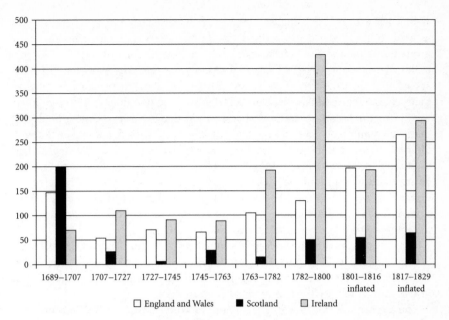

Figure 2.6 Geographical focus of 'other domestic' legislation passed by all
UK legislatures, 1689–1829

of all legislation of this kind targeted on one country only. It brings England into
the picture, and facilitates comparison between the experience of different countries in each time period. It illustrates how *relatively* active both Scottish and
Irish parliaments were, in the period immediately before union; also the by-now
familiar pattern, of shrinkage after union. Against the background of this graph,
I shall now probe more closely into first the Scottish and then the Irish case.

One observation which the latest graph prompts is that Scottish and Irish
unions took place in different legislative climates. The Scottish union, to take
that first, took place at a time when the output of general legislation concerned
with English domestic matters was declining too. There were good reasons for
this. The rage for 'reformation' that had followed the Glorious Revolution of
1688 was waning. At the same time, government managers were learning new
ways of controlling parliamentary business.[15] Still, though English 'other domestic'
legislation declined by more than 50 per cent between our first and second
periods, the collapse in Scottish legislation was more dramatic. There must have
been other forces at work.

Historians of Scotland have not noted this broader British context. But they
have identified other factors in play. In what follows I largely echo their analyses
– though the data at my disposal sometimes allows me to enlarge upon or to give
precision to their accounts.[16]

Significant weight surely attaches to attitudes to union (we shall see shortly
that these differed importantly in the Irish case). In the opening years of the

eighteenth century, the English sought union with Scotland not because they wanted to get involved in Scotland's domestic affairs, but rather because they wanted to stop the Scots from pursuing an independent dynastic or foreign policy: they sought union for national security reasons. The Scots for their part agreed to union mostly because they anticipated material benefits. Benefits to themselves as individuals, because British places or pensions might come their way, or to the nation, because Scotland would thereby gain access to England's maritime empire, or, more largely and vaguely, because in this way they threw in their lot with a rapidly commercialising society. In this context, the English had no special interest in Scots domestic affairs. The Scots for their part had no desire to allow them any say. On the contrary. Scots had previously balked at union because they feared the erosion of the Scottish institutional order. They agreed to parliamentary union at this point only in the context of guarantees that the integrity of other key institutions would be respected.[17]

Against this background, English ministers did not rush to legislate for Scotland. Scots, for their part, were also disinclined to act. Subjecting their wishes for Scotland to the uninformed judgment of a largely English legislature was not in the main a course that commended itself to them.

The hypothesis that they in effect chose to keep certain kinds of business out of the hands of the Westminster parliament gains weight from further analysis of the content of legislation. Table 2.1 breaks Scottish 'other domestic' legislation down into a series of topical categories. Among categories in which the fall-off in legislation was particularly marked were 'law' and 'religion'.[18] Law here means essentially substantive law. Not included under this heading are either legal administration, or measures concerned with civil disorder – which, not surprisingly, loomed large after both the Revolution and the two Jacobite risings. Legislation designed to change substantive law in cases not involving state security disappeared from the statute book in the decades after union, though began to reappear thereafter. Legislation about the kirk all but disappeared: the 'religious' legislation which appears in the post-union columns of the table of the graph included one controversial case (an act establishing lay patronage), a few acts relating to episcopal ministers (a problematically loyal group) and an act establishing a pension fund for ministers' widows and orphans.[19] Law and religion were matters most Scots were keen to keep out of English hands. The superior courts – the courts of Session and Justiciary – and the General Assembly of the Kirk provided alternative fora in which these classes of business could be addressed – and, after the union, these were preferred.

In the case of criminal law, it is possible to enlarge further on the new course Scots embarked on at this time. Edinburgh parliaments had passed numbers of statutes stating penalties for crimes, including for instance in the immediately pre-union period laws against duelling, and against 'the killers of blackfish and destroyers of the fry and smelts of salmond' – laws comparable in their particularity to much English criminal legislation of the period. Following the union, however, Scottish jurists developed the theory that judicial discretion in defining

Table 2.1 'Other domestic' acts relating to Scotland passed by Edinburgh and Westminster parliaments, 1689–1829, broken down by subject category

	Elections	Law	Legal admin.	Rebellion	Religion	Local govt.	Welfare	Economy	Communic.	Misc.
1689–1707 (E)	2	27	35	25	43	3	10	53	3	1
1707–27 (W)	2	0	8	5	2	0	0	6	1	0
1727–45 (W)	2	0	1	2	1	0	0	0	0	0
1745–63 (W)	0	2	4	13	2	1	0	5	1	0
1763–82 (W)	1	4	1	2	1	0	0	5	2	0
1782–1800 (W)	1	10	5	4	3	1	1	23	2	0
1808–16 (W)	0	2	10	0	3	1	2	17	11	0
1816–29 (W)	0	20	13	0	3	3	1	8	5	0

crimes and determining punishments was an essential feature of the genius of Scottish law.[20]

This abstentionism was not isolationism. Take criminal law again: Scots lawyers were perfectly prepared to consider English ways of defining crimes and conceiving of responsibility for criminal actions among sources for their own arguments. Yet they seem to have lacked confidence that parliament would behave with care and restraint if presented with proposals for the amendment of Scots law.[21]

How consistently did the English manage to leave well alone? I have noted that ministers did not enter into union with any grand plan for the reform of Scotland. Occasionally they ventured to interfere, especially when some faction among the Scots urged them on. The Tories' 1712 reinstatement of lay patronage in the Scottish church, for example, followed a Scots Jacobite initiative.[22] Ministers also intervened when they saw overriding fiscal or military reasons for doing so – and sat out the cries of breach of the terms of the union which inevitably followed. The most heavy-handed interventions came in the wake of the 1745 Jacobite rising. Many Scots defended the Hanoverian regime on this occasion, but the Highlands proved a weak link. Some in the British government camp thought terror and repression an adequate response. But numerous Scots, mobilised by the crisis, outlined alternative approaches: schemes to civilise the Highlands through a process of development. The English Lord Chancellor, Hardwicke, ushered some such measures through parliament.[23] Yet this episode was exceptional. It did not mark the establishment of any enduring system for generating Scottish legislation, nor did it immediately stimulate more Scots to bring projects of domestic improvement to Westminster. Attitudes would shift in time, as Figures 2.2 and 2.4 indicate, but not for several decades.

It remains to consider more closely sources – or potential sources – of legislative initiative. Who were the possible initiators of Scottish legislation – more specifically, of the forms of 'other domestic' legislation we have just been focusing upon – and did union have an impact upon these actors' ability or willingness to act?

At Westminster in this era, ministers did not expect their own measures to dominate the parliamentary timetable. Government spokesmen brought in a programme of bills each session, on fiscal and military matters and a few other topics. Until 1820 or so, however, it was assumed that bills relating to other economic issues, criminal and civil law, local government and so forth would emanate from interested private members – and thereafter initiatives from these sources declined rather than disappeared.[24] In addition, as Figures 2.2 and 2.3 have indicated, a growing proportion of legislation was narrowly local in scope. All MPs might bring proposals of this kind and shepherd them through increasingly conventionalised assessment processes.

The abolition of the Scottish privy council immediately after the union removed from the scene one potential source of initiative in Scottish affairs. There was, until the 1720s, and briefly in the 1740s, a Scottish Secretary of State, based in London. But this office never amounted to much. In the late eighteenth century, the senior Scottish law officer, the Lord Advocate (roughly equivalent to the Attorney General) emerged as a key channel for Scottish measures: sometimes initiating them, more often helping to shape them. His legal expertise meant that he was always likely to be consulted – as his English counterpart was in analogous matters. But he was not at first as important a figure as he became.[25]

Had there been more of an executive centre to Scottish government, it is possible that more Scottish legislation would have emerged. The Irish comparison, to be developed shortly, might suggest this. However, I would repeat that English ministers did not play much part in initiating English 'other domestic' legislation at this time. Such English initiatives as there were were largely the work of private members, sometimes acting for voluntary societies. Scotland had its own centres of initiative. Indeed, if anything, it was better equipped than England with national corporate bodies: in the form of its courts, General Assembly and Convention of Royal Burghs. And these bodies did help to set some measures in train: thus, in the 1720s the Convention of Royal Burghs, in association with the Society of Improvers in Agriculture, and under the auspices of the Argyll network, successfully lobbied for money to be assigned to a commission to promote Scottish manufactures and fisheries; in 1735, the General Assembly of the Kirk petitioned unsuccessfully for a repeal of the Patronage Act.[26] The Scots simply did not promote as many general measures as the English (despite proving perfectly competent at securing local ones).

Of course there were fewer of them – and perhaps the structure of Scottish public life differed significantly too. Many English independent legislators were active justices of the peace, by that means involved in the public life of their region. In Scotland, JPs were a recent import, sharing power with sheriffs and commissioners of supply. Perhaps Scotland was in this respect less well-placed than England to develop a vigorous civil society as traditional systems of governmental oversight declined.[27]

Historians sometimes suggest that Scots had difficulty getting the majority of English MPs to take an interest in their concerns. When they did propose measures, it is said, these tended to get lost in the press of parliamentary business, to discouraging effect.[28] However, this factor has probably been overplayed. That perception may have deterred Scots from making proposals. But it is not obvious that when they made them, English indifference was a special obstacle. Figure 2.7 draws on Julian Hoppit's compilation, *Failed legislation*, to examine Scottish experience in this respect in the period covered by that book: down to 1800. The graph does not suggest to me that low, indeed declining levels of Scottish legislation after the union reflected abundant Scots proposals falling before an indifferent or hostile parliament. On the contrary: by and large, when acts were few, failures were also few. This is not altogether surprising. A proportion of bills commonly failed, at least on a first attempt. It was normal, in this parliament at this period, for failures to shadow acts. The Scottish record overall does not look exceptionally poor. Furthermore, some failures represent the failure of English

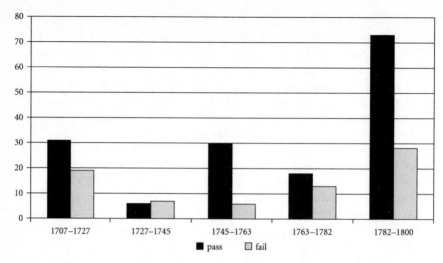

Figure 2.7 Scottish legislation proposed at Westminster, 1707–1800, distinguished into passes and fails

attempts to impose legislation upon Scotland (thus the Bishop of Worcester's attempt to regulate Gretna Green marriages)[29]; rather more reflect disagreements among Scots. Contemporaries noted that the General Assembly's 1735 petition against patronage did *not* command the support of most Scots MPs – they being the sort of people who exercised that patronage.[30] Only one issue here really has the flavour of a Scottish national cause, frustrated by English opposition: repeated attempts to obtain a Scottish militia act. Ministers long blocked that as not clearly conducive to national security interests. They finally conceded the point in 1797.[31]

It is true that the period 1727–45, a low point in Scottish legislation, also saw a very high proportion of fails, more than half the total. Insofar as the tiny number of proposals involved reflect anything of special note, this seems to have been willingness to provoke on the part of Scottish opponents of Walpole. Of the 1735 Lord Advocate's bill to extend the Scottish act against wrongous imprisonment, in the context of a recent election dispute – a proposal over which parliament divided four times – Walpole reputedly said that nothing that session had given him more concern.[32] This does not illustrate Scots MPs languishing in a state of forlorn neglect!

During the Walpolean era especially, to some extent through into the later eighteenth century, English backbenchers lamented the want of general domestic legislation bearing on English concerns. Nationalist explanations not being readily available to them, they instead opted for what in the eighteenth century was termed a 'patriot' diagnosis: ministers were not interested enough in the welfare of 'the country'.

Yet Ireland's experience was different. As Figures 2.5–2.6 have shown, legislation on Irish domestic affairs also declined with union, but recovered a little after the close of the Napoleonic wars, and in any case ran at a much higher level throughout. Why the difference?

First, the legislative climate was different. English and Scottish domestic legislation increased steadily from the 1760s, not even showing Ireland's wartime drop-back. This was the age of enlightenment and reform. Interest in legislation as an instrument of institutional, cultural and social change ran high throughout Europe. Populations grew and economies expanded – though not always enough, causing strains and tensions, which in turn were inquired into and engaged with in increasingly ambitious ways.[33]

The aims of British–Irish union also differed significantly from those of Anglo-Scottish union. Union with Ireland was also prompted by fears for national security, in the context of the French Revolutionary Wars. But in Ireland, the fear was not just that the governing elite might set their own foreign policy or dynastic course; it was also that they might lose control of the situation: that radical Protestants and alienated Catholics would combine with discontented peasants to destabilise the regime. The Irish Rebellion of 1798, though effectively suppressed, sounded a warning that later disturbances reinforced. In that context the British government *did* have an interest in becoming involved in Irish domestic affairs.[34]

Irish institutions more closely resembled English ones than Scottish – not surprisingly, given that they were the product of centuries of English rule. Irish common law, thus, was largely English common law. This made the assimilation of laws less problematic. Indeed, more than that, it was generally agreed, by ministers, British and Irish MPs that assimilation of English and Irish laws was one of the *objects* of union. Irish MP Sir John Newport in 1812 went so far as to state that he saw it as 'a solecism, that all the public bills introduced were not made to include the whole united kingdom'.[35] Few Scottish MPs, then or since, have taken this view. Even in the Irish case, apparent consensus shatters on closer inspection. There was plenty of scope for disagreement about just when different parts of the British Isles should be similarly treated. The slogan 'assimilation' was tactically used by all parties for particular purposes. Thus, Peel resisted taking special action against the Orange order on the grounds that the rule of law should operate in the same way throughout the UK – a consideration that had never deterred him from promoting special measures against troublesome Catholics.[36] It was a significant difference between Scottish and Irish unions, nonetheless, that in the Irish case shared rhetoric favoured assimilation.

What more substantively did Irish MPs want from the union? (at least, once it had become political reality – not all of them had wanted it at the start, and, insofar as it did not deliver what they wanted, some, with more or less heat and conviction, recurrently demanded its repeal). Of course, their wishes varied, but we might generalise them as the hope that it would help to resolve the 'condition of Ireland question'. Within Ireland, the late eighteenth century saw the rise of intense domestic discussion of domestic problems – in part a manifestation of the new culture of inquiry and reform developing throughout Europe, in part a response to a succession of rural disturbances, characterised by acts of 'outrage'. Many different elements of the Irish situation were diagnosed and debated: religious issues; issues to do with the state of the economy; to do with tenant rights; with the attitudes of the gentry and the character of local government institutions. Many contributors to this debate thought that British legislators, if they could be persuaded to develop an informed interest, might help identify solutions – or at least, be mobilised into political alliances that would break local deadlocks and make action (or alternatively definitive resistance to action) possible.[37] Given these concerns, we can begin to understand why – in contrast to the Scots, who commonly complained that Westminster did not leave them alone – the Irish commonly complained that Westminster did not attend to them enough.

The most striking feature of the Irish record is probably not any change that accompanied the union, but rather the great spike of legislation passed between 1782 and 1800. This was the era of 'Irish legislative independence', customarily termed 'Grattan's parliament' – the era inaugurated by the British parliament's agreement, under extreme Irish pressure, to abandon both the requirement that Irish legislation have the approval of the Irish privy council, and Westminster's own claim to legislate for Ireland.[38] The era of 'Grattan's parliament' was conceived by the Irish parliamentary class as an era of nation-building (even though that it was relatively recently that this mostly Anglo-Irish group had come to term themselves Irish).[39] During this era, the Irish parliament met more frequently than before – every year rather than every other year. We can appreciate that the passage from this era of expansive hopes to one in which space had to be created for Irish business was for many Irish MPs a frustrating passage – even if they hoped for compensating advantage.

Table 2.2 attempts to refine our understanding of the impact of union by probing changes in the composition of Irish legislation. It compares the proportions of legislation in particular subject categories passed in four periods. before and after legislative independence; after union and after the end of the Napoleonic wars. Of course this is a very blunt and crude way of measuring the changing character of legislation. Nonetheless, the results are suggestive, and not out of line with what a more detailed qualitative inquiry suggests.

The first finding of interest is that the huge expansion in the volume of legislation after 1782 was not linked with much change in its make-up. Change was only very noticeable in three categories. Grattan's parliament passed relatively fewer acts about elections, marginally fewer acts about religion and significantly *more* acts only about civil disorder. Perhaps we should not be too surprised that change is not more evident. Irish 'patriots' had been trying to promote Ireland's economic and social welfare for decades. In the era of legislative independence, they did more of the same.[40]

The union brought no immediate change in direction, but some change became evident. Following the union, even more legislation dealing with civil disorder

Table 2.2 'Other domestic' acts relating to Ireland passed by Dublin and Westminster parliaments, 1763–1829, broken down by subject category (% given in parentheses)

	Elections	Law	Legal admin.	Rebellion	Religion	Local govt.	Welfare	Economy	Communic.	Misc.
1763–82 (D)	11 (5)	29 (14)	15 (7)	4 (2)	34 (17)	15 (7)	6 (3)	63 (31)	15 (7)	12 (6)
1782–1800 (D)	9 (2)	65 (15)	40 (9)	22 (5)	52 (12)	27 (6)	25 (6)	152 (35)	37 (8)	8 (2)
1801–16 (W)	6 (4)	17 (11)	18 (11)	17 (11)	13 (8)	7 (4)	4 (2)	55 (34)	24 (15)	0 (0)
1817–29 (W)	7 (4)	35 (18)	37 (19)	16 (8)	15 (8)	24 (12)	6 (3)	43 (22)	13 (7)	0 (0)

was passed. Local government received little attention in the immediate post union years. But after the end of the war; interest in local government revived, and there was also more legislation focusing on legal administration. Much of this reflects attempts to reform courts and legal procedures, also made in England and Scotland. Some however relates to a diagnosis of the 'condition of Ireland question' popular at this time: the notion that Ireland would not be governed well until the personnel and conduct of its domestic and local government apparatus were reformed. This implied attention not only to policing (inaugurated before the union), but also to, for example, county grand juries, engines of Irish local government finance.[41]

To complete the comparison with Scotland, it remains to consider mechanisms: where did this Irish legislation come from? Some had expected that post-union Irish arrangements would echo Scottish: the Lord Lieutenancy would be discontinued; Ireland would cease to be treated like a conquered province, and instead be put on the same footing as the rest of the UK, without intermediary powers between central departments and local government. But these expectations were not realised. Lord Lieutenants argued for the retention of their post.[42]

What did shift was the balance of power between the Lord Lieutenant and his chief secretary. The secretary had customarily sat in the Irish Commons, serving as administration spokesman there. After the union, he sat at Westminster. His close involvement in Irish affairs and ready access to ministers positioned him at a key point in the web of power. It became the norm for him to agree a programme of Irish measures with government, and to guide these through parliament. Until the unification of fiscal administration in 1816, there was also an Irish chancellor of the exchequer, who proposed a budget, and oversaw fiscal legislation. Machinery did thus exist for promoting Irish legislation – and in an age of increasingly active central government, this proved a powerful statute-generating system.[43]

Not all Irish legislation was officially promoted. In the earliest years of the union, almost all acts reflected official concerns, mostly military or fiscal in character. Some independent Irish MPs proved vocal from the start in debates on these matters, as well as on issues of UK politics; by contrast, they took a time to get into their stride as legislators. Thus, Maurice Keatinge, who represented County Kildare at Westminster as he had in the Irish parliament, attempted in his first session to sponsor a scheme for Irish poor relief, but was 'hampered by his ignorance of English parliamentary procedures'.[44]

Within a few years, however, the Irish Lord Chancellor, Lord Redesdale (former English barrister and MP, John Freeman Mitford) was complaining about the activities of certain 'great manufacturers of Irish legislation'. These included Sir John Newport (already quoted above) who in 1804 succeeded in getting a select committee set up to consider provision for the Irish poor. Newport's attempt to secure public funding for lunatic asylums in Ireland bore fruit in 1806. From 1806, early activists were joined by Sir Henry Parnell. First elected immediately after the union, Parnell was initially silent, and gained confidence only after being appointed lord of the Irish Treasury under the Talents administration and having to speak in that role. He emerged as a pertinacious campaigner for tithe reform. Pittite and post-Pittite governments' views of these activists were not improved by the fact that most were supporters of some element of Whiggery.[45]

As in England, backbenchers' pertinacity nonetheless began, in the 1810s and 1820s, to provoke official action. In the Irish case, renewed rural disturbances, economic distress and epidemic disease set the scene. Officeholders seem to have concluded that since significant legislation looked likely to emerge one way or another, it had better be under their direction. Grand jury reform exemplifies the process. Richard Synge Cooper, MP for County Sligo, raised the issue at West-minster with several bills. When his 1812 bill passed the Commons, but was lost in the Lords, William Vesey Fitzgerald, then chancellor of the Irish exchequer, promised that the government would bring in reforming legislation. By 1825, we find the Irish chief secretary, Goulburn, apologising to the Home Secretary (Peel) for not having *more* to bring forward in the way of official proposals.[46]

Irish historiography is less illuminating than it might be on the character of the public culture out of which proposals for legislation emerged. However, it seems clear that there was what might be termed an 'Irish public sphere' as in England (and by this date in Scotland); that this was articulated in part by the apparatus of local government in town and country (which helped to define a class of local public figures, and provided fora for debate), in part by voluntary organisations, and in part by the press.[47]

In Scotland from the later eighteenth century county meetings claimed the right to be consulted on important Scottish legislation, wherever it might ori-ginate: how else, it was argued, could the will of Scotland be ascertained? No English extra-parliamentary bodies made quite these claims, though it did become common for bills bearing on English domestic government to be pro-posed at the end of a session, printed, and circulated to magistrates and the like during the summer for comment.[48] Irish extraparliamentary bodies made no such strong claims either. The consultative system probably best served defensive purposes: it provided a way of staving off, or at least securing the modification of, unwelcome attempts to legislate. It would not have served so well to force proposals upon parliament: the outcome Irishmen more often sought. Further-more the Irish political community was much more deeply fractured than the Scottish one: what set of bodies could plausibly have claimed to speak for post-union 'Ireland'? It would take the famine transiently to bring such a body into existence. In January 1847, a meeting of nobility and gentry was held in Dublin, attended by over 1,000 landowners, to attempt to guide British government response to the famine. A recent historian describes this as the first such 'aggregate' meeting since 1782–83.[49]

I have stressed how much legislation the Westminster parliament passed relating to Ireland. By comparison with what was passed relating to Scotland, it was very substantial. The scale of Irish general domestic legislation was indeed compar-able with that for England at the same date. Since some Irish issues were very controversial (notably Catholic Emancipation, though of course that was not wholly an Irish issue), much debating time was devoted to Irish affairs: at the end of the 1823 session, Peel observed that some forty-nine out of eighty-four days of business had been spent on Irish subjects.[50] Yet Irish MPs often complained that Ireland was neglected, and that perception helped to fuel demand for repeal of the union.[51]

In general, surely, what these high levels of frustration reflect is unusually high levels of expectation. MPs who complained loudest had especially high expectations. They saw Ireland as a society in crisis, needing radical reconstruction. Characteristically they supported Catholic Emancipation – the removal of remaining restrictions on Catholic participation in public life. They wanted to see the benefits of English laws and institutions extended to Ireland (in the abstract a common position, as I have noted). They were anxious too to see Ireland's distinctive problems – problems of economic underdevelopment, rural immiseration and cultural fragmentation – creatively addressed.[52]

This however was a very ambitious agenda. We should not be surprised that wartime governments balked at it, nor that attempts to grapple with it often foundered. It was also quite amorphously conceived. Though its proponents were sure that there was a 'condition of Ireland' question, they often were unsure how to tackle it. One reiterated demand was, consequently, for large-scale inquiries, to take the true measure of the situation, and chart ways forward. Ministers sometimes conceded such demands. Nonetheless they disliked and distrusted their fuzzy comprehensiveness. Peel's dislike of the inquiry into the state of Ireland set up in 1816 is clear from his mocking reference to it as the 'moralo-politico-agriculturo-judicialo-financial inquiry'. Wide-ranging select committee inquiries were then only beginning to catch on as ways of laying the groundwork for English legislation.[53]

Those whose demands led to the convening of such bodies hoped that they would prepare the ground for action. But action did not always follow. By 1830, this pattern had become cause for concern in its own right. Thus, when Anglesey, who had been Wellington's Lord Lieutenant, was restored to office by the Whigs in 1830 he wrote to Irish Whig Thomas Spring Rice about the need 'not merely to have *reports* on the wants of Ireland, but vigorously to set upon those that we already possess.'[54]

Thus far this essay been concerned with the ways in which the Westminster parliament dealt with Scotland and Ireland severally. This emphasis seems appropriate, because through this period, military and fiscal matters apart, that is mostly how they *were* dealt with. Legislation concerned with the general domestic affairs of England, Scotland and Ireland was, for the most part, locally generated – or at the very least, drew on local inquiry and consultation. Measures were openly debated (though debate was usually dominated by those who hailed from the region in question). The preponderant local view did not necessarily prevail, and this was potentially a source of tension between the nation legislated for, and

Westminster. But for minority opinion within the nations, it was also sometimes a source of opportunity.

There was however another side to the story, and one which became more important with the passage of time, as both ministers and private members took more interest in parallels and differences between structures and patterns of governance in the different nations, and made more ambitious attempts to align them upon some notion of best practice. In this final substantive section of my discussion, I shall attempt to illuminate this theme by considering patterns of what I shall term 'integrative' and 'parallel' legislation': integrative legislation being legislation bearing on more than one of the three kingdoms; parallel legislation being legislation for one kingdom echoing that for another.

General patterns of 'integrative' legislation were recorded in Figure 2.1.[55] Most such acts dealt fiscal or military matters. I will not say much about those here – though, had I accorded them a larger part in the story, the shape of the story might in some ways have changed. Much Scottish and Irish national effort at Westminster went into trying to modify fiscal legislation in particular, so as better to meet their countries' needs, and, if this effort were taken into account, Scots especially might very well appear more active at an earlier date than in my account. Perceptions of Westminster's responsiveness to local needs were no doubt as – or more significantly – shaped by these struggles as by the kinds of effort I have examined. This part of the picture therefore deserves more attention than I can give it here.[56]

Military, fiscal and other such central governmental concerns apart, the output of integrative legislation was meagre. It is represented in Table 2.3. It will be apparent that the amount of integrative 'other domestic' legislation rose in the 1780s. However, numbers of acts remained small. Not much movement was made in this period towards producing integrative legislation bearing on the domestic affairs of the three kingdoms.

Far and away the greatest number of integrative acts dealt with the domestic economy. Some of this really reflected state fiscal concerns: it was about the production of and trade in taxable commodities, such as salt and spirits. The growth of the illicit distilling industry in the later eighteenth century explains some of the expansion at that point.[57] In other cases, promoters of measures seem to have been heeding the geography of an industry. Legislation relating to linen and cotton, thus, was often given British form. International shipping, roads and turnpikes and postal services were among the subjects of a growing body of integrative 'communications' legislation. A swelling tide of emigration, especially from Scotland and Ireland, prompted the passage in the nineteenth century of a series of integrative passenger acts.[58]

The sizeable 'civil disorder' total reflects government decisions to promote legislation against threats to national security or civil order on a pan-British or UK basis. Country-specific measures were sometimes proposed: the Disarming Acts in Scotland; the Insurrection Acts in Ireland. But many such acts was given wider scope, a process inaugurated by the Treason Act of 1708, extending English treason

Table 2.3 'Integrative' legislation, 1707–1829, broken down by topic

		Elections	Law	Legal admin.	Rebellion	Religion	Local govt.	Welfare	Economy	Communic.	Totals	Tot. int. leg.
1707–27	GB	2	6	1	13	2	1	1	12	1	39	
	GBI	0	0	0	0	2	0	0	0	1	3	
	ENI	0	0	0	0	2	0	0	0	0	2	44
1727–45	GB	2	2	0	5	8	0	0	9	1	27	
	GBI	0	0	0	0	0	0	1	0	0	1	28
1745–63	GB	0	3	0	8	8	1	1	20	0	41	
	GBI	0	2	0	0	0	0	0	10	1	13	54
1763–82	GB	2	6	1	1	10	2	0	23	3	48	
	GBI	0	0	0	0	0	0	0	4	1	5	53
1782–1800	GB	5	4	0	12	7	2	1	59	18	108	
	GBI	2	1	0	0	0	0	0	0	3	6	114
1801–16	GB	1	7	1	6	1	1	2	24	5	48	
	GBI	6	4	7	0	0	0	1	25	0	43	
	ENI	0	4	2	0	3	3	0	1	0	13	
	SCI	0	0	1	0	0	0	0	0	0	1	105
1817–29	GB	0	4	3	5	0	4	1	18	6	41	
	GBI	3	7	3	5	4	4	3	40	15	84	
	ENI	1	8	3	0	0	0	0	4	1	17	
	SCI	0	0	0	0	0	0	0	0	1	1	143
Totals	GB	12	32	6	50	36	11	6	165	34	352	
	GBI	11	14	10	5	6	4	5	79	21	155	
	ENI	1	12	5	0	5	3	0	5	1	32	
	SCI	0	0	1	0	0	0	0	0	1	2	541

law to Scotland under the rubric of 'improving the union'.[59] Repressive legislation of the 1790s and post-war eras – the Two Acts and the Six Acts – was all given British or UK application. Integrative religious legislation, similarly, initially mostly reflected national security concerns: most of it focused on Catholics. From the later eighteenth century, new integrative legislation repealed earlier provisions.

A non-trivial number of integrative measures focused on criminal or civil law. Anglo-Scottish such acts were mainly criminal in focus, and dealt with crimes judged especially heinous, such as wrecking or murder.[60] This apart, attempts to assimilate English and Scottish laws were desultory.[61] Given common agreement that union in 1801 should set in train a process of assimilating English and Irish law, parliament's early achievements in this regard do not greatly impress. Statutes were issued to regulate procedures in debt and bankruptcy.[62] An 1820 act laid down procedures whereby English, Welsh and Irish landlords might speedily recover possession of lands and tenements; another made it possible summarily to punish wilful trespass. Acts facilitating misdemeanour and summary proceedings applied to both England and Ireland.[63]

Of related interest are parallel measures – measures enacting, in separate legislation, provisions echoing, more or less closely, those which applied elsewhere. Parallel measures figure among those surveyed in earlier sections of this discussion, inasmuch as formally they applied to one country only. Some measures particular to a country were also peculiar to it, but others were not. The subset of 'parallel measures' is not easily charted. To identify them, one would have to analyse the content of legislation more closely than I have done; even then, problems of definition would remain. What I shall say under this heading is therefore impressionistic.

It is clear that, throughout the eighteenth century, the Irish parliament often passed laws echoing enactments of the British parliament. This sometimes reflected deliberate government effort to keep the two in step, but often, it seems, nothing was officially engineered: rather, Irish MPs voluntarily followed English models. Such echoing legislation did not necessarily replicate. Thus, there was an Irish 'bloody code' – an array of statutes extending the application of the death penalty – as well as an English one, but Irish acts were fewer, and differed in other respects too.[64]

Though they shared the same parliament, Scots did not choose to echo much English legislation in the first decades after the union. From mid-century, this began to change. Mainly at first within the category of local acts: they began to enact turnpike and improvement acts, after English models.[65] A scattering of parallel general measures issued thereafter. Crewe's act, disfranchising revenue officers – an early achievement of the parliamentary reform movement – was extended to Scotland in 1797. In 1823, following English example, Scots obtained funds for the building of more churches. Like the English and Irish, they sought legislation relating to lunatic asylums in the early nineteenth century (though they did not seek to establish public institutions, limiting themselves to a system of inspection and allowances).[66]

These measures were, I suspect, adopted because wanted by numerous Scots. But during the early nineteenth century, as elsewhere, the co-ordinating hand of central government became more evident, sometimes to controversial effect. Measures to reform the court of session had their origins in an English desire to reduce Scottish appeals to the Lords, and initially provoked much local opposition. However, they drew some support from long-standing indigenous interest in juries playing a more extensive part in the Scottish, as in the English legal system. After the initial clash, Scottish and English judges and lawyers worked together for more than a decade to produce mutually acceptable reforms.[67]

These measures – and a few others one might add to the list – once again do not add up to a major effort to bring the laws and practices of the British kingdoms into line. However, the trend was clearly towards more parallel legislation. In Ireland, parallel acts continued to issue after the union, as before – legislation on prisons and lunatic asylums provide instances. Traffic was two way: in the late 1790s, English law on theft by servants of bankers and merchants was brought into line with Scottish; in the early nineteenth century, Irish practice was invoked in discussions of English charity administration.[68]

We can see that there were grounds for officeholders to argue that progress was being made in the assimilation of laws – yet, at the same time, why those who hoped for great things from this process felt that little was being achieved.[69] Irish attempts to enact *more* integrative and parallel legislation were, moreover, in practice sometimes frustrated – as repeatedly in the case of attempts to establish poor laws on the English model. The Scots, who showed less interest in imitating England, do not appear to have had this problem.[70]

I noted initially that, from the later eighteenth century, but most obviously from 1801, Westminster's legislative output became more plural than it had been before. This was more obviously an 'imperial parliament': a parliament superintending the affairs of several, interacting but distinct politico-cultural entities. The example of the British and Irish parliaments before the union shows that it was not necessary for two countries to share a legislature for cross-fertilisation between their legislative programmes to take place. Furthermore, it was certainly possible for MPs sharing a single chamber to ignore business which did not interest them: William Lamb, appointed Chief Secretary in Ireland under the Canning ministry, claimed that until that point he had not paid 'the least attention to any of the reports or debates upon Irish subjects.'[71] Yet coexistence within a single chamber surely had *some* effect in raising levels of mutual awareness on the part of at least some MPs, in this age of 'improvement' and 'reform', when opportunities to legislate were vigorously exploited.[72] Other forces were working to this end too: including developments in the newspaper and periodical press; the growth of empirical social inquiry, tourism, and emigration from Ireland and the Scottish Highlands to other parts of Britain – bringing the problems of poorer home to wealthier regions.

The effects of all this can be seen in the activities of some independent MPs: active backbenchers and parliamentary radicals. John Christian Curwen, a Whig from Cumberland who championed English tithe reform, and promoted a variety of self-help remedies for English poverty, visited Ireland between 1813 and 1816, and wrote a book about his findings (in 1822, he would serve on a select committee on the Irish poor).[73] Michael Sadler did not visit Ireland, but became interested because of his interest in the pros and cons of emigration. In 1828, he published an account: *Ireland: its evils and their remedies*; in 1830, he moved a resolution in favour of establishing a poor law for Ireland.[74] The sufferings of the Irish at the hands of an oppressive state and church provided an attractive theme for radicals. The Scot Joseph Hume, the only radical to be returned for a Scottish constituency before 1832, an obsessive House of Commons man, was interested in everything, but Ireland was one of his interests. He moved the disestablishment of the Irish Church in 1823. In 1837, when Hume lost his seat, Daniel O'Connell would get him returned for Kilkenny.[75] Scotland also attracted some attention from reform-minded MPs – thus Whig radical Samuel Romilly took an interest in Scottish law reform – but to a lesser extent: private members who were not Scots do not seem to have felt compelled to wrestle with the ills of Scotland in quite the same way that they felt compelled to wrestle with the ills of Ireland.[76]

This growth of mutual awareness had ambiguous effects. On the one hand, there was widespread interest in doing whatever might be done to allow the different parts of the UK to progress together. Yet increased mutual awareness also meant increased awareness of difference: the discourse of comparison was also a discourse of dissimilarity – as the record of debates on attempts to produce 'integrative' and 'parallel' legislation reveal. And attempts to make the nations march in step spurred some to try to break rank. The very ways in which comparisons were framed – around the entities 'England', 'Scotland' and 'Ireland' – helped to encourage preoccupation with national distinctiveness. Those who took an interest in such matters wavered uneasily, torn between the twin attractions of, on the one hand, participating in a broad-based improvement project, and, on the other, asserting national distinctiveness, and rights of self-rule.

The end of the twentieth century has been marked in Britain by constitutional re-engineering. In that context, this survey of Scotland and Ireland's early experience of throwing in their lot with English Lords and Commons at Westminster provides a perhaps useful reminder that formal constitutional arrangements play only a limited part in determining how legislative systems work in practice. The constitutional positions of Scotland and Ireland were not identical. The Scots had sought to protect numerous of their institutions against possible parliamentary assault; the terms of the union with Ireland entrenched – or attempted to entrench – only the Church of Ireland. In the period that I have been considering, Scotland had relatively little in the way of a local apparatus of executive government, Ireland rather more. These differences probably helped to shape the different ways in which Scots and Irish experienced their relations with Westminster. Yet other, extra-constitutional factors mattered as much or more, notably the character of political culture in the two kingdoms (including the cohesiveness or otherwise of that culture), and their ideas about what they wanted from Westminster.

Scottish and Irish historians often suggest that Scotland and Ireland lost out from incorporation into an English-dominated legislature. There is surely some truth in this. As we have seen, the quantity of legislation passed relating to each kingdom declined after union; their ability to gain endorsement for projects well supported locally became more dependent on their ability to gain support from non-local fellow MPs. Conversely, however, other historians have argued that we must compare Scottish and Irish experience at Westminster with their experience at the hands of some likely version of a local legislature: not some utopian body, perfectly responsive to national needs.[77] I would add that we should assess their experience comparatively: we must compare the experience of each with that of the other – and with that of England. Those who sought to legislate for England also often suffered frustration. Though the Irish complained that they were neglected, local acts apart, they were in fact the subject of more acts than the English in the early nineteenth century. In the mid-eighteenth century, general domestic legislation relating to Scotland – as we have seen – dropped away to a mere trickle. But English general domestic legislation dropped at the same time, and Scottish local legislation dropped less than general. Later, the volume of Scottish general domestic legislation would increase. These patterns surely had something to do with attitudes at Westminster, but also something to do with attitudes in Scotland. We need to analyse Scottish and Irish experience at Westminster as the product of choices Scots and Irish made within a matrix that did impose constraints, but also offered certain opportunities. After 1830, the scope for independent Scottish or Irish action would seem to have decreased (though it certainly did not disappear), as increasingly pro-active governments sought to shape legislative programmes – and as the House of Lords increasingly asserted itself as an anti-reforming force. It is nonetheless interesting to note that patterns of complaint from Scotland and Ireland had to a significant extent already been established, in rather different circumstances.

Inasmuch as the Westminster parliament provided a forum in which debates about how to legislate for three kingdoms took place, in its own way it helped to reinforce awareness of that difference. Debates about how these differences were best negotiated, both in terms of 'process' and in terms of 'approach', offered opportunities to rehearse ideas about national identity and its implications. Ideas about what it meant to be Scottish and what it meant to be Irish were formed in part in the context of debates about whether and how the legislative process could be made to serve local needs. In the 1840s, when they sponsored a provocative inquiry into educational provision in Wales, the Westminster parliament was indeed to help spark vigorous debate about what, until that point, had been the most submerged of all 'national' issues: what it meant to be Welsh.[78] The scene was set for the playing out of diverse nationalisms on the floor of the late nineteenth-century Palace of Westminster.

40

Notes

1 Thanks are due for help of various kinds to Sean Connolly, Grainne de Burca, Andrew Hann, Bob Harris, Douglas Hay, David Hayton, Holger Hoock, Julian Hoppit, Des Kenny, Bill Noblett, Tadgh O'Sullivan, Paul Pickering, Jennifer Ridden, and the staff of the Bodleian library, who have been more than ordinarily helpful in various small respects. I am also grateful to the Humanities Research Centre at the Australian National University for awarding me a visiting fellowship; it was in their hospitable quarters that I revised my original text for publication.

2 R. G. Thorne (ed.), *The history of parliament: House of Commons, 1790–1820*, 5 vols (1986), i, pp. 106–7 for Irish members. Scottish members were mocked for their heavy brogue; both Scots and Irish tended to serve as ministerial lobby fodder.

3 See chapter 11 in this volume.

4 This argument was already being made by A. V. Dicey and R. S. Rait in their *Thoughts on the Union between England and Scotland* (1920), see especially 292–9. They clearly wrote with the then burning issue of Anglo-Irish Union also in view. Recent influential accounts include N. Phillipson's thesis, *The Scottish Whigs and the reform of the Court of Session, 1785–1830* (Edinburgh, 1990) and L. Paterson, *The anatomy of modern Scotland* (Edinburgh, 1994). J. S. Shaw, in *The management of Scottish society 1707–1764: power, nobles, lawyers, Edinburgh agents and English influences* (Edinburgh, 1983), expresses scepticism, but his account is not structured around a contrast between Scots and English, but between 'home Scots' and London Scots; in his account Scottish MPs 'impose' legislation on home Scots.

5 I am very grateful for Julian Hoppit for allowing me to use databases of acts of the Westminster, Edinburgh and Dublin parliaments down to 1800 which he compiled. The Westminster database was extended down to 1830 by Andrew Hann, who was funded to do this by the British Academy and the University of Oxford, to all of whom I am also grateful. The category 'local' was not officially employed before 1797. I have categorised as 'local' not only formally 'local acts' and their earlier analogues, but also all other acts applying to sub-national areas or particular non-governmental institutions. The geographical categorisation of acts is mine. I relied on the titles of acts, when these were sufficiently unambiguous; the texts of acts when necessary. Acts applying to Scotland are a particularly hard group to demarcate nonetheless, since eighteenth-century English legislators especially often did not think very hard about whether they meant acts to apply to Scotland; when they did so intend, their knowledge of Scottish law and government was not always sufficient for them to give their wishes appropriate effect. I have counted as applying to Scotland all acts where the intention that they should so apply is explicit. For the shortcomings of parliamentary draftsmanship see [J. Swinton], *An abridgement of the public statutes in force and use relative to Scotland*, 2 vols (Edinburgh, 1755), i, v–vi (who, however, uses other criteria than mine).

6 The key acts of Union were 6 Anne *c.* 11 (Scottish acts Anne 1706 *c.* 6–8) and 40 George III *c.* 67 (Irish acts 40 George III *c.* 29 and *c.* 38). Some of these questions are enduringly controversial, see thus D. Walker, *A legal history of Scotland, V: the eighteenth century* (Edinburgh, 1988), 88–9, 135–6.

7 J. Innes, 'The local acts of a national parliament: the role of parliament in sanctioning local legislation', *Parliamentary History*, xvii (1998), 23–47 for a survey of patterns of local legislation in England and Scotland; P. Langford, *Public life and the propertied*

Englishman, 1689–1798 (Oxford, 1991), 166–206 for the ways in which English proposals were handled.

8 R. Sedgwick (ed.), *The history of parliament: the House of Commons, 1715–54*, 2 vols (1979), i, 523, 617; ii, 9, 98, 99 for some early examples of Scots sitting for English seats. For surveys of MPs of Scots and Irish origin, wherever sitting L. B. Namier and J. Brooke (eds), *The history of parliament: the House of Commons, 1754–90*, 3 vols (reprinted with corrections 1985), i, 163–7; Thorne (ed.), *Commons*, i, 328–9.

9 Some did so by making up their own rules of conduct. Thus John Foster wrote in 1811 that as an Irishman he made it a general rule not to interfere in British private bills: A. P. W. Malcolmson, *John Foster: the politics of the Anglo-Irish ascendancy* (Oxford, 1978), 432.

10 The graphs also exclude a small number of acts dealing with other countries, individuals or companies not susceptible to my form of analysis.

11 I have included in the Irish graph – partly in order to demonstrate its limited extent – legislation passed by the Westminster parliament relating to Ireland *only*. For a survey of this see J. C. Beckett and A. G. Donaldson, 'British legislation for Ireland between the enactment of the 'Sixth of George I' and its repeal', *Proceedings of the Belfast Natural History and Philosophical Society*, iv (1951), 17–37.

12 The subject categories I have employed are constructed out of the codes used in J. Hoppit (ed.), *Failed legislation, 1660–1800: extracted from the Commons and Lords Journals* (1997), but do not correspond precisely to categories used in that work. Thus, I split public finance measures from private ones (relating to debt and bankruptcy, or money and banking), and measures relating to central and colonial government from those relating to local government. There is an element of arbitrariness in all classifications and groupings of acts; I have attempted to employ reasonably commonsense categories that make sense in terms of the issues I am concerned to explore.

13 For the small role central government played either in initiating or assessing domestic legislation, J. Innes, 'Parliament and the shaping of eighteenth-century English social policy', *Transactions of the Royal Historical Society*, 5th series, xl (1990), 63–92.

14 Constraints of space do not allow me to elaborate on contrasting patterns of resort to local legislation. L. Rydz, *The parliamentary agents: a history* (1979), 68–9, 114 picks up the contrast from another angle.

15 J. Innes and J. Hoppit, 'Introduction' to Hoppit (ed.), *Failed legislation*, 5, 7–8.

16 See note 3 above.

17 See for recent accounts J. Robertson (ed.), *A union for empire: political thought and the Union of 1707* (Cambridge, 1995) and C. A. Whatley, 'Economic causes and consequences of the Union of 1707: a survey', *Scottish Historical Review*, lxviii (1989), 150–81.

18 Once again, groupings of statutes here make use of the codes employed in Hoppit (ed.), *Failed legislation*, but do not replicate categories employed in that work.

19 10 Anne *c.* 7, 10 Anne *c.* 12, 19 George II *c.* 38, 17 George II *c.* 11, 22 George II *c.* 21. For objections to the patronage act, and also the Yule Vacance Act of 1711 (repealed 1714), Dicey and Rait, *Thoughts on the Union*, 280–2; P. W. J. Riley, *The English ministers and Scotland, 1707–27* (1964), 233.

20 Scottish acts William 1696 *c.* 35 and *c.* 37. That this was a post-Union development is argued in L. Farmer, *Criminal law, tradition and legal order: crime and the genius of Scots law, 1747 to the present* (Cambridge, 1997).

21 J. W. Cairns, 'Scottish law, Scottish lawyers and the status of the Union' in Robertson (ed.), *A union for empire*, 243–68.

22 Riley, *English ministers*, 233. The fullest account of the religious tensions of this period remains W. L. Mathieson, *Scotland and the Union: a history of Scotland from 1695 to 1747* (Glasgow, 1905), ch. 5.

23 B. F. Jewell, 'The legislation relating to Scotland after the Forty Five' (University of North Carolina PhD thesis, 1975). See also C. Kidd, *Subverting Scotland's past: Scottish Whig historians and the creation of an Anglo-British identity, 1669–c. 1830* (Cambridge, 1993), 153–7.

24 Innes, 'Parliament and the shaping'; D. Eastwood, 'Men, morals and the machinery of social legislation, 1790–1840', *Parliamentary History*, xiii (1994), 190–205; M. Taylor, *The decline of British radicalism, 1847–60* (Oxford, 1995), especially ch. 1 and conclusion.

25 The basic structures of Scottish government are surveyed in Walker, *Legal history*, 140–64, 173–83; M. Fry, *The Dundas despotism* (Edinburgh, 1992) focuses on the man who did most to develop the Lord Advocate's role.

26 Early lobbying by the Convention is noted by Riley, *English ministers*, 120–2; for the complexities of this instance Shaw, *Management*, 124–32, for the Patronage Act, Cobbett, *Parliamentary History*, ix, col. 966.

27 A. Whetstone, *Scottish county government in the eighteenth and nineteenth centuries* (Edinburgh, 1981); see also Shaw, *Management*, 125–6.

28 To this effect, Shaw, *Management*, 126; Riley, *English ministers*, 172 – Riley is discussing a specific moment; the question is, how generalisable this is.

29 Hoppit (ed.), *Failed legislation*, bill ref. 94.019.

30 *Tory and Whig: the parliamentary papers of Edward Harley, third Earl of Oxford, and William Hay, MP for Seaford, 1716–53*, ed. C. Jones and S. Taylor (Woodbridge, 1998), 121.

31 J. Robertson, *The Scottish Enlightenment and the militia issue* (Edinburgh, 1985).

32 Hoppit (ed.), *Failed legislation*, bill ref. 73.014. *Tory and Whig*, ed. Jones and Taylor, 6, 110, 121. Walpole cited in Sedgwick (ed.), *Commons*, i, 629.

33 For attempts to provide for the anticipated impact of new Irish business, see O. C. Williams, *The clerical organisation of the House of Commons* (Oxford, 1954), 149–51, 205–7. No such provision was made in 1707 for an access of Scottish business.

34 For a recent overview, see essays on 'The British–Irish Union of 1801' in *Transactions of the Royal Historical Society*, 6th series, x (2000).

35 *Hansard* xxi, col. 400. Newport was moving the taking of a census for Ireland.

36 B. Jenkins, *Era of emancipation: the British government of Ireland, 1812–30* (Kingston and Montreal, 1988), 187–9.

37 For debate on what I have termed the 'condition of Ireland' question see R. B. McDowell, *Irish public opinion, 1750–1800* (1944) and W. J. McCormack, *The Dublin paper war of 1786–1788: a bibliographical inquiry including an account of the origins of Protestant Ascendancy and its 'baptism' in 1792* (Blackrock, 1993).

38 R. B. McDowell, *Ireland in the age of imperialism and revolution* (Oxford, 1979), ch. 6 provides an overview of this episode. For the legislative effects of 'dependency', Beckett and Donaldson, 'British legislation for Ireland' and G. P. O'Brien, *Anglo-Irish politics in the age of Grattan and Pitt* (Dublin, 1987), 28–32, 133–4, 175–6.

39 The 'nation building' formulation is mine. O'Brien, *Anglo-Irish politics*, ch. 4, especially 117, offers an account of patriot policies which makes passing reference to such projects.

40 Among unsuccessful proposals were Grattan's proposal to do something about tithes and Orde's educational proposals (for which see also D. H. Akenson, *The Irish*

education experiment. The national system of education in the nineteenth century (1970), 60–74) – which did at least lead to the institution of inquiries and prepare the ground for later action.

41 For grand juries, V. Crossman, *Local government in nineteenth-century Ireland* (Belfast, 1994), 25–39.

42 For post-Union Irish governmental arrangements, E. Brynn, *Crown and castle: British rule in Ireland, 1800–30* (Dublin, 1978) and R. B. McDowell, *The Irish administration, 1800–1914* (1964), especially ch. 2.

43 See as well as works in note 41 above discussion of early parliamentary provision in Malcolmson, *John Foster*, 433–7. In 1829, Lord Melville (Dundas' son and heir) represented to Peel that a similar 'establishment' – in the form at least of a responsible minister – was needed for Scotland, this work having 'hitherto improperly devolved on the Lord Advocate' (Fry, *Dundas despotism*, 377).

44 Thorne (ed.), *Commons*, iv, 328.

45 BL Add. MS. 49188, fo. 200, cited Thorne (ed.), *Commons*, iv, 664. For Newport, 663–7, for Parnell, 723–6.

46 Crossman, *Local government*, 33–4; Jenkins, *Era of emancipation*, 210.

47 R. B. McDowell, *Public opinion and government policy in Ireland, 1801–46* (1952) remains the only general account. Recent work focusing on popular protest has challenged McDowell's narrow focus – but has not offered a comprehensive overview. Accounts of the tithe debate provide some insight into a world not only of direct action but also of grand jury resolutions and county meetings, petitioning and pamphleteering: see E. Brynn, *The Church of Ireland in the age of Catholic emancipation* (New York, 1982), ch. 4; McDowell, *Public opinion*, 20, 72–3. See also references in F. O'Ferrall, *Catholic emancipation: Daniel O'Connell and the birth of Irish democracy* (Dublin, 1985), especially 78, 106, 110.

48 For Scotland, Phillipson, *Scottish Whigs*, 3–4, 66–71 and Whetstone, *Scottish county government*, 69–70. There seems to be no clear evidence that they played this role before mid century. Thus, they did not mobilise against early eighteenth-century Tory initiatives – perhaps in part because divisions within Scotland would have made them an uncertain instrument. For England, Innes, 'Parliament and the shaping', 88–9.

49 R. Sloan, *William Smith O'Brien and the Young Ireland rebellion of 1848* (Dublin, 2000), 180.

50 Jenkins, *Era of emancipation*, 177.

51 I regret not having more information about Irish failed bills. Peter Jupp's figures, in *British politics on the eve of reform: the Duke of Wellington's administration, 1828–30* (Basingstoke, 1988), 187–8, are not entirely comparable to mine, notably because he does not distinguish UK from English legislation. However, he reports that during 1828–30, while the ratio of 'private members' bills' to all bills was roughly the same in the UK and Ireland (at 32 per cent and 29 per cent), the failure rate was much higher for Irish private members' bills, such that whereas they made up 18 per cent of UK acts, they made up only 7 per cent of Irish acts. Most of the private members' bills concerned 'law and order' or 'social issues'. Jupp appears to designate as government bills all bills which an officeholder introduced or reported on at some stage, though he notes that many bills apparently arose out of cooperation between officeholders and private members. For repeal sentiment in the 1830s and 40s, A. Macintyre, *The liberator: Daniel O'Connell and the Irish party, 1830–1847* (1965) and Sloan, *William Smith O'Brien*.

52 Thus Lord Holland, supporting Stanhope's motion for change in the law of distraint, with a view to improving the situation of Irish peasants. 'The Union with Ireland had existed for several years; and he recollected one great argument for it was, the profound attention which would be given to the affairs of Ireland. It was with pain that he witnessed how little that expectation had been answered': *Hansard*, xxii, col. 400.

53 For such demands, e.g. Cobbett, *Parliamentary History*, xxvi, col. 1704 ff; *Hansard*, i, cols. 1766–7; xxi. cols. 494–514. For Peel, R. C. Shipkey, *Sir Robert Peel's Irish policy* (New York, 1987), 128. Royal commissions of inquiry, also novelties, were also more common at an early date in Ireland (and indeed in Scotland) than in England The point was presumably to devolve policy-making to local experts: thus the Scottish commission on courts was set up only after an initial attempt to legislate had failed.

54 Jenkins, *Era of emancipation*, 298. Jenkins' book is essentially a study of the failure of this first phase of post-Union effort to 'reform' Ireland.

55 For a list of pre-1782 Westminster acts applying to Britain and Ireland, see Beckett and Donaldson, 'British legislation for Ireland', 31–7.

56 For the effect of frustrations in this sphere on Scottish morale in the early eighteenth century, Riley, *English ministers*, 172ff. Peter Jupp notes that Newport and Parnell, whom I have highlighted as active Irish MPs, believed that reform in Ireland should commence on the administrative and economic front, both supporting union of the two economies: Jupp, 'Irish MPs at Westminster in the early nineteenth century', *Historical Studies*, ix (1969), 80.

57 For unlicensed distilling, T. Devine, *Clanship to crofter's war: the social transformation of the Scottish Highlands* (Manchester, 1994), ch. 9 and K. H. Connell, *Irish peasant society: four historical essays* (Oxford, 1968), ch. 1.

58 O. Macdonagh, *A pattern of government growth, 1800–60: the passenger acts and their enforcement* (1961) – the study which stimulated Macdonagh's interest in general issues of government growth. Given his parallel interest in Anglo-Irish relations, it is striking that he was not more interested in the problems of legislating for three kingdoms.

59 7 Anne *c.* 21. On this act, Riley, *English ministers*, 119.

60 4 George I *c.* 12; 25 George II *c.* 37.

61 Occasional re-jigging of an existing line of legislation to ensure that it could be applied in Scotland I suspect usually reflects some Scottish initiative. Glasgow lobbying at the Convention of Royal Burghs thus may have helped prompt the incorporation of Scotland in licensing acts from 1756 (I owe this information to Bob Harris). I suspect that the same was true for an act of 1763 (3 George III *c.* 6), addressing the problem that, though the assize of bread, as reissued in 1710, was intended to apply to Scotland, thought had not been given to how it was to operate in those parts of Scotland not equipped with markets.

62 50 George III *c.* 47 – the Insolvent Debtors' Ireland Act, 1810 – includes in its preamble an interesting commentary, explaining what concerns inform its attempt to assimilate the laws of Ireland to those of England.

63 60 George III and 1 George IV *c.* 4, 1 George IV *c.* 56, 1 George IV *c.* 87, 3 George IV *c.* 23.

64 S. Connolly, 'Albion's fatal twigs: justice and law in the eighteenth century' in R. Mitchison and P. Roebuck (eds), *Economy and society in Scotland and Ireland, 1500–1939* (Edinburgh, 1988), 117–25 and N. Garnham, *The courts, crime and criminal law in Ireland, 1692–1760* (Blackrock, 1996).

65 The first turnpike act was 25 George II *c.* 28. 32 George II *c.* 15 provided general regulations for Scottish turnpikes. The Edinburgh Streets Act 1771 (11 George III *c.* 36) appears to have been the first English-type improvement act. Earlier acts had provided, according to Scottish tradition, for the levying of ale duties to pay for local improvements.

66 37 George III *c.* 138, 55 George III *c.* 69, 4 George IV *c.* 79, 9 George IV *c.* 34.

67 Phillipson, *Scottish Whigs*. For the ambiguities of early nineteenth-century Scottish attitudes, see also Phillipson, 'Nationalism and ideology' in J. N. Wolfe (ed.), *Government and nationalism in Scotland* (Edinburgh, 1969), 167–88.

68 Major Irish prison acts were: 50 George III *c.* 103, 59 George III *c.* 100, 1 and 2 George IV *c.* 57, 3 George IV *c.* 64, 7 George I *c.* 74; for lunatic asylums: 57 George III *c.* 106, 1 George IV *c.* 98, 1 and 2 George IV *c.* 33. Theft from bankers and merchants: 39 George III *c.* 85. R. S. Tompson, *The Charity Commission and the age of reform* (1979), 84, 90. See also S. Lynam, *Humanity Dick: a biography of Richard Martin MP, 1754–1834* (1975), 139 for Irish anti-bull-baiting legislation invoked as a model for England.

69 One change evident to anyone who studies the statute book, in which I suspect the hand of central government, consisted in improved standards of legislative draftsmanship – in the sense that there is generally more clarity at this period than there had been earlier as to *where* in the UK statutes applied. In that context, the question, should they apply more widely, and what if any changes would then be needed would more naturally have occurred. Note against this background Peel's promise, as Irish secretary, to bring in Irish legislation to parallel one of Romilly's proposed criminal law reforms, if its English version secured approval (S. Romilly, *Memoirs of the life of Sir Samuel Romilly*, 3 vols (1840), iii, 334).

70 Scottish poor law policy has been magisterially surveyed in R. Mitchison, *The old poor law in Scotland: the experience of poverty, 1574–1845* (Edinburgh, 2000). For debate on the pros and cons of extending the poor law to Ireland, R. C. D. Black, *Economic thought and the Irish question 1817–70* (Cambridge, 1960), ch. 4; Macintyre, *The Liberator*, ch. 4. I briefly review pan-British debate on this subject in 'The distinctiveness of the English poor laws, 1750–1850' in P. O'Brien and D. Winch (eds), *The political economy of British historical experience 1688–1914* (Oxford, 2002).

71 Jenkins, *Era of emancipation*, 249.

72 Members appointed to select committees inquiring into legislation relating to other parts of the UK would have special opportunities to learn about those countries' concerns – and the more so as these committees became more probing and investigative.

73 E. Hughes, *North country life in the eighteenth century*, 2 vols (1952–65), ii, 273–89.

74 K. Lawes, *Paternalism and politics: the revival of paternalism in early nineteenth century Britain* (Basingstoke, 2000) is essentially a political biography of Sadler.

75 R. K. Huch and P. R. Ziegler, *Joseph Hume, the people's MP* (Philadelphia, 1985).

76 Romilly, *Memoirs*, ii, 165–70, 248–9, 257; iii, 162–4, 278–82 (where he protests that that the implications of the Habeas Corpus suspension bill for Scotland have not been thought through), 286–9, 304–7, 329 (largely on the repercussions of that intervention).

77 L. Kennedy and D. S. Johnson, 'The union of Britain and Ireland, 1801–1922', in D. G. Boyce and A. O'Day (eds), *The making of modern Irish history* (1996), 60–3.

78 As originally delivered, this paper included a number of references to Welsh experience, but I have removed these to save space and because they were anyway underdeveloped. For the episode referred to here, see P. Morgan, 'From long knives to blue books' in R. R. Davies and G. Williams (eds), *Welsh society and nationhood: historical essays presented to Glanmor Williams* (Cardiff, 1994) and I. G. Jones, *Mid-Victorian Wales: the observers and the observed* (Cardiff, 1992).

3

Local identities and a national parliament, c. 1688–1835[1]

Rosemary Sweet

The increase in parliamentary activity following the Glorious Revolution of 1688 is one of the most conspicuous features of the eighteenth-century landscape, and a large proportion of the growing volume of legislation arose from local bills. More recently, historians have also been alerted to the significance of failed legislation which reveals even higher levels of business emanating from the localities.[2] Legislation of both kinds, national and local, attracted an even greater volume of petitions for and against, and the growth of petitioning activity was a crucial element in the development of an increasingly sophisticated political nation outside Westminster.[3] As John Spranger remarked in 1754: 'It is our peculiar felicity to live in an Age, in which the Ears of King and Parliament are open to all the Petitions and Remonstrances of the People, it must therefore be our own Faults, if any one Thing be wanting to compleat the Public Weal.'[4] In order to secure the passage of legislation which would benefit the interests of a specific locality, or to prevent the passage of legislation detrimental to local concerns, the paths of communication between Westminster and the localities were becoming increasingly well-trodden and familiar. In turn, legislation became more business-like and formulaic; the wording of parliamentary activity became increasingly standardised, and the spread of permissive legislation, whether for poor law incorporation, turnpikes or street lighting, rendered the process of acquiring legislation smoother, swifter and more efficient.

Parliament's role, from the perspective of the localities, was primarily an enabling one. Parliament was expected to delegate powers necessary to achieve specific aims within a locally defined area; it was expected to bestow legitimacy and authority upon the exercise of power to groups of individuals chosen by the urban or county communities rather than those appointed by a national execut-ive; it sanctioned the levying of local taxation for locally specific aims. Those in positions of authority and influence in the regions therefore acquired a wider range of powers and responsibilities, and developed a wider sense of group identity through their interaction with each other in activities sanctioned by parliamentary statute and by the possession of specific rights or privileges. This identity could be related to property (for example, the landed interest as discussed by Hoppit in this volume) but was almost always defined in geographical terms, being located in a specific town, county or region. In many ways, therefore, it could be argued that the growth of the domestic side of the fiscal-military state during the eighteenth century tended not only to develop a sense of British national consciousness but also to enhance local and regional identities. Improvements in transport, the growth of a national press and the rise of public opinion outside Westminster facilitated the creation of national networks of communication, but they also simultaneously facilitated and contributed to the formation and articulation of local and regional consciousness.[5] These developments raise important questions concerning the mode in which the British perceived parliament in relation to their own locality, and how the interests of a particular local community were constructed or expressed in relation to a national parliamentary one. From the perspective of parliament, it must also be asked how the petitions and counter petitions seeking legislation articulated (or failed to articulate) local identities in the framework of parliamentary legislation; and whether the wording of petitions suggests the existence of a strong sense of common local interest based upon a geographically specific area in whose interests it was anticipated that the legislation would operate.

Such an enquiry, however, presupposes the existence of urban or other local identities within a culture for which some historians have suggested a growing sense of nationalism to be a dominant trait. The construction of urban identities in eighteenth-century England, once supposed to be a somewhat anaemic and insignificant factor in provincial society, has recently attracted rather more sympathetic treatment.[6] Local issues dominated the political culture of Britain outside Westminster, and could be of crucial significance in determining the outcome of parliamentary elections. Party alignments, even in an era of increasingly nationalised political culture, often owed more to local divisions and differences than to the opposition of Whig and Tory at Westminster.[7] Local identities could draw on many sources: a historical foundation myth, a religious cult, a particular landscape or a common economy. The key to urban identity, throughout the eighteenth century, lay in the possession of particular rights and privileges granted by charter, which distinguished the recipient town from its hinterland and from other potential competitors.[8] Historical or prescriptive possession of these rights reinforced their imaginative power. Although in the new political economy charters of incorporation and the associated restrictive trading practices were rapidly becoming tinged with the negative traits of monopoly, corruption and backwardness, rights and privileges could take other forms, and as a species of property enjoyed the same kind of ideological sanctity as did the possession of broad acres. Even in the non-incorporated towns the structure of the unreformed local government system was a composite of fragmented local rights, privileges and exemptions. If there was indeed a 'national' parliamentary identity, there was behind it a complex range of locally defined identities, including the county, town, civic, corporate and customary.

The petitions to parliament for leave to bring in a bill (and the counter petitions which they often provoked) are of particular interest as representing the interface where a town, or some other local community, represented to parliament local needs, requests or reactions.[9] Less frequently the pamphlets in which proposed changes were discussed and dissected have survived and offer a less formalised insight into the way in which the issues were debated and the representation of the relationship between locality and parliament outside Westminster. What we are left with in the *Common Journals*, where many of these petitions are to be found, is a necessarily abbreviated and compressed view of the parliamentary process. The language of these petitions and the related procedures is highly formulaic and shows little, if any, variation in vocabulary or phrasing from one end of the century to the other. The petitions were expressive of local concerns and interests, but the inflexibility of the wording also locked the local petitioners into a specific rhetorical relationship with the centre and fixed the terms by which the petitioners conceptualised their own role in the wider nation. Petitioners were rarely as disinterested as their language would suggest, and their claims to embody a particular community must be treated with caution. The impression of identities which can be gleaned from petitions is in this sense an artificial one, but although we may be unclear as to precisely *whose* identity is being expressed through these debates, the material is suggestive as to how the localities perceived themselves in relation to a parliament with whom they were being drawn into ever closer contact.

According to the theory of virtual representation parliament assembled in Westminster to embody the nation collectively. MPs were not supposedly directly accountable to their constituents, but represented their interests. Hence propertied interests, despite the uneven geographical distribution of MPs, were, as Langford has shown, well represented in the House of Commons, if one takes into account the patterns of property holding amongst those same MPs. Members of parliament were responsive to a great variety of different pressures and means of persuasion, many of which originated from either their original constituency or from the regions where their own proprietary interests lay. This set up a tension, or rather, encouraged two possible tactics in framing a petition for local improvements. One was to appeal to the 'virtual' notion of parliament as the promoter of the national good and to present the sought after measures as being ultimately conducive to the overall improvement and advantage of the nation. By extension, it would also be necessary to present the petition as emanating from a united community; the outcome of a common understanding of the public good. (The doctrine of virtual representation could be effectively deployed by urban elites for use at the local as well as the national level.) Alternatively, petitions could be framed in terms of the preservation, confirmation or expansion of local rights and privileges; counter petitions could challenge the claims to unanimous consent and the common good, and assert by contrast the prior possession of rights and privileges.[10] If a stronger sense of nationhood was emerging in the eighteenth century, it was simultaneously being exploited by much narrower interest groups in less edifying power struggles. It is not surprising, therefore, to find that in parliamentary petitions, at either end of the eighteenth century, there was a recurrent emphasis on the public benefit or public advantage which the proposed changes would bring. The term 'local' was never one which commanded much credibility in political contexts; it carried with it a heavy baggage of associated meanings of narrowness, limitation and private interest and seemed to be incompatible with the ethos of public spirit and patriotic virtue which was supposed to characterise the ruling class of eighteenth-century Britain.

Petitions for leave to bring in local improvement bills were rather less likely to draw on the language of the national good than were petitions which sought to improve trade and communications (through river navigations, turnpikes, canals) which represented a significant proportion of the local legislation coming before the House of Commons.[11] It was easy enough to present such measures as benefiting the public good: swifter communication lowered costs and encouraged trade, and therefore prosperity. As the petition for the Avon to Froom navigation put it: 'nothing tends more to the promoting the Strength and Wealth of the Kingdom than Trade and Navigation having Communication with Places that tend to Maritime Ports.'[12] The nation's commercial and defensive strength hinged on the quality of her ports and harbours and any place with pretensions to water borne trade could claim to be a nursery for seamen.[13] Scottish ports had to adopt the same strategy of appealing to the language of the national good or public utility for the improvement of their facilities once their interests came also to be represented in Westminster.[14] Similarly, the populousness of a town had important implications for the nation, and after 1801, for the Empire as a whole. A comment upon the size of the town or its population was an indirect way of stating the town's national importance. There was effectively a hierarchy of towns which were likely to appeal to the national interest or the public good; the commercial ports, the dockyards, the manufacturing towns had a much more plausible case to make, and these were generally also the ones with the largest populations. But the language of nation or kingdom was available also at the other extreme to decaying south coast towns where the issue of defence as well as the local economy was involved. A petition from the decayed port of Rye in 1700 concluded: 'That such Course may be taken for restoring the said Harbour to its ancient Goodness, as shall be thought fit; that so considerable a Harbour for the Benefit of the whole Kingdom may not be lost.'[15]

The word 'public' could be adopted by petitioners with even greater flexibility and was deployed with much greater frequency. By the early nineteenth century the trend towards greater standardisation in the wording of petitions and their reporting in the *Commons Journals* means that there is barely a piece of local legislation which does not present itself as being of great 'public utility'. The exact parameters of 'the public' were nicely imprecise, and whilst the term could be interpreted to mean that the scheme would operate to the benefit of the nation at large, the public might also legitimately refer to the public, as in the propertied inhabitants of that particular town or county only (the terms country and county often being used synonymously). Even Paving and Lighting Acts, which were obviously confined in their application, argued almost without exception that the proposed measures would not only further the convenience and comfort of the inhabitants, but 'of those who resort there'. The 1771 Mileways Act for Oxford made the case that 'it would tend to the Benefit and Health of the Inhabitants of the said University, City and all Persons resorting thereto' and that 'it would be of great Advantage to the Public' if the market were to be removed elsewhere. Petitioning against the proposed legislation, the gentlemen, clergy and freeholders of Oxfordshire and Buckinghamshire expressed the rather general fear that their property might be affected, and in a second petition made the more pointed complaint that the proposed tolls, which were to be used for embellishing and ornamenting the town, were an imposition and inconsistent with the laws for repairing the highways. It was, they suggested, a tax upon the land for the 'local improvement' of a rich and opulent town and university, and would present an intolerable grievance to them. Local thus appears here in its pejorative, confined sense, and the county gentlemen appealed, though unsuc-cessfully, to parliament as the upholder of the general laws of the kingdom not to be swayed by the consideration of local and particular interests. Their petition failed, perhaps because the opposition was itself too 'local' in its criticisms. Similarly, when certain citizens of the town of Reading applied for equivalent powers for their town in 1785, the opponents of the plan played down Read-ing's importance: it was 'not a Place of public Resort' and its 'Trade is much confined.' They were undermining the traditional arguments for *public* utility or *national* benefit, by denying Reading's claims to be a town of any national significance. Moreover, these petitioners also presented the promoters of the improvement bill as self-interested 'a few opulent Individuals', who wished to indulge themselves in 'unnecessary luxury', and presented their own side of the argument as the majority view of public meetings.[16]

The yawning gap between private interest and the 'public' good and the strenu-ous efforts which were made to cover this up in securing the necessary parlia-mentary legislation are highlighted in the protracted negotiations surrounding the provision and expansion of modern port facilities in Hull.[17] Hull was the only major port in Britain which had no public quay; instead the business of the port was conducted through the private staithes of the individual merchants. This raised problems not only for those who sought the expansion of port facilities, but also for the government's commissioners of customs, who had no legal quay through which they could regulate the trade coming through Hull. The 'national' interest was further implicated in that the only available land for expansion of the docks was where the garrison had been based; it would therefore be necessary to secure a parliamentary grant of land before dock construction could even begin, not to mention the grant of powers to levy rates in order to pay for the improvements. Thus the government was directly involved in Hull in a way in which it was not in other port towns, and this was reflected in the language of the pamphlets generated in the controversies, as well as the wording of the more formal documents of parliamentary business.

From the 1750s onwards there was recurrent debate, firstly on how to expand the port facilities, and once a new dock was built, the further expansion. The merchants petitioning for legislation in 1774 took care to present their own cause as synonymous with the interests of the whole town. The Hull Dock Act stated that the improvements would be 'beneficial with respect to his Majesty's revenue, useful to navigation, and conducive to the advancement and security of commerce'. Opponents, however, consistently attempted to prove that the merchants (who from 1774 were incorporated as the Dock Company), were simply self-interested monopolists and acting against the public interest of Hull and the nation at large. Petitioners from the nearby town of Beverley opposed the measure, arguing that the intended sufferance quays were 'calculated only for the convenience and private emolument of the some few of the merchants of the said town'; a complaint which was echoed by other groups of merchants from within Hull, who were not included in the membership of the proposed new Dock Company. Fracturing the facade of a united Hull interest created by the merchant propaganda, they declared that they were 'sensible' that the 'same can no ways tend either to promote the Benefit of Trade in general, or the Revenue of his Majesty's Customs in particular within the said Port.'[18] Hence the battle between local interest groups was fought out primarily in the language of the national good and parliament was appealed to as a disinterested body, which would, with the wisdom of Solomon, be able to divine the course of the greatest public benefit.

The struggles in Hull did not end with the formation of the Dock Company. Within ten years of constructing the new dock it became apparent that it was insufficient to cope with the ever expanding volume of shipping. The Dock Company faced pressing demands from other interests in Hull that some of their profits should be invested in the expansion of the docks to relieve the pressure on the already over-crowded harbour. The merchants were reluctant to comply with proposals which might diminish their profits in this way;[19] and in the subsequent quarrels the opposing parties modified the manner in which they presented their cases to the public and to parliament. The critics of the Company refused to allow that the proprietors represented the best interests of Hull and appealed to parliament against them: 'For, considering the opulent circumstances of the Company, and the urgent demands of the public on them, it may reasonably be presumed, that parliament, under the sanction of their authority, will not permit the Company to make such exorbitant gains and repeated accumulations of private property, to the *detriment of trade and navigation of the kingdom.*' The critics of the Company presented the interests of Hull as identical with those of the nation, and sought to bolster their case against the proprietors of the Dock Company by aligning themselves with a national interest, which was given expression in parliamentary legislation: 'The *public good* is the object of all these laws.' The purpose of the act which had established the Dock was not, they argued, the convenience or private profit of individuals, but the good of the public, moreover 'It is a principal implied in all grants, by which the country in general may be affected.' In response, the Dock Company tried to lay claim to the same high ground of public good: 'The public spirit and exertions of the Dock Company, in compliance with the views of the Legislature, for the public good, have been unexampled, and remain unrivalled by any similar undertaking.' They described their dock as 'one of the greatest national improvements of the age'.[20] Private interest was thus attempting to hide behind the cloak of national pride, to obscure the fact that, impressive though the dock undoubtedly was, it was essentially being run as a private monopoly.

This issue of monopoly brought an additional layer of complexity to the debate.[21] For those whose interests were not represented by the Dock Company, the company's refusal to use its revenues to extend the port facilities seemed wilfully short sighted and self interested; the Company was trying to exert a monopoly over the trade through Hull, and was more concerned with increasing the dividends from shares than with increasing the business of the port. The Dock Company, however, appealed to parliament upon an entirely different basis. The original act, they argued, had bestowed upon the Dock Company certain rights and privileges, sanctioned by parliamentary authority: 'the Rights and Interests of the Dock Company, as a Corporate body, given and granted to them by the said Act, which were intended to be permanent, cannot be altered or taken away in the Manner as prayed by the above-mentioned petition, without annulling the Faith of Parliament.' Again we find the same pattern of argument: from the private to the public, from the local to the national. Had the Dock Company not resisted the attack of its critics and had they not 'in the intrepid consciousness of a just cause, disdained to submit the honour and faith of Parliament to menaces' their pusillanimity in the face of such a disgraceful compromise 'would have betrayed the future cause of all public improvements derived from parliamentary sanction.'[22]

The controversy, which was at its peak in the years 1787–89, contained close parallels to the furore over the structural reform of the East India Company only a few years previously.[23] The same questions as to whether parliament had the authority to interfere in rights and privileges which had been granted in a charter were raised. Was the charter protecting rights which belonged to a private body or was it a means of promoting the public good? If the latter, parliament was justified in remodelling it in what it saw to be the public interest. If, however, the charter was a legal instrument ratifying privileges which belonged to that body, parliament could do no such thing. At one point in the debate over Fox's East India Bill it was claimed that 'there would not only be an end of the rights and privileges of the East India Company, but an end of all rights held on the sanction of parliamentary faith, and an end even of the independence of Parliament itself.'[24] Considerable mileage was extracted from the notion that the rights and privileges of the company were being violated, and the East India Company itself appealed to the corporations of England to make common cause in the defence of chartered rights and privileges.

The battle over the expression of local interests or identities in terms of the possession of chartered rights or privileges was highlighted even more obviously in the debate over the extension of the London Docks in the 1790s. The promoters of the new dock company, predictably, used the language of public good to the full, but the proposals encountered widespread opposition, both from within London (from the individual parishes, the ferrymen, the livery companies and others) who feared the consequences of the diversion of trade and business to the new dockland areas, and also from other bodies and groups who held property in the area of the old docks. The common theme running through all the petitions against the bill was parliament's duty to uphold their rights and privileges. The Corporation of London argued that theirs would be 'invaded' 'infringed' and 'violated'; that they would be unable to exercise their responsibility in safeguarding the 'Rights and Welfare' of their Fellow Citizens – and that the trade and commerce of London, which belonged to it by virtue of these chartered rights and privileges would be diverted elsewhere, with ruinous economic consequences. The company of carmen feared that they 'would be deprived of that exclusive Privilege they apprehended to be secured to them when they entered into and embarked their capitals in their Business'. The companies of cordwainers and fishmongers appealed to parliament to 'preserve those Rights and Privileges which the Citizens of London have hitherto enjoyed, and which they have been taught to consider as inviolable.' Even those opposing the bill who were ostensibly unconnected with the corporation of London and the other privileged bodies which stood to lose by the proposals, used the same tactics. The fellows of Balliol College argued that the rights and privileges enjoyed by the citizens of London since time immemorial would be invaded. Faith in parliamentary authority, it was argued would be undermined, if parliament failed to uphold the rights and privileges of the petitioners, or to uphold grants that had been made upon an earlier occasion. Ironically the bill was also opposed on the grounds that it would create exclusive privileges of the very kind which parliament was simultaneously being asked to protect. Whilst pleading for the protection of the privileges of the City of London – in itself a form of monopoly – the Corporation objected that the proposed bill was 'founded on a system of monopoly'.[25]

This emphasis on chartered rights, liberties and the connection with the expression of local identity is worth exploring further. It was in the preamble that petitioners would sketch out some sense of the particular character of the town and its claims on parliamentary attention. One of the most frequent statements concerned the antiquity of the town and its historic importance, its rights, privileges, and customs held from time immemorial. This is a reflection both of the significance of the past in constructing the identity of a town, but also the importance of framing petitions for additional powers, or extension of powers, or relief from other legislation, in terms of history and historical precedent. The appeal to parliament on the basis of a town's historic identity, its traditional position in the nation's commercial framework and its ancient privileges run consistently through the petitions to parliament, up until the 1790s when the reporting of petitions in the pages of the *Commons Journals* becomes considerably condensed. When Chester petitioned for improvements to the navigation of the River Dee, its first appeal was to its status as an 'ancient' sea port which had been allowed to fall into decay; the second was the benefits such improvements would confer upon the town and the public in general. Meanwhile, the town of Bewdley, which opposed schemes for improving the navigation of the Severn from Stourport to Gloucester in 1785, referred to itself as 'an ancient Borough' and stressed the historic credentials of its key position in the trade passing along the Severn to Bristol.[26] The port of Great Grimsby, whose economic role in the region had long since been usurped by Hull, stated in a petition of 1796 that 'Great Grimsby is a very ancient port', and requested parliament to remedy a situation whereby Grimsby's traditional role had been allowed to fall into decay.[27]

This historic identity, expressed in petitions presented to parliament, was a muted and abbreviated version of the rather more strident assertions of local pride and one-up-manship which could be articulated away from the parliamentary arena. From the perspective of the planners and promoters of local improvement – whether of streets, pavements, roads, harbours or canals – parliament existed to offer the means by which a town or a region (or equally a particular commercial or manufacturing interest) could enhance or improve its facilities or more effectively manage its affairs, the better to compete with other towns or other branches of trade. Intra-urban rivalry, and on occasions, quite aggressive competition in both cultural and economic terms rather than slavish emulation of a metropolis, was increasingly apparent amongst the towns of provincial England and the pursuit of statutory authority through parliament offered the means to further that rivalry and competition.[28]

The port of Bristol was subject to numerous proposals intended to improve the provision of facilities for ships using the harbour. Between 1764 and 1812, barely a year passed in which some scheme was not proposed.[29] The debates surrounding the proposals heavily exploited the notion of Bristol's historic identity as a port: the improvements would restore Bristol to a place in the nation's trading and commercial economy which belonged to the city by right.[30] The language of the pamphlets which were published in Bristol as successive schemes were aired reflected the encomiastic descriptions of the city found in the urban histories of the period, a genre in which Bristol outdid any other provincial town in terms of volume. The promoters of a scheme in 1787 claimed that whilst at present Bristol was inferior to Liverpool and Hull, it was capable of being made greatly superior to both in elegance and utility. The improvements would 'restore to the City of Bristol that superiority as a Port which nature seems to have intended.'[31]

The plans for the harbour development which eventually reached the statute books in 1803 were not uncontroversial, and in order to persuade uncommitted opinion the promoters appealed quite explicitly to the civic pride of Bristolians, urging them to act to prevent Bristol from sliding into a place of mediocrity in the nation's commerce. The improvements, it was argued, would rescue Bristol from the disrepute which had long fallen upon it, and 'lowered its estimation among the other commercial towns of England'.[32] Again, the 'natural advantages' of the port were referred to and Bristol's rightful place as second city of the kingdom. Bristolians were exhorted not to let the port 'suffer itself to be surpassed by other towns far inferior to it' and to use the opportunities presented to regain pre-eminence.[33] Claims for Bristol's supposed superiority over the other ports of the kingdom were not appropriate for framing a parliamentary petition for a harbour improvement scheme and such explicit appeals to local sentiment and pride were dropped; what was important was to represent the scheme as being in the interests of the city as a whole. Predictably this was the point contested by the opposition.[34]

Scottish petitioners were ready to use the language of nationhood and empire, but they also shared exactly the same language of historic rights and privileges although the rights which were presented as needing protection had been granted whilst Scotland was a separate kingdom.[35] The language and procedure of the state overrode the historical differences between the two nations. This is seen most clearly in the movement for reform of the Scottish burghs in 1818. The petitions to parliament presented the case for reform in terms of both the 'free constitution of the British Empire' *and* the restoration of lost rights and privileges which had been usurped by other interest groups, even though these were not rights which had been granted by the English crown or ratified by English parliament.[36]

There was some ambiguity about the role of parliament in its relationship to the constituent parts of the nation. Parliament, as the highest court of appeal in the land, existed to uphold the constitution and to protect rights and privileges. As such, it could also be used to uphold a very particularist outlook; it could be seen as the upholder of a corporate view of the nation, which ran directly against a trend towards a centralised and centralising body, seeking to draw the country together into a common national identity. On the one hand parliament was expected to uphold the myriad of local privileges, rights and customs which offered the foundation for a sense of local identity within a composite kingdom, and presented a barrier to the imposition of national policy or state sponsored intervention in local affairs. On the other hand parliament was also a body which could be creative and interventionist and which could sanction activity which might otherwise be controversial. The wording of petitions, particularly those concerning urban improvement and other areas of governance such as the management of poor relief, shows that urban authorities turned to parliament for the confirmation or extension of their own powers. Frequent recourse to parliament did not necessarily entail a curtailment of local liberties and privileges; on the contrary it could consolidate and enlarge them and authorise the structural framework through which they could be further developed.

However, it cannot be assumed that this relationship between centre and locality was wholly in balance. Indeed, as the nineteenth century progressed, parliament's role was tending towards a more pro-active, though still largely responsive stance. Parliamentary inquiries into poor relief, charitable provision, or gaols were providing the raw materials for establishing national benchmarks and more standardised criteria for local government.[37] The inexorable increase in local statutes concomitant upon the rise in population and urban growth had anyway necessitated increasing use of standing orders and clauses acts in areas such as urban improvement or gas lighting bills.[38] Permissive legislation (in areas such as poor relief, turnpikes, lighting and watching) similarly cut down on the need for each town to frame an individual petition to parliament but at the same time diminished the opportunities for the articulation of specific local needs or idiosyncrasies.[39] Some petitions, particularly those pertaining to transport bills, began to frame the proposals with reference to other turnpike trusts or canal companies, presenting the scheme as a means of consolidating and uniting the variety of trusts and companies which had evolved, and paving the way for a more co-ordinated view of local improvement and development.[40] In the early nineteenth century the phrase 'local government', a stranger to the parliamentary language of the eighteenth century, was cropping up in debates with increasing regularity, and had become accepted as an area of parliamentary intervention by the time of the Municipal Reform Act.[41] One could hardly talk of an invasive and centralising state, but opposition could still be provoked, in terms of the invasion of traditional rights and privileges.[42] The implicit assumption in the local response to such legislation, as expressed through petitions to parliament, was that parliament existed to support and uphold those to whom power had been delegated, and who were best placed to judge how that authority should be implemented; it did not direct how it should be exercised. Thus, even with the expansion of parliamentary business, considerable local autonomy and account-ability, along with local rights and privileges (all of which were elements in the construction of local identities) were sustained and enhanced.

Ultimately, the locally specific rights and privileges which have been identified as a defining element between centre and locality were fundamentally challenged in the reform legislation of the 1830s. Even so, we do not find outraged tirades asserting local identities as such. Opposition to reform was framed primarily in party political terms, as both the Great Reform Act and the Municipal Reform Act were primarily party measures, both with respect to their conception and how they were perceived by the wider public.[43] However, when the municipal reform bill was debated in the House of Lords in 1835, there was rather more discussion than there had been in the House of Commons, where it had gone through unexpectedly smoothly; more weight was given to the arguments of those who resisted the proposed changes. There were some who did indeed see the inquiry by the Royal Commission and the resulting bill as a measure of unprecedented parliamentary interference into local affairs, and who argued against a general bill. Sir Robert Inglis suggested that it would be better to ask each borough what reforms they required rather than impose a general measure upon them all: he would have preferred to have conferred powers upon those in authority in the cities and boroughs, leaving it to the majority decision of the inhabitants to say what reforms they themselves required rather than compelling them to accept a general measure suggested by third parties.[44] The most strenuous opposition was expressed in the terms of chartered rights and privileges. In the petitions to the House of Lords from the corporations, few questioned the right of parliament to impose general reforms or to issue directives on watching, lighting, or the constitution of towns councils. Rather, the Municipal Reform Act was depicted an invasion of the traditional rights of the chartered corporations. Objections were framed, again, primarily in terms of the loss of local rights and privileges, which it was parliament's duty to uphold. The mayor and aldermen of Grantham requested that 'the soke of Grantham be not curtailed or interfered with in any way, inasmuch as they have exercised the same for many centuries by grants from the sovereign' whilst the freemen of Oxford urged the need for provisions which would secure to them their electoral privileges and right of property, 'which the Petitioners submit are as much their undeniable Right as any kind of private Property'. Meanwhile the corporation of Colchester pleaded for the preservation of their chartered rights, warning that the loss of such local privileges could only be a prelude to constitutional melt-down and the loss of British liberties generally.[45] Even petitions which were in favour of the proposed reforms expressed their support in terms of *restoring* the rights of election to the inhabitants of the town and a reinvigoration of the forces of local government. The typical phrasing was a request that the House should 'enact such laws as will give the Petitioners the power to elect their own magisterial and local authorities.' The reform was perceived as a restoration of the rights of the inhabitant house-holders of specific towns, rather than as a remodelling of local government by central authorities.

The significance of chartered rights and privileges in providing the structural framework for the conceptualisation of local identity should not be under-estimated. Parliament's role was less that of a body instituted to co-ordinate and impose policy on a national basis, than to ratify and uphold the legal structure of rights and privileges. Identity was defined by the possession of property; an individual's public persona was overwhelmingly determined by virtue of the possession of property, of which rights, such as freemen's privileges or chartered monopolies, were but one variant. [46] Thus, towns constructed their identities upon the rights granted to them in charters of incorporation, and the local identity of freemen was based upon the possession of the privileges which they held.[47] Appeals were not made to parliament on the grounds of some nebulous concept of a locality, but through the much more tangible structures of charters, rights and privileges. Local improvement was essentially carried out by creating a myriad of interest groups – turnpike trustees, canal companies, improvement commissioners, poor law guardians, all of which held specific rights and powers. To undermine those would be to undermine the credibility of parliament as the guardian of law and the constitution. However, in the absence of consensus within a community, where there was a clash of local interests, it was also important to be able to appeal to that function of parliament as the virtual embodiment of the entire nation, and therefore an impartial adjudicator, whose wisdom and equity would discern the course of action best suited to the public good.

The stress on a town's antiquity and it historic status undoubtedly operated on one level as a statement of its importance, locating it in the narrative of British constitutional development, of which parliament was also a part. In most cases it was also a prelude to the assertion of chartered rights or historic privileges which were either endangered, in need of renewal or otherwise requiring some kind of parliamentary affirmation. In such cases parliament was being used to reinforce the very structures through which the expression of localism could be expressed. Although as a body parliament was suspicious of monopoly and restrictive practices, it was also bound to uphold the creed of liberty and property, and as long as rights and privileges of any kind could be construed as a form of property, it was vulnerable to charges of undermining liberties, property and its own parliamentary faith. Hence parliament had a duty to protect local interests; not because of any perceived virtue in local identities *per se*, but because such chartered rights and local liberties were fundamental to the British constitution as it was then understood. Whatever influence Benthamite notions of the greatest good for the greatest number may have had over MPs in the first decades of the nineteenth century, such ideologies had still to compete with strongly entrenched particularist views of rights and interests.

Notes

1 I would like to thank Julian Hoppit and other participants at the Neale Colloquium for comments on this piece, and in particular Robert Colls for perceptive advice.

2 S. Handley, 'Local legislative initiatives for economic and social development in Lancashire, 1689–1731', *Parliamentary History*, ix (1990), 14–37; J. Hoppit, 'Patterns of parliamentary legislation, 1660–1800', *Historical Journal*, xxxix (1996), 109–31; J. Hoppit (ed.), *Failed legislation 1600–1800: extracted from the Commons and Lords Journals* (1997); J. Innes, 'The domestic face of the military-fiscal state: government and society in eighteenth-century Britain' in L. Stone (ed.), *An imperial state at war: Britain from 1689 to 1815* (1994), 96–127 and 'The local acts of a national parliament: parliament's role in sanctioning local action in eighteenth-century England', *Parliamentary History*, xvii (1998), 23–47 and in particular her essay in this volume (chapter 2).

3 Petitioning activity beyond the realm of parliamentary reform has been little studied; a noteworthy exception for the earlier part of the century is P. Gauci, *The politics of trade: the overseas merchant in state and society, 1660–1720* (Oxford, 2001), especially 195–233. I am extremely grateful for being allowed to see sections of this in draft before publication.

4 J. Spranger, *A proposal or a plan . . . for the city and liberty of Westminster* (1754), preface.

5 J. Brewer, *The sinews of power war, money and the English state, 1688–1783* (1989); L. Colley, *Britons: forging the nation, 1707–1837* (New Haven and London, 1992); Innes, 'Domestic face'. On regional consciousness see e.g. J. Barry, 'The press and

the politics of culture in Bristol, 1660–1775' in J. Black and J. Gregory (eds), *Culture, politics and society in Britain, 1660–1800* (Manchester, 1991), 49–81; J. Money, *Experience and identity: Birmingham and the West Midlands, 1760–1800* (Manchester, 1977); H. Barker, 'Catering for provincial tastes: newspapers, readership and profit in late eighteenth-century England', *Historical Research*, lxix (1996), 43–61 and *Newspapers, politics and public opinion in late eighteenth century England* (Oxford, 1998).

6 J. Barry, 'The cultural life of Bristol, 1640–1775' (University of Oxford, D.Phil thesis, 1985), 'Provincial town culture, 1640–1760: urbane or civic?' in J. Pittock and A. Wear (eds), *Interpretation and cultural history* (Basingstoke, 1991), 198–234 and 'Bristol pride: civic identity in Bristol, c. 1640–1775' in M. Dresser and P. Ollerenshaw, *The making of modern Bristol* (Bristol, 1996), 25–47; P. Borsay, 'The London connection: cultural diffusion and the eighteenth-century provincial town', *London Journal*, xix (1994), 21–35; J. Ellis, 'Regional and county centres 1700–1840' in P. Clark (ed.), *The Cambridge urban history of Britain, II: 1540–1840* (Cambridge, 2000), 673–704; Money, *Experience and identity*; S. Poole, 'To be a Bristollian: civic identity and the social order, 1750–1850', in Dresser and Ollerenshaw (eds), *Modern Bristol*, 76–95; R. Sweet, *The writing of urban histories in eighteenth-century England* (Oxford, 1997). For an overview of some of these issues see D. Wahrmann, 'National society, provincial culture: an argument about the recent historiography of eighteenth-century Britain', *Social History*, xvii (1992), 43–72.

7 H. T. Dickinson, *The politics of the people in eighteenth-century Britain* (1994); F. O'Gorman, *Voters, patrons and parties: the unreformed electoral system of Hanoverian England, 1734–1832* (Oxford, 1989) and 'Campaign rituals and ceremonies: the social meaning of elections in England, 1780–1860', *Past and Present*, 135 (May 1992), 79–115; N. Rogers, *Whigs and cities: popular politics in the age of Walpole and Pitt* (Oxford, 1989); K. Wilson, *The sense of the people: politics, culture and imperialism in England, 1715–1785* (Cambridge, 1995).

8 R. Sweet, 'Freemen and independence in English borough politics, c. 1770–1830', *Past and Present*, 161 (Nov. 1998), 84–115.

9 On the volume of local legislation see J. Innes and N. Rogers, 'Politics and government 1700–1840' in Clark (ed.), *Cambridge urban history*, 536–8, 572–3 and Hoppit, 'Patterns of parliamentary legislation'.

10 On the parliamentary procedure see O. C. Williams, *The historical development of private bill procedure in the House of Commons* (1949) and S. Lambert, *Bills and acts: legislative procedure in eighteenth-century England* (Cambridge, 1971).

11 See Innes in this volume (chapter 2) and 'Local acts of a national parliament', 27–8.

12 *CJ*, xiii, 100.

13 P. Langford, 'Property and virtual representation in eighteenth-century England', *Historical Journal*, xxxi (1988), 111.

14 See for example the petition from Glasgow, *CJ*, xxxiii, 421, 498; petitions from Perth, Edinburgh and Fife in 1810 *CJ*, lxv, 16, 41.

15 *CJ*, xiii, 67. See also the petition from Dover *CJ*, xiii, 100, 201: 'the restoring the said Harbour of *Dover* to its former State and Condition, will be of great Service to the Nation, and Benefit to Trade and Navigation.'

16 *CJ*, xxxiii, 199; xl, 585.

17 For the provision of modern port facilities in Hull see G. Jackson, *Hull in the eighteenth century: a study in economic and social history* (Oxford, 1972), 235–61.

18 *CJ*, xxxiv, 471, 604, 653.

19 Jackson, *Hull*; G. Hadley, *History and antiquities of the town and county of the town of Kingston upon Hull* (Hull, 1788).

20 Hadley, *Hull*, 590–2, 603.

21 As Gauci shows, parliament was already regarded at the national arbiter on commerce and was being used to attack company charters granted under royal authority by the late seventeenth century (*Politics of trade*, 218).

22 *CJ*, xlii, 537; Hadley, *Hull*, 605.

23 Cobbett, *Parliamentary History*, xxiii, cols. 1225–1434. See in particular the petitions presented by Sir Henry Fletcher, cols. 1247 and 1249.

24 Cobbett, *Parliamentary History*, xxiii, col. 1287.

25 *CJ*, li, 431, 439, 483, 486.

26 *CJ*, xxxiii, 419; lx, 759.

27 *CJ*, li, 365.

28 J. Ellis, '"For the honour of the town": comparison, competition and civic identity in eighteenth-century England', paper given at University of Leicester, November 1999; see also Sweet, *Writing urban histories*, 236–41.

29 A. F. Williams, 'Bristol port plans and improvement schemes of the eighteenth century', *Transactions of the Bristol and Gloucestershire Archaeological Society*, lxxxi (1962), 138–88.

30 The assumption that a town or city's geographical location somehow endowed it with inalienable commercial privileges, which should be defended by the legislature in the same way that chartered rights were, was not confined to Bristol. The university and the city of Oxford used similar arguments in 1785, arguing that proposals for a canal between Lechlade and Abingdon would deprive them of the benefits of the navigation of the Isis 'which their natural Situation entitles them to, and which they have enjoyed for many years.' *CJ*, lx, 825.

31 Barry, 'Cultural life of Bristol'; Sweet, *Writing urban histories*, 76–8; W. Barrett, *The history and antiquities of Bristol* (Bristol, 1789), 164–90 on the trade of Bristol.

32 The use of 'England' here rather than 'Britain' is significant in this context, reflecting Bristol's traditional importance as a port in English history prior to union with Scotland.

33 'An answer to the objections raised by "citizen" against the embankment of the river Avon, within the port of Bristol' quoted in Williams, 'Bristol port plans', 158–9.

34 *CJ*, lxiii, 393: the proposals, 'if carried into effect, will be beneficial to Individuals only, and not to the Public at large'.

35 Although, as Harris shows later in this volume, the General Assembly and the Convention of Royal Burghs could be used as an alternative to parliament in Scotland, there was nevertheless a significant volume of petitions relating to measures of local improvement from Scottish towns. See Innes in this volume and 'Politics and government', 536 and 'Local acts of a national parliament', 27–8.

36 *CJ*, lxxiii, 61, 109, 122, 237, 408, 414, 418.

37 D. Eastwood, *Governing rural England: tradition and transformation in local government, 1780–1840* (Oxford, 1994); *Government and community in the English provinces, 1700–1870* (Basingstoke, 1997).

38 By this time the recording of petitions for this type of legislation in the *Commons Journals* had become considerably abbreviated and formulaic in comparison with the earlier part of the eighteenth century. This greater brevity renders attempts to draw conclusions concerning changes over time perilous.

39 Innes, 'Local acts of a national parliament', 29; J. Prest, *Liberty and locality: parliament, permissive legislation and ratepayers' democracies in the mid-nineteenth century* (Oxford, 1990), 208–20. Innes, 'Local acts of a national parliament', 45, comments on the difficulties MPs faced in bringing in general measures.

40 For example, the petition in 1810 from trustees from several different acts in West Riding and Lancashire: 'it would be of public utility if the Acts relating to both the said Roads were repealed, and the powers thereof consolidated in one Act, and under one Trust' *CJ*, lxv, 49.

41 The phrase is slow to appear and municipal government was often used in preference to local government: e.g. R. P. Cruden, *Observations upon municipal bodies in cities and towns incorporated by royal charters* (1826). The report of the Royal Commissioners for Municipal Reform, the subsequent parliamentary debates and accompanying media discussion mark a turning point in the shift from viewing local government in particularist terms to conceptualising it as a part of a national system: *Hansard*, 3rd series, xxviii, cols. 831–2; xix, col. 668; *Report of the Royal Commission on municipal corporations* (PP 1835, XXIII), 5–49; H. A. Merewether and A. J. Stephens, *The history of the boroughs and municipal corporations of the United Kingdom, from the earliest to the present time*, 3 vols (1835).

42 Directives from the centre, such as Pitt's notorious bill for the reform of the Poor Laws in 1796, could be expected to provoke a response framed in terms of local interests, local identities, and local rights. The petition from Carmarthen drew a contrast between the needs of opulent manufacturing towns and its own needs (as a small market town). In similar vein, the corporation of Lincoln petitioned against the bill claiming that the current local act was better adapted to the circumstances of the parish, and was more effective than the proposed changes. *Pace* Carmarthen's objections, a number of London parishes also petitioned against it, but on the grounds that the regulations were 'framed chiefly for the Relief of Labourers in Husbandry, and not calculated or suitable for the Poor of a large, commercial and manufacturing City possessed of peculiar Privileges': *CJ*, lii, 346, 376–7.

43 On the political context to the Municipal Reform Act see G. B. A. M. Finlayson, 'The politics of municipal reform in 1835', *English Historical Review*, lxxxi (1966), 673–92 and 'The Municipal Corporation Commission and report, 1833–35', *Bulletin of the Institute of Historical Research*, xxxvi (1963), 36–52.

44 *Hansard*, 3rd series, xxvii (1835), col. 753.

45 *CJ*, lxxxviii, 413; *LJ*, lxvii, 549, 319. See also *LJ*, lxvii, 313–77 and 550–4.

46 P. Langford, *Public life and the propertied Englishman, 1689–1797* (Oxford, 1991).

47 Sweet, *Writing urban histories*, 264–73 and 'Freemen and independence'.

4

Church, parliament and national identity, c. 1770–c. 1830[1]

G. M. Ditchfield

There can be no doubt of the central nature of parliament in debates as to the religious nature of English, and increasingly of British, national identity between 1770 and 1830. The supremacy of statute law carried almost universal acceptance and attempts to influence parliamentary opinion dominated the efforts of those who sought to promote or resist ecclesiastical change. The belief that legislation could influence theological opinion was widespread. When advocating the Unitarian petition of 1792 John Disney alleged that 'The people of this country would not, at this time of day, hold the belief in ONE GOD, the sole creator and governor of the world, to be a wicked or heretical opinion, if an act of parliament had not called it "blasphemy and profaneness"'.[2] Appeals to legislation as a means to secure the reformation of morals and manners frequently invoked an idealised sense of historic national identity to suggest that there was something recent and un-English about vice. 'It was not till *Britain* became one of the most degenerate, that she ceased to be the happiest of nations', complained George Davis, as he championed the national Fast in February 1758 with the words 'Now the Evils with which we are threatened, are no less than the loss of Every thing that is dear and valuable to us . . . as Men, as *Britons*, as Christians, or as Protestants.'[3] That legislation could cause or repair an imagined deterioration in the national character was frequently asserted. Lord Auckland when promoting the Adultery Bill of 1800 believed that it would counteract the tendency whereby 'it had long been the object of the French writers, [and] it is at this day the object of the German Theatre, to give fascinating portraits of adultery, to corrupt the institution of marriage'.[4]

The purpose of this paper is to examine the ways in which notions of national identity were used in applications to, and debates within, parliament on religious matters. It was in such applications and debates, affecting the privileges of the Church of England, relations with foreign Protestants and the legal position of non-Anglicans in the British Isles, that these issues were raised in what was often their most elaborate and sophisticated form. Religious pressure groups sought to identify their own aspirations with a supposed national character and history, and to claim consistency with both. Even when claims and counter-claims did not explicitly evoke images of national identity, they carried implications of relative advantage and disadvantage which concerned national and state interests. Traditional arguments all carried this implication. It applied in general terms, as with the balance between authority and liberty, between individual and institutional rights, and in more specific terms, as with allegations that Catholics could not be regarded as loyal citizens and that the property of the national Church was endangered.[5] The very expression 'national interest' bore implications as to the qualities which were supposedly 'English' or 'British'.

This essay suggests that images of national identity to which appeal was made in religious debates during this period fall into one or more of three broad categories. These categories may be defined as the Protestant image, the Anglican image and the pluralist, or libertarian, image. That the three categories could, and did, overlap indicates the highly contested nature of the religious dimensions of national identity, as well as the porous character of the categories themselves. Partly because of the intensity of that contest, it will be suggested that none of these images alone presents an adequate reflection of the religious terms in which national identity was invoked in the parliamentary sphere.

The notion of a Protestant identity is based primarily upon the enduring strength of British anti-Catholicism. Linda Colley has stressed the influence of Protestantism, together with success in wars of imperial expansion, as decisive in the exertion of a unifying influence on English, Welsh and Scottish people, making it increasingly possible for them to define themselves as 'Britons', as distinct from 'The other', which meant, above all, French Catholicism. As Linda Colley puts it, Protestantism 'gave the majority of men and women a sense of their place in history and a sense of worth'. It was associated with liberty and prosperity, in sharp contrast to the superstition and deprivation of Catholic Europe and, significantly, it involved a veneration of parliament, as part of the 'Protestant inheritance'. Similarly, Gerald Newman contended that the key feature of English national identity in the eighteenth century was a Francophobia which involved a Hogarthian demonisation of all things French, as well as of such members of the aristocracy who adopted foreign fashions.[6]

There is no shortage of evidence as to the breadth and vehemence of anti-Catholicism in this period. The defensive perception of Protestantism as the antithesis of, and shield against, Catholicism could be cited both by Anglican and Dissenter. When attacking the Catholic petition to parliament of 1810, Isaac Huntingford, Bishop of Gloucester, wrote 'In the British Empire particularly, the firm establishment of Protestant Religion is essential to the existence of a Protestant Government.'[7] Anglican and Dissenter could both argue that the English Protestant identity was the epitome of toleration: Anglicans when defending the existing system, Dissenters when advocating its reform. Dissenters frequently claimed that legislation which excluded them from office, and particularly the Test Act of 1673, was designed primarily against Catholics. In 1790, William Bristow, urging the repeal of the sacramental test, put the matter clearly:

The oaths of allegiance, and renunciation of the absurdities and intolerance of the Roman Catholic religion, seem sufficient sureties for any description of Protestants, employed in public offices; all further exclusions are in their nature impolitic, and inconsistent with the spirit of the law of this country.[8]

Samuel Heywood, too, accepted the principle of Protestant exclusivity: the sacramental test could be removed 'without the smallest risque to the established church from the admission of Papists; for these might be excluded as effectually as they ever have been, by the test still to remain'.[9] After 1789, moreover, there developed a Francophobic continuum in which anti-Catholicism was supplemented by anti-Jacobinism. When Sir William Scott successfully opposed James Adair's Quaker Relief Bill on 24 February 1797 by comparing its implications with the French attack on ecclesiastical rights of property, he was simply extending a traditional Protestant horror at the French example.[10] On the death of George III in 1820, the vehemently anti-Catholic Joseph Mendham of Sutton Coldfield eulogised the late king as a Protestant, rather than a specifically Anglican, monarch, while the London Independent minister Andrew Reed likewise praised him for a benign reign which had witnessed a considerable extension of Dissenting civil liberties – and for not being a Catholic Stuart.[11]

Yet anti-Catholicism, however passionate, fell far short of a positive Protestant consensus.[12] At least four problems arise from any assumption of such a consensus. In the first place, there were very different, and conflicting, motives for seeking to exploit anti-Catholicism for political purposes. Those who wished to persuade parliament to preserve an Anglican hegemony called upon Dissenters to show unity in the face of internal and external Catholic threats. This amounted to an appeal to an overriding 'national' security against Catholic 'internationalism'. 'Would to God we could be united against such an insidious and powerful adversary as Rome is!', wrote an Anglican pamphleteer when opposing the repeal of the Test and Corporation Acts in 1790.[13] The Catholic petition of 1810 inspired Huntingford to be even more emphatic:

All Protestants should unite in support of Reformed Religion. If the spiritual light, which illumines this Empire, be indeed so threatened with a return of mental darkness, from the Catholics of England, from the Catholics of Ireland, from much the greater part of Europe... Protestants... resigning to a higher concern the subordinate consideration of sect or party, should make it a Common Cause to labour for the ascendancy of Protestant Christianity.[14]

In 1825, Bishop Blomfield of Chester made a similar appeal in the House of Lords when introducing a petition from Dissenters against the Catholic Relief Bill.[15]

A Protestant identity, however, could also be claimed by Dissenters whose objective was to undermine, rather than to preserve, the Anglican constitution and its theoretical monopoly of public office. With distant echoes of earlier schemes for 'comprehension', Dissenting writers built on fundamental Reformation principles. Joseph Smith, minister of Renshaw Street Chapel, Liverpool, was expressing a common opinion in 1790 when he claimed 'We believe the bible to contain the religion of Protestants, and the right of private judgment, which justified a separation from the Romish Church, is the foundation of our Dissent from the establishment of this kingdom.'[16] The strong sense of anti-Catholicism, in its anti-Papal sense, even encouraged elements of the Catholic elite to pay an indirect tribute to a sense of Protestant identity by devising the expression 'Protesting Catholic Dissenters' to promote their claims for toleration in the late 1780s.[17] There was still an echo of this invocation of a sense of national, rather than universal, identity in the petition to parliament of the English Catholics on 4 March 1819; they described themselves as 'British Roman Catholics'.[18]

A second problem concerns the status of foreign Protestants who were or who became subjects of the King of Great Britain. There was no national consensus as to the identity of 'the other'. Resentment at William III's favours to his Dutch adherents led directly to that ungenerous post-1714 treatment of Hanoverians which illustrates the difficulties of perceiving a broader sense of Protestantism within the King's domains. Hanover was not only a Protestant entity but the source of the only available Protestant dynasty. Yet parliament, by the Act of Settlement (1701), effectively defined Hanoverians as foreigners, excluding them (even if naturalised) from the Privy Council, from membership of either House of Parliament, from civil and military offices and from receiving grants of land from the crown. These provisions remained largely unrepealed during the Hanoverian period.[19] The Hanoverian monarchs were expressly required to conform to the Anglican, and not the German Lutheran, definition of the Protestant religion. British subjects were not admitted to the Hanoverian service. The parliamentary designation, and the public perception, of Hanoverians as foreigners hardly sustains an impression of a broader Protestantism among the non-English subjects of George III.

The same is true of other foreign Protestants in the service, or inhabiting the domains, of the King of Great Britain. Even at the height of the Seven Years' War there was strong parliamentary opposition to the granting to them of military commissions. In February 1756, Pitt the Elder denounced the Newcastle ministry's bill to allow foreign Protestants to serve in America as a 'poison to the constitution'. In the Lords the following month Talbot and Temple signed a protest to the effect that such a proposal would 'excite and spread a deep and universal disgust and apprehension in the minds of his majesty's most loyal and deserving American subjects'. Far from regarding foreign Protestants as symbols of libertarianism, they feared 'the entire overthrow of the present Constitution, and . . . the subversion of the liberties of *Great Britain*'.[20] Other measures which granted such commissions did so under jealous regulation; the Acts of 1798 and 1799, even when manpower was desperately needed, were carefully restricted to service in America.[21] Moravians – for all their ancient episcopal orders – were also specifically defined by parliament as a foreign church. The Act of 1749 which legitimised their missions in the British North American colonies was a complete negation of all Count Zinzendorf's aspirations for a close co-operation, amounting almost to union, with the Church of England.[22] John Wesley and other Methodists were not paying a compliment when they referred to Moravians as 'the Germans'.[23]

Thirdly, the legal status of the Church of Scotland presents further difficulties with regard to any notion of a shared Protestant identity. A Dissenting affinity, and in many cases a shared educational background, with Scottish Presbyterianism on the one hand was matched by a High Church sympathy with the Scottish Episcopalians on the other.[24] When English Dissenters made common cause with the Scottish Presbyterian Church over the repeal of the Test Act in 1790–1, they referred to a Scottish national identity as opposed not to 'Popery' but to an oppressive Anglican hegemony. 'The test act is equally injurious to the Scottish nation', claimed a Dissenting meeting at Nottingham in 1790.[25] That sense of a separate Scottish Protestant, rather than a united British, non-Anglican identity is hardly surprising. The Kirk was, after all, an established church. In the campaign of 1790–1 to repeal the Test Act as it affected Scotland, the 'Memorial' of the General Assembly to parliament referred in vigorous terms to national identity, denouncing the infringements of 'The Rights and Dignities of a High Spirited People'. It clearly identified the people of Scotland with the Presbyterian Church and described the General Assembly as 'the National Assembly of the Church of Scotland',[26] at the very time when a National Assembly in France was causing alarm in Britain, and when the death of the Young Pretender (1788) had made possible a Toleration Bill for their historic Episcopalian enemies.

Sir Gilbert Elliot, moving the motion for repeal in the House of Commons on 10 May 1791, argued that Scotland had 'a right, both by treaty and by law, to enjoy her civil and religious privileges in equal participation with the subjects of England'. Scotland, with a separate church establishment, was asserting its rights within the union. William Pulteney declared 'It came . . . to this short proposition; that 'The church of Scotland and the church of England, being equally established by law, and both being equally the national religion, whether, under these circumstances, the members of both churches had not an equal right to the participation of every privilege and advantage?' But this was an appeal to a parallel, not to a common, Protestantism. There was a markedly defensive note in Sir Adam Fergusson's claim that 'There certainly were settled by the treaty of union two distinct churches for Scotland and England; but he did not believe that any man would say there were two different religions established in Great Britain.'[27] But while the 'Memorial' referred to the 'Sister Churches' as in agreement 'in all the great and fundamental principles of Christianity' and as 'parts of One Empire', it also proclaimed diversity by drawing attention to differences over the sacrament.[28] There was a potential ambiguity between the assertion of the identity of a proud-spirited people as against England, and the demand for better terms within the Union, and empire, on the basis of a shared Protestantism. When Fox spoke in favour of the Catholic Petition on 13 May 1805 he drew the opposite conclusion; making a virtue of diversity rather than a shared Anglo-Scottish Protestantism, he declared of the Kirk 'Surely the presbyterian doctrine and discipline of it are at least as repugnant to the established religion of this country as the opinions of the Roman catholics are.'[29] Henry Brougham drew upon his own Scottish experience in 1828 when he told the Commons 'that not one Presbyterian in a thousand would, on any terms, take the Sacrament of the Church of England'.[30] These were only slight exaggerations. Opponents of repeal of the Test Act for Scotland depicted Scottish Presbyterianism as Dissent, claimed that repeal would stimulate English Dissenting attacks upon the Church and denied its parallel status with the Church of England. Richard Pepper Arden claimed that the Act of Union rendered the Test Act 'irrepealable'.[31] The role of the Act of Union as an argument in defence of the Test Act went further; its repeal was held to carry dangerous implications for the break-up of the British state, while advocates of repeal were accused of sedition.[32] This argument was of sufficient power in parliament to prevail until 1828.

Fourthly, there were serious disputes as to the full and precise meaning of the Protestant image of national identity. The decline of parliamentary anti-Catholicism and the gradual process whereby Catholics yielded to radical Dissenters as the principal enemy was bound to have profound consequences for any Protestant sense of common identity.[33] By this time Unitarians in particular constituted an internal version of 'the other'. The intense debates over the Trinity went to the very centre of Christian belief and amounted to something far more serious and fundamental than 'subtle divisions' within a non-existent single 'Protestant community'.[34] Some Dissenters, many Anglicans and most Catholics feared the spread of Unitarian influence and refused to regard Unitarians as Christians at all. Some Unitarians felt a sense of abandonment when the defeat of Lord Sidmouth's bill and the repeal of the Five Mile and Conventicle Acts (1812) did not give them immediate relief. Catholics, moreover, were not the 'other' perceived by those, notably Lord Sidmouth, who sought to place parliamentary curbs on popular, unlettered, and possibly subversive, evangelical preaching during the first decade of the nineteenth century.

Some Protestants, moreover, saw 'Popery' as residing principally in the Church of England. As John Disney put it, 'Penal laws in matters of religion in protestant countries are like the rack and the wheel in popish ones; they are only different names for the same thing.' Dissenters incurred criticism for complaining about 'the *imaginary* Popery of our church; which most foreign Protestants have ever looked up to, as their firmest bulwark against Rome'[35]. The strongly anti-Unitarian William Cobbett went further: 'England was great and free when our fathers were Catholics.' He alleged that Methodist preachers 'join most cordially with the Clergy of the establishment in expressing an abhorrence of popish principles, though the principles of the former are worse than the worst part of those taught by the rankest of papists'.[36] The Dissenting perception of an 'Anglican' popery was deepened by the High Church revival and even more so by the Oxford Movement; no longer could the established church be regarded as a firm 'bulwark against Rome'.

The parliamentary debates of 1828–29 show how great were the differences between the ways in which the Protestant identity could be interpreted. On

19 February 1829 William Smith MP urged the Commons to grant Catholic Emancipation without 'securities' by evoking a tolerant, broadly inclusive, image of Protestantism; he 'would not . . . suffer any gentlemen to assume to themselves the exclusive name of the Protestants, because they would confine the Roman Catholics within limits in which, he thought, no sect of religionists ought to be confined'. Eleven days later, Colonel Sibthorp had words of praise for anti-emancipation opinion: 'All these petitions came from persons of real John Bull feeling; and, as an agriculturalist, he would say, that their desire was to have the real British breed, and no cross one from the Popish.'[37]

The notion of a common Protestant sense of identity, especially after the mid-eighteenth century, is something of a myth. That identity may be categorised either as an ideal, prescriptive vision or as a tactical weapon, caricaturing some sort of external or internal enemy, but not always the same enemy. The problems of maintaining that identity are seen in the difficulty of co-operation between Anglicans and Dissenters over anti-Catholic campaigns in the 1840s. As the *Church of England Quarterly Review* observed in 1844, 'It is quite impossible for Churchmen to unite with Dissenters in a Reformation Society.'[38] It was a judgment accurate in retrospect as well as at the height of the agitation over the Corn Laws and the church rates. It reflected more than half a century of conflict, which included the subscription debates of the 1770s, the Test Act controversies and the increasing propensity of Dissenters to vote for opposition candidates in parliamentary elections.[39]

A more plausible interpretation of national identity in religious terms may be claimed for an Anglican image. It was always likely to be of some effect in a House of Commons which was largely, and an upper chamber which was almost exclusively, composed of members of the established church. The assumption that the Church of England was coterminous with society as a whole, and that membership of, and loyalty to, the Church amounted to a fundamental duty of citizenship, was widely held. As the High Churchman George Horne put it in 1760, 'The churchman is the true patriot.'[40] Spencer Madan expressed the same view more bluntly, and more defensively, thirty years later:

> It is evident that this national church cannot subsist in security, or discharge its engagements in the contract formed between church and state for their mutual support and prosperity, if the state should equally encourage and promote *other* systems of religion essentially repugnant to the tenets of that national church.[41]

Hence to Anglican writers any parliamentary attack on the property of the church, such as the tithe system, had to be resisted. In February 1828 Sir Robert Inglis, opposing the repeal of the Test and Corporation Acts, allowed Dissenters 'the fullest rights of conscience' but insisted that 'it is perfectly clear, that the principles of Dissenters conscientiously opposed to the Church, can never give the same undivided allegiance to the constitution in church and state which a churchman does'.[42] The expressions 'schism' and 'schismatic' still carried subversive overtones.

The Anglican image, moreover, began to be more explicitly identified with monarchy from the 1770s. 'It is further to be considered that the Presbyterian principles are unquestionably republican', complained Spencer Madan, while George Croft, chaplain to the Earl of Elgin, described Dissent as the 'enemy to the English constitution'.[43] The assertion of an Anglican national identity involved a vilification of the 'other' just as much as did the assertion of a common Protestantism. A meeting of clergy and their sympathisers at Bolton-le-Moors on 18 February 1790 defended the Test and Corporation Acts in terms which are notable for their omission of any reference to papists:

> A repeal of these acts would certainly open a door for men of all descriptions inimical to the Christian religion – Jews, Turks, Infidels, Hereticks, to come into places of power and profit, in the disposal of the magistrate, and consequently endanger our establishment.[44]

Parliamentary defences of Anglicanism constantly appealed to Englishness, English liberties and national stability. An Anglican writer in 1790 denounced Dissenting pressure groups as 'Committees of Correspondence' and 'a measure of *American* complexion'.[45] The Anglican *via media*, was represented as national equipoise, 'national tranquillity', 'the public tranquillity'.[46] The resultant damage from the removal of the legislative bulwarks of the Church would not be confined to Anglicans: it would be 'fatal to the interests of the Protestant religion, at least in this kingdom'.[47] The Anglican image was frequently equated with English liberty. 'The moderation of the Church of England was her boast and her chief pride', declared Shute Barrington, Bishop of Salisbury, in the Regency debate of 17 February 1789.[48]

Some of the strongest testimony to the enduring power of the Anglican image of national identity is evident in the implicit and sometimes explicit recognition of it which may be found in the rhetoric of its critics. Dissenters argued with monotonous regularity that repeal of the Test and Corporation Acts would not harm the interests of the Church. There was a defensive nervousness, a sense of urgent tactical necessity, in the pleading of a Dissenting pamphleteer in 1790:

> And we think the HONOUR of the CHURCH (which we regard as one of the most natural and effectual SECURITIES) would be essentially maintained by the removal of a TEST, which many of her ablest and best members have considered as a shocking PERVERSION of an ordinance of religion.[49]

Fox in March 1790, and Lord Holland when expressing reservations about the New Churches Bill in 1818, also recognised the identification, at least in nominal terms, of Anglicanism with the majority of the English people.[50] In 1813 the Unitarian minister Thomas Belsham urged the Church's supporters in parliament to 'give the nonconformists, both catholic and protestant, all they ask ... Then you may bid defiance to every attempt to shake the established church ... by division you will reign secure.'[51] William Plunket, moving the Catholic petition of 17 April 1823, strenuously denied a necessary connection between Catholic

Emancipation and repeal of the Test and Corporation Acts. Robert Fergusson, supporting that repeal five years later, used his membership of an established church in Scotland to assert that 'His opinion was favourable to a national church' and to deny that repeal would harm the Church of England.[52]

Yet problems remain with the Anglican definition of national identity. William Gibson effectively delineates three unifying roles for Anglicanism: the survival of the idea of the state and government as a national construct, a shared cultural experience through the Bible and the Book of Common Prayer, and the Church's role in the realm of philanthropy.[53] However, a high proportion of Dr Gibson's evidence is drawn from the early and middle years of the eighteenth century, rather than from the later, post-Jacobite and more aggressively sectarian, period. Bishop Hoadly's appeal to a common Protestantism in 1710,[54] based on a benign establishment and toleration for Protestant non-Anglicans, could be effective Whig propaganda at a time of war with Catholic France and the immediate prospect of a Stuart restoration, but such appeals carried far less conviction after 1770. The eirenical image of Anglicanism was more convincing when the public profile of Dissent was represented by Isaac Watts and Philip Doddridge than when the image of Dissent constantly invoked in parliament was that of Richard Price and Joseph Priestley.

Anglicanism proclaimed a form of theological, as well as ethnic or territorial, identity. But the range of doctrinal opinion within the Church of England renders the term insufficiently precise to be an effective index of national identity. There remained an influential and articulate Latitudinarian element, which countenanced, even when it did not fully embrace, heterodoxy, and which retained a strong suspicion of 'priestcraft'. The academic re-discovery of Anglican high churchmanship reveals that any sense of uniformity spread by the Prayer Book was not matched by uniformity of liturgical and ceremonial practice, or of sermons preached or published.[55] It is noteworthy that two recent studies of later eighteenth-century Church thought and practice have emphasised 'variations'.[56] Moreover it has been suggested that the religious dimensions of philanthropy began to carry more sharply denominational implications, especially after about 1800.[57] The renewed stress upon the Trinity divided Anglicans themselves. In many parts of the country, there were local contrasts between heterodox and high church clergy. It became increasingly necessary for the orthodox to appeal to nationality to buttress Trinitarianism. 'Now the Doctrine of the trinity, we know, is a most sacred and fundamental article of the national creed', insisted Spencer Madan in 1790.[58] Even Cobbett appeared to concede that this was so when he berated William Smith for the very limited nature of the Trinity Bill of 1813. Attacks on Christianity would still be illegal because, said Smith, 'Christianity is the *religion of the country*'; yet, replied Cobbett, 'For this characteristic to have any weight . . . the Christianity here spoken of must be the Christianity of the Church. That is the religion *of the country*, and the Unitarian doctrine is a direct attack upon that religion.'[59] Lord Calthorpe, helping to secure the defeat of the Unitarian Marriages Relief Bill on 2 April 1824, spoke of Unitarian doctrines as 'at variance with what the English church considered as constituting the very essence of Christianity'.[60] As long as the Church of England made Trinitarianism 'the very essence of christianity', it provoked divisiveness by invoking a perceived (and allegedly un-English) enemy. It was for this reason that the Catholic polemicist John Milner was able to exploit the growth of Socinianism and the enduring legacy of 'Hoadlyism', conveyed through Francis Blackburne and others, as a sign not of Protestant unity but of Anglican disunity.[61] As Sir George Savile pointed out in the debate (6 February 1772) on the Feathers Tavern Petition, the Church was vulnerable to the argument that it could not consistently justify its secession from Rome and at the same time censure as un-English and heretical those who had seceded from and remained, outside its own ranks.[62]

The 'relative unity' of the Church of England[63] was only preserved by a practical and sensible acceptance of diversity, notably at parish level. There were very few prosecutions for heresy, and, before 1830, relatively few clerical secessions; even so determined and heterodox a critic as John Jebb expressed an acceptance of the principle of a national church.[64] As one of those seceders, John Disney put it:

> An outward profession of faith in the church of England will, and oftentimes does, conceal and cover a great discordance of opinion; and, like other established churches, is doubtless the sanctuary and retreat of much infidelity. How little agreed have been some of the most distinguished advocates of its particular constitution and doctrines?[65]

Nor were the key ministries of the period, notably that of the Younger Pitt (1783–1801), intent on the preservation, let alone the extension, of an Anglican agenda.[66] There was neither a High Church nor a Latitudinarian consensus; the notion of the Thirty-nine Articles as 'Articles of peace' allowed numerous different interpretations of them to be aired. The Calvinist and anti-Calvinist debate over the predestinarian implications of Article 17, for instance, was of lengthy duration. So was the debate over Evangelicalism within the Church.[67] What requires explanation is not an Anglican unanimity which did not exist, but the success with which the Church used parliamentary and other means to preserve its own structural unity in the light of these theological and devotional differences. As Dr Young puts it, England's 'national church harboured variations, both catholic and proto-unitarian, which led its members to identify with things and places other than and beyond England'.[68]

The rising numbers of Dissenters, moreover, made an Anglican correlation with English, let alone British, identity far more difficult to justify. Following the death of John Wesley, Methodists gradually became associated with Dissent and over Sidmouth's bill in 1810–11 they co-operated effectively with the older Dissent for the first time. There was a large difference between assertions of Anglican identity in 1770 and in 1830. During that period those assertions acquired an increasing sense of anxiety.[69] 'An establishment with a toleration is the only conceivable mode of supporting something of true religion in the present degenerate state of nature', was the somewhat nervous plea of an Anglican writer in 1790.[70] There was also something rather desperate about the sermon of William Carey, sub-almoner to George III, before the Commons in 1809, when he insisted that 'There are some points in which as a Christian nation, we must be all agreed . . . we humbly hope, that we have in some degree at least profited by the spirit of Christianity, and that it is not totally extinguished and lost among us.'[71] When opposing the Reform Bill in the Commons on 13 July 1831, J. E. Gordon was under no illusions as to the dangers to the Church which would follow from even a modest enfranchisement: 'It is a generally acknowledged fact, that about one half of the gross population of England are dissenters from the national Establishment; and it follows, that at least 200,000 of the newly created voters will be of this description.'[72]

The third type of image of national identity was that of pluralism and libertarianism. Its main characteristic was a historically sited, self-congratulatory assertion of traditional English, occasionally British, liberties. The Unitarian minister Charles Wellbeloved of York based his sympathy for Catholic relief upon what was becoming an increasingly familiar distinction between English Catholics, imbued with English traditions, and 'Popery', which was foreign and professed by 'persons who have not by their intercourse with Englishmen, and by habits acquired in a land of freedom, lost as our Catholic countrymen have, much of what is offensive, and all that is politically alarming in the doctrines of the Romish Church'.[73]

Those seeking changes to the religious constitution frequently claimed that such changes were consistent with a historically evolving development of British liberty. 'Our reverence of Britain, her government and laws is only in subordination to our reverence of God and of human nature', proclaimed a Dissenting meeting at Nottingham in 1790. This image of national identity owed something to earlier eighteenth-century ideas of patriotism as essentially constitutionalist and libertarian; hence it attracted opposition Whigs and Dissenters, who were beginning to rediscover their 'country' roots under George III. Fox on the Unitarian Petition in 1792 declared: 'The people of this country were neither indifferent about religion, nor were they blindly attached to any particular faith; they were not pagans, nor popish bigots. For us there was no excuse for persecution.'[74] To Joseph Smith of Liverpool this libertarian mentality was closely linked to active citizenship: 'An Englishman cannot be reduced to a more unhappy condition, than to be put by law under an incapacity of serving his Prince and Country, and therefore nothing but a crime of the most detestable nature ought to put him under such a disability.'[75] The Memorial of the Church of Scotland in 1790 invoked this image when it referred approvingly to the defeat in the Scottish parliament of a proposal for an equivalent to the English Corporation Act.[76] So did Bishop Horsley in 1800 when he spoke of his country's 'natural proneness to toleration'.[77] The 'repeal committee' of the Dissenting Deputies urged in 1827 that 'those rights of conscience secure from the ensnaring interference of human authority' which they sought, were 'founded on the divine law natural and revealed and congenial . . . to the spirit of the British constitution'.[78]

The expansion of empire in general and the Act of Union with Ireland in particular appeared to provide a stimulus to the pluralist image. The Memorial of the Church of Scotland in 1790 had referred to the benefits which would flow to what it called the 'Empire of Great Britain' if, by the repeal of the Test Act, the King were to be enabled to call upon the services of all his (Protestant) subjects.[79] The growing perception of Britain as an imperial state with imperial needs, together with the urgent demands of warfare, enhanced this appeal. John Milner exploited the needs of the empire when complaining that a refusal to allow them to practise their religion might deter Irish Catholics from joining the British army. When, in 1805, he wrote 'Not only Gentlemen are precluded from holding military commissions in England, without abjuring transubstantiation; but also a common man is not permitted by law to shoulder a musket in the militia, unless he can swear that he *is a Protestant*', Milner was merely broadening the complaint of Samuel Heywood eighteen years earlier, that 'Not even a bug can be destroyed within the purlieus of the royal household but by the hallowed fingers of a communicant.'[80] Similar arguments were heard over the Catholic relief bill which brought down the Talents ministry in 1807, while the Catholic Petition of 1810, pointing out that Catholics formed 'more than one-fourth of the whole mass of the subjects of the United Empire', added:

> Whatever there is of genius of talent, or of energy among them, is absolutely lost for public use, and this at a time when the United Empire is engaged in a conflict formidable beyond example; and it therefore seems important . . . that she should call into action, without qualification, or limit, or any religious test, or declaration, the genius, talents, and energies of all her subjects.[81]

The petition for religious liberty organised by Christopher Wyvill in 1807 cited 'the present perilous juncture of Affairs in which our Continental Allies have been compelled to sue the French Emperor for an Armistice' as a compelling reason why 'All Men . . . ought not to be injured by exclusion from the service of their Country, by bearing arms in its defence, at a crisis of great national danger, *such* as that which is now impending over the British Empire.'[82] In the same year the Earl of Darnley warned 'Had Lord Wellington's parents been unfortunately Catholics, our victories in Spain might have been dreamt of, but never realized.'[83] The Whig clergyman Henry Bathurst, soon to be bishop of Norwich, urged Lord Grenville to 'put a finishing hand to that noble monument of wisdom and beneficence, the Union of Ireland with England, by granting a full and complete toleration to those, without whose co-operation this monument could never have been erected'.[84] Thomas Belsham looked forward to a day when 'we see Whig and Tory, Churchman and Dissenter, Protestant and Catholic, Peer and Commoner, Rich and Poor, all joining hand and heart, agreeing to forget all invidious distinctions, and . . . uniting in a firm invincible phalanx to save the country'.[85] Bishop Watson, too, dreamed of a patriotic unity in 1813:

> The struggle for the liberty of Europe, has been most nobly sustained by Great Britain, and might it not at this period be successfully terminated by our Government granting emancipation to the Catholics, and a repeal of the test and corporation acts to the Dissenters? These concessions would be more powerful means of defence, than all the conscriptions of our enemy can ever be to the contrary.[86]

There were numerous claims that Catholic Emancipation would contribute to the peace and security of the empire.[87] Sir Francis Burdett and Luke White both used this argument in the Commons' debate on the Catholic petition on 17 April 1823.[88] Lord Ebrington made the assertion that emancipation would be 'a benefit to the empire at large' the central point of his speech on 19 February 1829.[89]

The Act of Union allowed religious reformers to cite a larger non-Anglican population under the jurisdiction of the parliament of the United Kingdom in order to argue for a 'Universal Toleration'. This was the principal feature of Wyvill's campaigns of 1807–13. He hoped 'that Millions in Ireland will cooperate in the attempt which will be made in the next Session by liberal Christians of all Denominations in England, to extinguish Intolerance finally and completely, on the true principles of our Religion'.[90] Wyvill appealed to a generalised, non-denominational Christianity, couching his petitions in terms of 'the principles of Gospel Freedom', 'The great and just principle of Universal Liberty of Conscience', and asserting that his supporters 'belong to no party but that of humanity and the gospel'.[91] When Lord Lansdowne introduced a petition of Dublin Protestants in favour of Catholic Emancipation on 24 February 1825 he claimed 'that this great question was not a Catholic or a Protestant, but an Irish question; that it was not a question whether or not several millions of Catholics should be admitted to an equal share of the benefits of the constitution, but how long that practical community, in which here as in every other country all over the globe, Catholics as well as Protestants, should enjoy a participation of civil rights, was to be deferred'.[92] This led to an attitude which sought to combine an overriding British patriotism with a cross-denominational universalism. Ralph Leycester, MP for Shaftesbury, on 19 February 1829, described Emancipation as 'A measure of justice, of policy, of charity. It was not an English measure, nor a Scotch measure, nor an Irish measure – it was a British measure. It was not a Protestant measure, nor a Popish measure, – it was a Christian measure.'[93]

But the pluralist image, too, could be invoked with very different motives. There was bound to be a debate as to the forms which such pluralism should take. Was it, for instance, a matter of right or of privilege generously (and conditionally) conferred? It could be used to resist further change: what further change could be needed? 'A Country Freeholder', defending the Test laws, appealed to the lenity and tolerance of English legislation which 'seldom or never provides against evils, until they have appeared and wrought some mischief'.[94] Spencer Madan insisted that 'The British government, in church and state *already* allows to *all* its subjects every civil and religious liberty which *can be* consistent with its own security.'[95] But foreign comparisons with English traditions could be used for purposes other than self-congratulation. According to the *Case of the Protestant*

Dissenters (1787), Britain was peculiar in the extent of its religious discrimination: 'In no other country is the sacramental test required as a qualification for civil employments.'[96] Three years later a Dissenter added 'England should not, must not, and cannot on any principle of sound policy, stoop to France in treating her subjects with lenity.'[97] The supposed distinctiveness of the English national character could be invoked by reformers and their opponents alike.

The libertarian interpretation of national identity had severe limitations. The effects in parliament of its invocation did not go far. By 1815 the war was won without legislation for religious equality. Wyvill failed to secure Catholic co-operation for his campaigns in favour of universal toleration; his aspirations for such co-operation were far too optimistic. Orthodox Dissenters, particularly Methodists, petitioned parliament against Catholic Emancipation in large numbers, while Catholics regarded Rational Dissenters less as fellow-victims of intolerance than as purveyors of Socinian heresy.[98] The Act of Union, of which Article 5 referred to 'one Protestant Episcopal Church, to be called *The United Church of England and Ireland*', was interpreted as an extension of Anglican hegemony as well as a harbinger of pluralism. In 1829 Archbishop Beresford of Armagh strongly opposed Catholic Emancipation from an 'ultra' perspective and some bishops of the Church of Ireland addressed George IV to urge him to withhold the Royal Assent from that measure.[99] As Sir Robert Inglis put it in his speech on the Catholic question on 10 May 1825, 'Sir, there is no Church of Ireland: the Church of Ireland ceased to exist at the Union; it is now for ever one with the Church of England; they form one undivided Establishment: any attack on the one is an attack on the other.' On 9 May 1828 Inglis went to considerable lengths to refute O'Connell's reference to 'the legislature of England [*sic*]' as 'a foreign parliament', asserting 'It is no more "foreign" to Dublin, than it is to Cornwall or to Cumberland.'[100] The decisive factor in the enactment of Catholic Emancipation was the fear of serious disorder in Ireland as much as intellectual conviction, and the measure was accompanied by elaborate 'securities' and the disenfranchisement of many Catholic freeholders. In terms of membership of parliament, as well as in other respects, moreover, the pluralist image of national identity did not extend to the emancipation of adherents of the Jewish religion.

Images of empire, too, were subject to differing interpretations. As Professor Wilson showed, 'discourses of empire' produced contradictions as well as unities. The expansion of empire and of commercial wealth could be interpreted as a vindication of constitutional liberties. But if there was a stronger national self-confidence after the Seven Years' War, there was also a sense of national hubris over the loss of the American colonies, and a sense of guilt over the impeachment of Warren Hastings, while the slave trade was increasingly construed as a justified cause of divine punishment. In 1804 the Unitarian Robert Aspland shrewdly linked the 'multiplied oaths' of religion which surrounded 'Every Department of our Civil and Ecclesiastical Administration' to the slave trade and 'our conquests (both treacherous and bloody) in the East Indies' as reasons for 'our present sufferings and apprehensions'.[101] Belief in a sense of progress was far from universal. If there was a developing cult of 'rationalism', there was also a strong body of anti-rationalism which argued that rationalism led to deism and infidelity. There was much more to English views of empire, moreover, than those associated with Protestant evangelicalism.[102] Empire produced not one but a multi-faceted 'other', which could include, for instance, Irish Protestants.[103] Of the three broad types of national identity postulated in parliamentary debate, that of religious pluralism comes closest to the category of the 'imagined' or 'invented'.

Political discourse suggests that the British parliamentary elite still perceived the country as fundamentally Christian. Religious allegiance was still crucial to the determination of political reliability, fitness for office, access to universities and the promotion of morality. Attempts to annex a sense of national identity which was associated with religious values and appeals to the past were fundamental to parliamentary debate in this period. But it was an identity open to numerous interpretations. Many sought to appropriate it and to harness it to their own advancement – by interlocking it with a common Protestantism, or with a national Church, or with complete toleration or even equality. Each of these identities was idealised, sometimes heavily so. But religious controversy within and beyond parliament allowed the proponents of each to construct an image which could be supported by historical evidence and which could draw upon international comparisons. The (rather limited) extension in parliamentary debate of 'national identity' from 'English' to 'British', especially after 1800, could be used not only to emphasise a patriotic Protestantism but also a level of diversity which that Protestantism could not contain. The increase in non-Anglican numbers led not to a consensual pluralism but to an aggressive denominationalism and parliamentary battles over dogma, over material advantages and, perhaps most bitterly, over education. Religion remained crucial in the formation of national as well as personal identity but its effects were much more divisive than unifying.

Notes

1 I am grateful to Jeremy Black and Julian Hoppit for helpful comments on this chapter and to the British Academy for a grant which helped to finance the necessary research.

2 J. Disney, *A dialogue between a clergyman of the Church of England and a lay-gentleman* (1792), 8.

3 G. Davis, *A discourse preached . . . on February 12, 1758. Being the Sunday of the general fast* (1758), 9, 5.

4 J. Debrett, *The Parliamentary Register*, 45 vols (1781–96), 3rd series, xi, 617.

5 Among many examples, see Sir Harry Inglis, *On the Roman Catholic question. Substance of two speeches delivered in the House of Commons, on May 10, 1825, and May 9, 1828* (1828).

6 L. Colley, *Britons: forging the nation, 1707–1837* (New Haven and London, 1992), ch. 1, especially 52–3; G. Newman, *The rise of English nationalism: a cultural history, 1740–1830* (rev. edn, 1998).

7 I. Huntingford, *The petition of the English Roman Catholics considered* (2nd edn, 1812), 36.

8 W. Bristow, *Cursory reflections on the policy, justice and expediency of repealing the Test and Corporation Acts* (1790), 24.

9 S. Heywood, *The right of Protestant dissenters* (1787), 159.

10 Cobbett, *Parliamentary History*, xxxii, col. 1512.

11 J. Mendham, *The Protestant king* (Birmingham, 1820), 9–10; A. Reed, *Lamentations for the dead!* (1820), 14–15.

12 See J. Black, 'Confessional state or elect nation? Religion and identity in eighteenth-century England' in T. Claydon and I. McBride (eds), *Protestantism and national identity: Britain and Ireland, c. 1650–c. 1850* (Cambridge, 1998), 53–74.

13 'A country freeholder', *The danger of repealing the Test-Act: in a letter to a Member of Parliament* (1790), 9.

14 G. I. Huntingford, *Petition of the English Roman Catholics*, 17–18. See also Huntingford's *A call for union with the established Church, addressed to English Protestants* (Winchester, 1800).

15 Hansard, *Parliamentary Debates*, new series, xiii, col. 62.

16 J. Smith, *Some remarks on the resolutions, which were formed at a meeting of the archdeaconry of Chester . . . 15 February 1790* (Liverpool, 1790), 30.

17 E. Duffy, 'Ecclesiastical Democracy Detected: I (1779–1787)', *Recusant History*, x (1970), 309–29.

18 Hansard, *Parliamentary Debates*, xxxix, cols. 858ff. (4 May 1819).

19 12 and 13 William III *c.* 2. For the handful of exceptions, see K. L. Ellis, 'The administrative connections between Britain and Hanover', *Journal of the Society of Archivists*, iii (1965–69), 548 and n. 10.

20 J. Black, *Pitt the Elder: the great commoner* (rev. edn Cambridge, 1999), 102; *LJ*, xxviii, 513.

21 38 George III *c.* 13 and 39 George III *c.* 104.

22 C. Podmore, *The Moravian church in England, 1728–1760* (Oxford, 1998), chs 8 and 9.

23 Quoted in C. W. Towlson, *Moravian and Methodist: relationships and influences in the eighteenth century* (Epworth, 1957), 141–2.

24 G. M. Ditchfield, 'The Scottish Campaign against the Test Act, 1790–1791', *Historical Journal*, xxiii (1980), 37–61; F. C. Mather, 'Church, parliament and penal laws: some Anglo-Scottish interactions in the eighteenth century', *English Historical Review*, xcii (1977), 540–72; P. Nockles, ' "Our brethren of the north": the Oxford movement and the Scottish episcopal church', *Journal of Ecclesiastical History*, xlvii (1996), 1–28.

25 Cited in S. Madan, *The principal claims of the dissenters considered* (Birmingham, 1790), 31.

26 Scottish Record Office [SRO], 1/5/124: 'Memorial', 28, 51–2.

27 Cobbett, *Parliamentary History*, xxix, cols. 491, 494, 498.

28 SRO, 'Memorial', 12, 15.

29 Cobbett, *Parliamentary History*, iv, col. 841.

30 Hansard, *Parliamentary Debates*, new series, xviii, col. 770.

31 Cobbett, *Parliamentary History*, xxix, col. 498.

32 Madan, *Principal claims*, 27, note K.

33 C. Haydon, *Anti-Catholicism in eighteenth-century England: a political and social study* (Manchester, 1993), chs 5 and 7.

34 Colley, *Britons*, 18.
35 Disney, *Dialogue*, 23; 'A country freeholder', 52.
36 *Cobbett's Political Register*, xxiii, 19 May, 13 Feb., 1813.
37 Hansard, *Parliamentary Debates*, xx, 426, 651.
38 *Church of England Quarterly Review*, xvi (1844), 202. See E. R. Norman, *Anti-Catholicism in Victorian England* (1968), 44ff.
39 J. Phillips, *Electoral behaviour in unreformed England: plumpers, splitters and straights* (Princeton, 1982).
40 Quoted in J. C. D. Clark, *English society 1660–1832. religion, ideology and politics during the ancien regime* (Cambridge, 2000), 266. The case for an Anglican identity is effectively stated in J. C. D. Clark, 'Protestantism, nationalism and national identity, 1660–1832', *Historical Journal*, xliii (2000), 249–76.
41 Madan, *Principal claims*, 7.
42 Hansard, *Parliamentary Debates*, new series, xviii, col. 714.
43 Madan, *Principal claims*, 55; G. Croft, *The test laws defended* (Birmingham, 1790), v. For further examples, see Clark, *English society*, 310.
44 Bolton-le-Moors meeting, 18 Feb. 1790: 'A collection of the resolutions passed at the meetings of the Church of England', 32; *Tracts on test laws*, Cambridge University Library, 8.23.43[4].
45 'Country Freeholder', *Repealing the Test Act*, 2.
46 'A Collection of the Resolutions', 32–3 and 28–9.
47 'A Country Freeholder', *Repealing the Test Act*, 16.
48 Cobbett, *Parliamentary History*, xxvii, col. 1282.
49 *A vindication of the short history of the Corporation and Test Acts* (1790), 33.
50 Cobbett, *Parliamentary History*, xxviii, 396–7; Hansard, *Parliamentary Debates*, xxxviii, cols. 715–16 (15 May 1818).
51 T. Belsham, *A plea for the Catholic claims* (1813), 31–2.
52 Hansard, *Parliamentary Debates*, new series, viii, col. 1113; xviii, col. 722.
53 W. Gibson, *The Church of England 1688–1832: unity and accord* (2001), especially ch. 7.
54 Quoted in Gibson, *Church of England*, 219.
55 F. C. Mather, 'Georgian churchmanship reconsidered: some variations in Anglican public worship, 1714–1830', *Journal of Ecclesiastical History*, xxxvi (1985), 255–83; P. Nockles, *The Oxford Movement in context: Anglican high churchmanship, 1760–1857* (Cambridge, 1994).
56 Mather, 'Georgian churchmanship'; B. Young, 'A history of variations: the identity of the eighteenth-century Church of England', in Claydon and McBride (eds), *Protestantism and national identity*, 105–28.
57 G. M. Ditchfield, 'English rational Dissent and philanthropy, c. 1760–c. 1810' in H. Cunningham and J. Innes (eds), *Charity, philanthropy and reform 1690s–1850* (Basingstoke, 1998), 193–207.
58 Madan, *Principal claims*, 19.
59 *Cobbett's Political Register*, xxiv, 199 (14 Aug. 1813).
60 Hansard, *Parliamentary Debates*, new series, xi, col. 85.
61 J. Milner, *Letters to a prebendary: being an answer to reflections on popery by the Rev. John Sturges, LL.D* (2nd edn, 1801).
62 Cobbett, *Parliamentary History*, xxvii, cols. 291–2.
63 Clark, *English society*, 301, n. 204.
64 J. Jebb, *Works*, 3 vols (1787), i, 106.

65 Disney, *Dialogue*, 14.
66 G. M. Ditchfield, 'Ecclesiastical policy during the ministry of the Younger Pitt, 1783–1801', *Parliamentary History*, xix (2000), 64–80.
67 Some 200 Evangelical clergymen seceded from the Church in the first half of the nineteenth century; G. Carter, 'The case of the Reverend James Shore', *Journal of Ecclesiastical History*, xlvii (1996), 478–504.
68 Young, 'A history of variations', 128.
69 As Clark notes, *English society*, 302, n. 206.
70 'Country freeholder', *Repealing the Test Act*, 49.
71 W. Carey, *A sermon preached before the honourable House of Commons . . . 8 February 1809* (1809), 11–12.
72 J. E. Gordon, *Substance of a speech . . .* (1831), 9; see also 11–12.
73 C. Wellbeloved, *The principles of Roman Catholics and Unitarians compared* (York, 1800), 15.
74 Cobbett, *Parliamentary History*, xxix, col. 1374.
75 Smith, *Some remarks*, 17n.
76 SRO, 'Memorial', 17.
77 Debrett, *Parliamentary Register*, xii, 343.
78 T. W. Davis (ed.), *Minutes for repeal of the Test and Corporation Acts: minutes 1786–90 and 1827–8* (London Record Society, xiv, 1978), 83.
79 SRO, 'Memorial', 16, 23.
80 Milner, *Short view*, (1805), 48–9; Heywood, *Right of Dissenters*, 76.
81 *CJ*, lxv, 123.
82 North Yorkshire County Record Office [NYCRO], ZFW 7/2/195/2 (Wyvill petition to the Commons, 13 July 1807); *CJ*, lxviii, 206 (23 Feb. 1813).
83 *Cobbett's Political Register*, xxiii, 210 (Kent county meeting, 6 Feb. 1813).
84 *Memoirs of the late Dr Henry Bathurst, Lord Bishop of Norwich. By the Rev. Henry Bathurst . . . Archdeacon of Norwich*, 2 vols (1837), ii, 246.
85 T. Belsham, *The situation, the prospects, and the duties, of Britons in the present crisis* (1803), 11.
86 *Anecdotes of the life of Richard Watson, Bishop of Llandaff, written by himself*, 2 vols (2nd edn, 1818), ii, 439.
87 See, for instance, the pro-emancipation speech of the Earl of Thanet at the Kent county meeting, 6 Feb. 1813; *Cobbett's Political. Register*, xxiii, 206.
88 Hansard, *Parliamentary Debates*, new series, viii, cols. 1071, 1073.
89 Hansard, *Parliamentary Debates*, xx, col. 428.
90 NYCRO, ZFW 7/2/238/2: Wyvill to Silvertop, 15 Aug. 1812.
91 NYCRO, ZFW 214/2, 238/1, 237/14.
92 Hansard, *Parliamentary Debates*, new series, xii, col. 645.
93 Hansard, *Parliamentary Debates*, xx, col. 421.
94 'Country freeholder', *Repealing the Test Act*, 7–8.
95 Madan, *Principal claims*, 24.
96 *Case of the Protestant Dissenters* (1787), 4.
97 *Observations on the origin and effect of the Test Act . . . By a Dissenter* (1790), 40.
98 R. W. Davis, *Dissent in politics 1780–1830: the political career of William Smith, MP* (Epworth, 1971), chs. 11 and 12; G. M. Ditchfield, ' "Incompatible with the very name of Christian": English Catholics and Unitarians in the age of Milner', *Recusant History*, xxv (2000), 52–73.

99 F. O'Ferrell, *Catholic emancipation: Daniel O'Connell and the Birth of Irish Democracy 1820–30* (Dublin, 1985), 255–6.

100 Inglis, *Substance of two speeches*, 53, 138.

101 Aspland, *Divine judgments on guilty nations* (1804), 21–3.

102 K. Wilson, 'The island race: Captain Cook, protestant evangelicalism and the construction of English national identity, 1760–1800' in Claydon and McBride (eds), *Protestantism and national identity*, 265–90. The works on evangelicalism cited by the author (p. 284, n. 44) have a somewhat dated appearance.

103 See, for instance, *Cobbett's Political Register*, xxiii, 779.

5

The landed interest and the national interest, 1660–1800[1]

Julian Hoppit

It is a commonplace that the two centuries following the Restoration of Charles II saw the apogee of landed power in Britain. At heart this view rests upon two related notions, of the rise of great estates and of the growing political importance of a parliament dominated by landowners. Moreover, in this view the landed are frequently characterised as being distinctively cohesive, often fighting for their interest with a passionate sense of common cause. So, for example, Sydney Checkland noted how 'The state was largely in the hands of the landed interest. It consisted of the aristocracy and gentry, men whose concern lay with agriculture rather than industry and commerce. They dominated parliament, the civil service, the army and navy, the church, the educational system and local government in the shires.'[2] In parliament this domination is often said to have led to the sacrifice of all else at the altar of property, especially landed property. To Douglas Hay, for example, 'The Glorious Revolution of 1688 established the freedom not of men, but of men of property . . . interests of state and Divine Will had disappeared. Property had swallowed them all.'[3] By implication, therefore, the national interest very often was the landed interest and *vice versa*. Josiah Tucker for one believed that 'the LANDED INTEREST . . . have *the most at Stake*; and their Interest, and the Interest of the Public, must necessarily coincide'.[4] It has, therefore, seemed reasonable to argue that the state in general and parliament in particular did what the landed wanted and, in doing so, defined the national interest or public good in their terms.

This paper considers this view by exploring how private landowners sought legislation in parliament, and what light their successes and failures shed on both their power and the claim that their and the nation's interests were largely synonymous.[5] It is shown that landed control of legislative authority was more partial and more conditional than is often allowed and that there were important differences within the English landed interest and between that interest and those of Scotland and Ireland. When put alongside other questions which have been raised about the integrity of the landed interest the very utility of the concept as a mode of analysis is severely questioned and the difficulties or limitations of defining *a* national interest in this period are underlined. Within the British Isles there was not one landed interest, but several, who by making use of statutory authority in very different ways were well aware of that lack of unity and common identity.

Landed authority in Britain in this period has been emphasised with good reason.[6] Amongst forms of wealth it was the most highly prized, conferring upon its holders a distinctive and enviable status. The connection between ownership of or access to property as a condition of full citizenship, the right to vote and much office holding was not only sacrosanct but further underlined with measures such as the Qualification Act of 1711, which required county and borough MPs to own property of certain values. Equally, membership of the House of Lords and Commons may have broadened socially by 1800, but even then landowners comfortably predominated. And landowners were certainly keen to use parliament to enhance their status and income, as with the passage of game and corn laws and by keeping a firm grip on how they and their wealth were taxed. Parliament was mainly composed of landowners who frequently exercised its authority for their benefit. If this was masked it was because, from this position of enormous strength, landowners in parliament were happy to attach themselves to what Colley has called a 'cult of commerce'.[7] But allowing for that, did landowners use their legislative power with little restraint by defining the national interest in their own image?

Certainly, from the late seventeenth century some contemporaries developed the concept of a 'landed interest' and gave it an unmatched supremacy. In this 'country' view landed wealth had a purity and permanence which allowed its holders to adopt a disinterestedness in public affairs which made them peculiarly suitable to exercise high office: 'A Gentleman of an Estate is undoubtedly the only proper Representative of his Country, for a Man of small Fortune is liable to the Temptation of a Bribe, or a Pension.'[8] It is important to note, however, that the concept of the landed interest was developed as a reaction to the emergence of two other supposed interests, most immediately to that of a moneyed interest consequent upon the efflorescence of public finances after 1688 and more generally to that of a trading or commercial interest through the seventeenth century.[9] If there is no question that during the 1690s and 1700s the 'landed interest' was frequently employed, especially by the Tories, to make political argument and to attempt to define the public good, it is important to emphasise that this was based as much upon what that interest was not as what it was.[10] Moreover, if it was justly noted in 1724 that 'It is not many Years ago, since an unhappy Distinction was sent on Foot, between the Landed and the Money'd Interest' there was something distinctly ephemeral about that distinction, such language appearing to have slipped out of common usage in the 1720s.[11] With the institution of Whig one-party rule after the accession of George I in 1714 and the stabilisation of public finances after the South Sea Bubble of 1720 its utility dramatically dwindled. Furthermore, some began to query whether the divisions between agriculture, trade and finance which underpinned this language of interest groups really made sense, for did not their 'Welfare *mutually* depend on each other'?[12] Did not agriculture provide raw materials for many industries and did not much of its output depend upon foreign markets? That said, after several decades of quiescence, the language of interests did begin to reemerge in the 1780s. In part, as in the 1690s, this was provoked by attempts to rethink public finances, especially by Pitt the Younger's hopes of taxing wealth in various forms. But it was also partly a product of the emergence of political radicalism with its hopes for rights and liberties that challenged those political privileges that were enjoyed by the landed above all others.[13] For radicals, new ideas of citizenship would inevitably promote a new and more inclusive idea of the national interest.

Of course in the eighteenth century there could have been a landed interest that was protean and subtle rather than fixed and direct, employed flexibly and furtively not rigidly and robustly. In the parliamentary context this possibility might be examined in several ways, but here consideration is given to the sorts of legislation that landowners sought and enacted at Westminster in the period, particularly in relation to estates, enclosure and land registries. Because these three areas concerned landed property very directly, looking at how each was legislated for should say much about how far landowners used parliament for their own ends and how successful they were in defining the national interest and public good in their own image. As will be seen, this leads, in turn, to a comparison with legislation undertaken on the same issues by landowners at the Dublin and Edinburgh parliaments, which raises important questions about the relationship between legislative authority and national identity. Such a study is avowedly selective, allowing certain issues to be considered in some depth, but at the cost of leaving out much, especially with regard to the practice of politics, the distribution of patronage, appeals to the Lords, developments in the criminal law, 'metropolitanism' and vital constitutional (including religious) questions.

The first point to note is that only two of the three areas of legislation examined here led to many acts of parliament. Vast numbers of estates and enclosure acts were passed, only a handful regarding land registries. The broad patterns for estates and enclosure statutes are set out in Table 5.1.

Table 5.1   Estate and enclosure acts passed at Westminster, 1660–1800

	All acts	Estate	as %	Enclosure	as %
1660–88	564	181	32	3	1
1689–1714	1,752	655	37	4	0
1714–60	3,549	790	22	254	7
1760–82	4,195	508	12	1,084	26
1782–1800	4,157	322	8	832	20
Total	14,217	2,456	17	2,177	15

Source: O. Ruffhead (ed.), *Statutes at large*, 18 vols (1769–1800), i–xviii.
Note: 'estate' means acts directly relating to estate ownership and excludes, for example, legislation relating to guardianship; 'enclosure' also includes a very small number of acts relating to the cultivation of wastelands.

If this table tells a conventional tale with regard to enclosure legislation, the pattern of estate acts it reveals is little known.[14] Indeed, estate acts were the most numerous single category of legislation for the whole period, surpassing in volume those for both enclosure and turnpike. By the narrow definition employed in Table 5.1 nearly one-third of all legislation passed at Westminster in this period was prompted by the highly particular requests of individual landowners; though if a wider definition of legislation relating to the landed is employed, including all acts dealing with wealth holding, the land and agriculture, then the proportion rises to 44 per cent.[15] Obviously to count acts is not a straightforward measure of importance, nor does it reckon the value or acreage of land involved, but it does demonstrate just how far the legislative process was being employed by landed society. Parliament was even more deeply involved in patterns of landownership within the country than is usually thought.

It is not difficult to see why landowners turned to parliament to buttress their estates or to enclose their lands. Estate acts were sought to help them deal with the web of contract which frequently enveloped their property. The overwhelming majority dealt with individuals or families and mostly concerned issues of landownership, more especially transferring land from one generation to another, including within that marriage. They dealt then with strict settlements, marriage agreements, wills, trusts and guardianships, often looking to alter arrangements which had been made in increasing numbers since the Restoration (many of which were being thrown into doubt by the elite's difficulties in finding the heirs demanded by an attachment to male primogeniture and some of which were being questioned because mounting debts required greater financial flexibility than they allowed).[16] Many dealt with large estates, but only about a quarter related to those of the rank of knight or above, nearly two-thirds of lesser rank and the remainder of women and the clergy – which is to say that this was legislation for the squirearchy as well as aristocracy.[17] For many, 'The private estate act was cheaper to obtain and a much faster process than a suit in Chancery. Instead of being at the mercy of the lawyers, an estate bill went before two bodies of men who were almost exclusively landowners themselves.'[18] Chancery suits might consume estates; estate acts preserved them. Similarly, enclosure legislation provided landowners with the authority to impose new definitions of proprietorship and land use, allowing opposing formal and informal rights to be marginalised, in most cases in the quest for agricultural 'improvement'. Parliamentary enclosure was an investment aiming at fattened rent rolls.

Striking though the sheer volume of estate and enclosure legislation is, and though it clearly shows the eagerness with which the landed employed legislative authority, closer examination demonstrates that their power was far from absolute. Here it is helpful to examine the specific chronology involved and the question of just how receptive parliament was to the demand for legislation from landowners. In Figure 5.1 the number of acts per parliamentary session for estates and enclosure have been charted, using a moving average to clarify the trends.[19] Looking first at estate acts, this graph makes clear that the volume of estate acts grew significantly

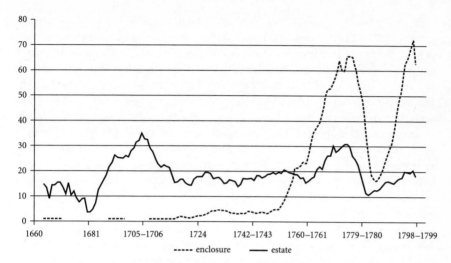

Figure 5.1 Westminster estate and enclosure acts, 1660–1800
(seven session moving average)

after the Glorious Revolution, peaking in the first half of Anne's reign before falling back and being fairly steady for the rest of the period, save for another rise and fall in the era of the American War of Independence. To explain this requires an understanding of the demand for such acts and parliament's willingness and capacity to meet that. Some sense of that relationship is obtained by comparing attempts to pass acts with those enacted. This is not easy to do, not least because what constituted an attempt might be variously defined. Here, drawing on earlier work, consideration is given only to those attempts which left some record in the *Journals* of the Commons and Lords. From this it is possible to calculate the success rate for attempts at estate acts, as in Table 5.2.

Table 5.2 Success rate for estate legislation at Westminster, 1660–1800

	Estate			Non-estate
	Acts	failures	% success	acts % success
1660–88	181	196	48	24
1689–1714	655	249	72	43
1714–60	790	254	76	69
1760–82	508	53	91	77
1782–1800	322	27	92	85
Total	2,456	779	76	68

Sources: Ruffhead (ed.), *Statutes at large*; J. Hoppit (ed.), *Failed legislation, 1660–1800: extracted from the Commons and Lords Journals* (1997).

Elsewhere I have noted how the Glorious Revolution led to longer, more predictable and better organised parliamentary sessions that meant fewer initiatives fell by the wayside, attracting more people to seek statutory authority.[20] Certainly 1688–89 was a watershed with regard to estate legislation, the success rate rising from under one-half to nearly three-quarters. But the rise of the number of acts was as much due to more initiatives being put Westminster's way, though these two factors probably fed off one another. As Table 5.2 makes clear, before 1714 parliament was much more prepared to pass estate than other types of acts, probably because their highly specific nature involved very restricted property rights and did not impinge upon the community at large. When parliament passed estate acts it could be confident that it was not treading on any toes. That said, it quickly felt the burden of business the landed were putting its way. In 1692, for example, two MPs 'spoke mightily against private bills, the number and multitude of them' and later that year another 'inveighed much against private bills ... this House was taken up with private bills to destroy the settlement of estates in England.'[21] Soon the Lords, where most estate bills were first considered, addressed the problem and, through a series of standing orders, sought to control the amount of private bill legislation in general and estate legislation specifically being put its way. In particular, on 16 February 1706 five standing orders were established, of which the most important were that: the petition initiating private bills now had to have the consent of all interested parties; two judges were to hear those parties and report to the House; careful land valuations were to be undertaken where the exchange of estates was the object; and trustees had personally to appear before the House to accept their new responsibilities.[22] As Figure 5.1 showed, these measures, designed to require applicants to prepare bills more thoroughly, halved numbers of estate acts. They made legislation more time consuming and costly and might have made the Lords appear less receptive to estate legislation (though the success rate, already relatively high, continued to move upwards).

Parliament's legislative caution with regard to the landed was also evident over enclosure. As Figure 5.1 showed, enclosure acts were very rare before about 1740, with numbers rising rapidly after 1750, though falling back sharply during the American War of Independence before recovering thereafter. This chronology prompts a number of questions. The first is why it was not until the middle of the eighteenth century that the landed commonly employed statutes to enclose? After all, enclosure by other routes had burgeoned since the early seventeenth century. One means, the use of actions (sometimes fictitious) at Chancery, appears to have been common, though Thirsk has noted that 'This procedure was not entirely satisfactory, inasmuch as the descendants of landholders subscribing to agreements could, and did, go back on them.'[23] Given this, and the uncertain costs of a Chancery suit, why did landowners not immediately after the Glorious Revolution turn to use statutory authority for enclosure as they had for estates? A clue to the answer to this question is provided in Table 5.3.

Table 5.3   Success rate for enclosure legislation at Westminster, 1660–1800

	Enclosure			Non-enclosure
	Acts	failures	% success	acts % success
1660–88	3	11	21	28
1689–1714	4	6	40	51
1714–60	254	41	86	73
1760–82	1,084	267	80	78
1782–1800	832	299	74	74
Total	2,177	624	78	65

Sources: Ruffhead (ed.), *Statutes at large*; Hoppit (ed.), *Failed legislation*.

It is clear that before 1714 very few landowners looked to parliament for enclosure legislation and those that did were very often thwarted. It is well known that in the sixteenth century parliament was generally hostile to enclosure, not least because of the resistance it encountered and disorder it provoked. If in the seventeenth century many landowners became increasingly enamoured with the personal financial and general economic benefits of enclosure, there were still those, even amongst the propertied, who were worried by its effects upon employment prospects and the self-sufficiency of commoners. To them it could not be achieved 'without prejudice to the Poor'.[24] Perhaps it was only with declining food prices and rising corn exports in the second quarter of the eighteenth century that such worries could be pushed to the margins. Certainly it was then that the balance between success and failure amongst enclosure legislation shifted decisively. Even so, landowners were certainly not granted a blank cheque under George II. In the first place it is important to note that after 1760 the success rate for enclosure legislation was not unusual and that, like estate legislation, many attempts still failed. There was no absolute certainty in the legislative process for landowners. Second, in 1781 the Commons introduced two new standing orders regarding enclosure bills – relating to the maintenance of roads and the need for salaried surveyors – which were part of a sharp decline to 60 per cent in the success rate for enclosure legislation in the early 1780s.[25] So, as with the Lords and estate bills, the Commons introduced new standards of due process upon bills, designed to improve their quality and legitimacy but at a short-term cost of more failed attempts.

About a quarter of attempts to pass estate and enclosure acts failed, a small but significant fraction involving some 1,400 initiatives. It is clear that parliamentary procedure partly explains this. Certainly, the introduction in the House of Lords of standing orders with regard to private bills generally, and estate bills specifically, in 1705 and 1706 dramatically changed the ways such bills were considered. Looking at failures only, prior to then some 95 per cent of estate bills obtained a first reading and fully 50 per cent a third reading in the first house;

after then, however, only 20 per cent of estate and enclosure bills obtained a first reading and 3 per cent a third reading.[26] Until 1705–6 private bills usually fell at the committee stage in either the first or the second house; thereafter most fell at the point of initial scrutiny, frequently by the judges in the Lords. Parliament appears to have been reasonably scrupulous in the ways bills were considered. Moreover, it was open to external opponents of measures. Because of its very nature, estate legislation rarely encountered extra-parliamentary opposition, but enclosure legislation did, opposition which sometimes expressed itself by counter-petitioning to the Commons. For the period 1730–1839, for example, one comprehensive study has found a failure rate for enclosure legislation of 26 per cent and that 10 per cent of bills were subject to counter-petitions.[27]

At heart parliamentary enclosure was the provision of the means to some landowners within a community to impose their view and will upon others. Especially where this involved the eradication of commons and wastes this often had profound social dimensions, with villages turned upside down. Famously, for E. P. Thompson 'Enclosure (when all the sophistications are allowed for) was a plain enough case of class robbery, played according to fair rules of property and law laid down by a parliament of property-owners and lawyers.'[28] But those rules were not entirely self-serving, for it did cramp what landowners could do and provided opportunities which opponents of enclosure appreciated and exploited, even if the effect was more usually to delay enclosure than prevent it outright.[29] Enclosure was certainly often imposed, but it required subscription to apparently universal principles if it was to have sufficient credibility to work in the face of resistance. As Thompson remarked in another context, 'The essential precondition for the effectiveness of law, in its function as ideology, is that it shall display an independence from gross manipulation and shall seem to be just. It cannot seem to be so without upholding its own logic and criteria of equity; indeed, on occasion, by actually *being* just.'[30]

A further point about the nature of parliament's handling of enclosure is worth considering. If parliament was dominated by landowners, doing what they wanted, why did it proceed on a case-by-case basis, creating bespoke legislation so consuming of time and money, rather than pass a general enclosure act? Failed attempts at such a general act – to ease enclosure of the commons, confirm Chancery decrees, or increase the regulation of commons – had begun in earnest in the 1660s.[31] General measures of a sort were passed in 1756, 1773 and 1801 (the last the product of two failed attempts), but these were distinctly limited in scope and effect, in good measure because of opposition from within the ranks of the social elite, notably the episcopal bench worried about the consequences for tithes.[32] In fact not until 1836, when only a small rump of unenclosed land remained, was the right to impose an enclosure without recourse to specific legislation generally granted.[33] Eighteenth-century parliaments were in fact usually unwilling to endorse one person's right at the expense of another's, even for landowners. They were willing to legislate specifically but not generally because they feared unintended consequences and, paradoxical as it may seem, because of their attachment to the rhetoric of property. This last point has often been overlooked: ideological commitments to property found it hard to distinguish between different types, sizes or amounts of property in an overtly value-laden way.

Estate and enclosure legislation was often highly specific and usually pursued for personal rather than public reasons. Land registries, as a piece of public policy, provides an important comparison here. Five land registries, where deeds and conveyances were recorded, were instituted in England in this period – for the Bedford Level in 1663, the West Riding in 1704, the East Riding in 1708, Middlesex in 1709 and, finally, the North Riding in 1736 – and remained operational until this century.[34] However, there were also 24 failed bills attempting to establish land or deed registries in England between 1660 and 1800, three-quarters of which were attempted between 1689 and 1750. Before 1700 the failed bills usually aimed to institute nationwide registries; from 1700 to 1730 the focus was upon on specific counties – Berkshire, Wiltshire, Surrey, Huntingdonshire and Derbyshire were all unsuccessful; thereafter attention usually returned to attempting to establish registries across the nation, notably in 1739 and 1740 when two attempts nearly succeeded.

Arguments for the utility of registries first began to be aired in earnest in the 1640s. John Lilburne wrote in 1648 that 'for the preventing of frauds, thefts and deceits, there be forthwith in every country or shire in England and the Dominion of Wales erected a country record for the perfect registering of all conveyances, bills and bonds, upon a severe and strict penalty'.[35] The Hale Commission, which investigated law reform in 1652, proposed county registries. And there were failed bills in 1650, 1653 and 1656. In 1669 one analysis of Dutch economic superiority noted 'Their keeping up publick Registers . . . whereby many charge-able Law-Suits are prevented, and the securities of Lands and Houses rendered indeed, such as we commonly call them Real Securities.'[36] The House of Lords and John Locke were thinking about the value of registers at the same time.[37] Similarly, according to Andrew Yarranton in 1677 'A Register will quicken Trade, and the Land Registered will be equal as Cash in a mans hands, and the Credit thereof will go and do in Trade what Ready Moneys now doth.'[38] In other words he saw the virtue of registers in terms of the enhanced security they would provide for the mortgage market. This was precisely the point made in the preamble to the statute creating the West Riding register. For Middlesex, however, the preamble's justification returned to Lilburne's emphasis upon the need to find a means of preventing fraud in the land market.

At first glance it would appear that landowners must have welcomed registries because the legal security they would provide for their property would have allowed them greater financial flexibility and kept them away from rapacious lawyers. Yet as the record of failed proposals attests such arguments rarely held sway. Why did a parliament of landowners not legislate registries into being? Hale had himself outlined some of the problems. He stressed the considerable bureaucratic problems of keeping adequate registers: the paperwork would be vast, making problems of indexing highly complex; a central registry might be unpopular with provincial landowners because of the time and money involved in making use of it; but a county based system would struggle to deal with estates that were split across two or more counties. Hale further worried that if deeds were registered children might discover their parents' intentions 'which may breed great unquietness and animosity'.[39] A century later Blackstone also queried the value of land registries. He believed that 'however plausible the provisions of these acts may appear in theory, it hath been doubted by very competent judges whether more disputes have not arisen in those counties, by the inattentions and omissions of parties, than prevented by the use of registers'.[40]

However, in true eighteenth-century fashion the defeat of so many attempts to establish registries was not just a question of practicality, cost and privacy but also of vested interests. After the failure of three bills in as many years in the 1690s Evelyn wondered 'Will ever those swarms of *locusts*, lawyers and attorney, who fill so many seats [in the Commons], vote for a public *Register*, by which men may be secured of their titles and possessions, and an infinity of suits and frauds prevented?'[41] When in 1703 the bill to establish the West Riding registry was making its way through parliament the clerks of enrolment of Chancery petitioned against it, complaining that it would take business away from their court, and presumably hit their fee income – theoretically by 'the statute of enrolments of 1535 land could only be exchanged if it was indented, sealed and enrolled in the king's court of record at Westminster, or in the counties'.[42] This objection did not succeed in this case, but when the Middlesex registry was established it was to be run not by officials elected by the Quarter Sessions, as was the case in Yorkshire, but by clerks from the central courts – Chancery, Queen's Bench, Common Pleas and Exchequer.[43] The defeat of the major measures of 1739 and 1740 – the latter introduced by the Lord Chief Justice King's Bench – appears to have centred upon whether offices were to be administered at the county level by the Clerks of the Peace or be part the Enrolment office of Chancery, under the direction and control of the Master of the Rolls, the first option gaining support from the Commons, the second from the Lords.[44] In the local context resistance came from similar quarters. For example, the bill to establish a registry for Berkshire was in part defeated by petitions from Abingdon, Newbury, Wallingford and Windsor, all claiming that they already had a court of record for deed registration.[45] Parliament showed considerable deference in these instances to other forms of 'property' and was quite prepared to allow what was by then a highly ad hoc system to survive rather than institute the sort of co-ordinated institution which many amongst the landed wished: 'Parliament remained for most purposes a kind of glorified umpire, adjudicating the disputes of propertied interests.'[46] In this case the landed lost, but arguably they partly attained the end of establishing categorical title by having ownership inscribed in land tax returns and all of those estate and enclosure acts.[47] If so, that would help to explain the muted demand for registries after mid-century.[48]

The failure to establish land registries in England on either a county-by-county or national basis is the more striking when put in a wider context, for Scotland

had had a national registry since the mid-seventeenth century and one was instituted for Ireland in 1708.[49] Commentators in England sometimes noted the
Scottish registry and did not attach to it the sorts of concerns expressed by Hale
and Blackstone. Similarly, the Irish registry, based at Dublin but with national
jurisdiction, was instituted without much opposition and did much business
through the eighteenth and nineteenth centuries. As might be expected, it was created partly to supplement the penal laws that buttressed the Protestant interest.[50]
For decades Protestants had appropriated and accumulated land from Catholics
at a spectacular rate – Protestants held 41 per cent of land in Ireland in 1640,
78 per cent in 1688 and 86 per cent in 1703.[51] The land registry was one means,
explicitly stated at its foundation, to confirm that transfer. Indeed, more generally
the Irish parliament's 'hey-day coincided with the ascendancy of the protestant
landowning class who had gathered the fruits of the Williamite victory and who
found in it an instrument for the protection and promotion of their interests'.[52]
In this instance at least the landed interest was the national interest, though
what that national interest was remained contested. Many landowners, even the
beneficiaries of forfeitures, had generations of ancestors from Ireland, whilst in
the early eighteenth century there were conscious attempts to forge a distinct and
separate identity, part English, part Irish, at once amphibious and uncertain.[53]

The presence of national registries in Ireland and Scotland but not in England
hints that the nature of the landed interest in the three kingdoms took different
forms. This can be explored further by comparing the patterns of estate and
enclosure acts at Westminster with those passed at Dublin and Edinburgh in
the period, some simple counts of which are set out in Tables 5.4 and 5.5.
Several points emerge from this evidence. Most obviously, both the Dublin
and Edinburgh parliaments produced considerable numbers of acts, providing
a form of authority that landowners might and did utilise.[54] Although lack of
evidence makes it impossible to estimate success rates, the fecundity of the
Edinburgh parliament is particularly notable in this regard, though Table 5.4

Table 5.4   Estate and enclosure acts passed at Dublin, 1660–1800

	All acts	Estate	as %	Enclosure	as %
1660–88	58	8	14	0	0
1689–1714	214	46	21	0	0
1714–60	516	74	14	2	0
1760–82	485	56	12	0	0
1782–1800	1,054	64	6	5	0
Total	2,327	248	11	7	0

Sources: *The statutes at large, passed in the parliaments held in Ireland*, i–xxi; *Journals of
the House of Commons of the kingdom of Ireland, from 18th May, 1613*, 19 vols in 21
(1796–1800), xviii–xix.

Table 5.5   Estate and enclosure acts passed at Edinburgh, 1660–1706

	All acts	Estate	as %	Enclosure	as %
1660–88	1,388	311	22	8	0
1689–1706	829	81	10	4	0
Total	2,217	392	18	12	1

Source: *The acts of the parliaments of Scotland*, 12 vols (1820–75), vii–xi.

also makes clear how new eras of legislative activity were ushered in at Dublin with the Glorious Revolution and then with independence in 1782. Second, the proportions of estate legislation passed at Dublin and Edinburgh approximated to the 17 per cent figure for Westminster seen earlier in Table 5.1. Third, if the small number of enclosure acts passed at Edinburgh before its abolition is unexpected their almost total insignificance at Dublin is somewhat surprising – and there were *no* enclosure acts for either Ireland or Scotland passed at Westminster in this period. Finally, it was shown earlier that at Westminster some 44 per of all legislation fairly directly concerned either the landed personally or agriculture more generally; but at Dublin and Edinburgh the proportions were just 17 and 28 per cent respectively.

The most striking differences between the use landowners made of legislation in the three kingdoms relates to enclosure. In England about one-fifth of land was enclosed by statute, but in Ireland and Scotland virtually none was.[55] One consequence is that it is unclear just how much land was enclosed in Ireland and Scotland, or what its chronological and geographical patterns were. Lack of evidence is most marked in the Irish case. There much waste and unproductive land was not liable to enclosure, but how enclosure was undertaken elsewhere is uncertain.[56] It is clear, however, that identifying a 'landed interest' in Ireland is fraught with difficulty. If Protestant landowners had some sense of affinity as a consequence of their grip over economic and political power, that identity was also confused and sometimes fractured. Looking only at land issues, it is important to note that many of the decisions driving agricultural change in Ireland were taken not by landlords but by middlemen, many of them Catholic. In many places long leases (often for three lives) on large estates was the norm, with substantial middlemen sub-letting, frequently to very small farmers. This left landowners surprisingly powerless, something only heightened by high levels of absenteeism, reckoned to be about 42 per cent at the start of the nineteenth century by one study.[57] It is interesting to note that landowners in Ireland were unable aggressively to promote improvement in the ways common in England and Scotland and that the language of agrarian capitalism was markedly more muted there.[58] Landowners may, therefore, have had a sense of common cause, but it was not derived in a very meaningful sense from the actual *practice* (rather than fact) of landownership. One major consequence was to hinder the development of a simple 'landed interest'. As has been noted, 'In England, the appeal to the land and its organic continuities had a seductive effect, a soothing sedative to excitable and deracinated radicalism. In Ireland . . . the jagged edges of the land question chafed at the superficially smooth patina of eighteenth-century life.'[59]

The nature of and significance of enclosure in Scotland is rather clearer. There little enclosure had taken place by 1700 and much land in the Scottish lowlands was tied up as 'commonties, areas of rough grazing in shared ownership between two or more proprietors and grazed in common'.[60] Much enclosure took place subsequently, especially in the late eighteenth century, but this was achieved not via bespoke legislation but by employing general enabling acts, particularly two from 1695, the 'Act anent lands lying run-rigs' (c. 36) and the 'Act concerning the dividing of the commonties' (c. 69).[61] Though little enclosure took place before 1750, the contrast with the English case here is nonetheless striking. Scottish landowners had, from an early date, the law squarely on their side, and 'The state did not try to limit the rate of consolidation or the evictions associated with it. No restraints were placed upon Improvers.'[62] Just as important, with regard to their estates landowners saw virtually no need to adjust or dilute Scottish law by seeking new legislation passed at Westminster.[63] Not only with regard to land, the integrity of Scottish national law was undiminished after the Union. As Blackstone put it, 'the many diversities, subsisting between the [English and Scottish] laws at present, may be well enough accounted for, from a diversity of practice in two large and uncommunicating jurisdictions, and from the acts of two distinct and independent parliaments'.[64]

Scotland provides the best case for the existence of a landed interest within the British Isles in the eighteenth century. Large Scottish landowners were perhaps more dominant within their society than their counterparts in England and Ireland. According to Smout 'Scottish landowners were the most absolute in Britain'.[65] They exerted considerable control over county and burgh elections, in local government 'the landowning class again had total power' and much of Scotland's economy was under their control, even if the growth of industry and trade was eroding that.[66] Necessarily, after 1706 the absence at Westminster and the court of many of the most notable Scottish landowners changed the nature of that dominance in local terms, but it did not significantly undermine it. Moreover, amongst landowners an attachment to 'improvement' as a national and patriotic venture, a belief in the need for Scotland to develop economically by vigorously exploiting land as well as trade and industry, provided a manifesto to which many happily subscribed in the period 1720–90.[67] A notable aspect of this was that Scottish landowners launched institutions to this end, for example the Society of Improvers in the Knowledge of Agriculture in Scotland in 1723, Highland Societies in London and Edinburgh in 1778 and 1784 respectively, the British Fisheries Society in 1786, and a Society for the Improvement of British Wool, founded at Edinburgh in 1791. As the titles of some of these suggest, in such ventures Scottish landowners sometimes sought to build bridges to their English counterparts, or at least to mask their Scottish origins or focus.

In the late eighteenth century Scottish landowners more willingly thought of themselves as a landed interest than those in England and Ireland and occasionally voiced the need for a British identity amongst agriculturists (i.e. English and Scottish). One example nicely brings out the difficulties involved in this. On 16 December 1785 'a general meeting of the landed interest of Scotland' took place at Edinburgh. An element of hyperbole was involved here, for the meeting was called to object to parliament of the damage being done to small Scottish distillers by new excise regulations, regulations which it was believed favoured large distillers in London. It was said that the London distillers sought 'a monopoly of the manufacture of corn-spirits in Britain' and would rob Scottish *farmers* of a valuable source of income.[68] But if Scottish protestors readily talked of 'the landed interest of Great Britain', and of England and Scotland as 'sister kingdoms', differences between north and south Britain were also acknowledged, as with the declaration that 'the Landed Interest of England, shall be invited to join the Landed Interest of Scotland'.[69] That this was based on some sense of inferiority is clear, for the general meeting believed English landowners 'are possessed of superior wealth, superior industry, a warmer sun, and a richer soil'.[70] But perhaps it was not so clear cut.

> When a Scots farmer, crossing the Tweed, views the native fertility of the soil, and compares the rich crops with the low rent of the land, he is at first struck with astonishment. But when he begins to reflect on the burthens which the English farmers labour under, from the restrictions inserted in their leases; the still more oppressive laws of King Melchisedeck; the great load of poor rates; the inconveniences attending the militia in time of peace; he thanks his stars he was born on the north side of the Tweed.[71]

As this points up, if the Union provided Scottish landowners with access to English markets it had done nothing to erode distinctions based upon differences in natural environments, tenurial arrangements, legal contexts, religious burdens and social obligations. However close their economic aspirations were, the Scottish and the English landed interests were, in many fundamentals, distinct. Much the same was true in relation to Ireland, except that it was dramatically exacerbated by the exclusion of first Irish cattle and then Irish wool from English markets.[72] Here at least the landed interest was conceived in national terms.

As is now clear, interest groups, landed or otherwise, are the product of much more than the distribution of economic power or particular ideologies. But it is also clear that such groups exist only in relation to issues which provide common cause, though such causes can be addressed differently in different contexts.[73] In England what is striking was the relative absence of general issues which might form or stimulate *a* landed interest. Two issues did partially provide this however. The first was the growing debate over the corn laws after *c.* 1750. In particular, until 1773 legislation favoured producers, especially via bounties, but then the balance shifted in favour of price maintenance. By 1791 the battlelines had been sketched that framed the ideological warfare between protectionism and free trade waged after 1815.[74] But, of course, the corn laws did not neatly unite the landed interest, for predominantly pastoral areas pursued rather different ends from their predominantly arable counterparts. Second, the land tax, which came of age as a discrete entity in 1692, apparently provided a fiscal identity to the landed, an identity made only the stronger by their ability to control the administration of the tax and to champion it as the antithesis of the excise.[75] That the relative burden of the tax declined over the eighteenth century presumably also served to underpin its attractions. But from a very early stage it was recognised that the burden of the land tax was geographically very unequal, divisively driving a wedge between the north and the west and the south and the east (and incidentally between England and Scotland).[76]

Centrally, the landed interest struggled to coalesce because of the absence of what might be called government agricultural policy. Arthur Young lamented in 1793 that 'ministers . . . never did, and never will do anything for the plough'.[77] If that was untrue, Sir John Sinclair, proselytising for his projected Board of Agriculture, rightly compared agriculture's unfavourable treatment to that of other interests catered for by the creation of the Royal Society in 1662, the Board of Trade in 1696 and the Board of Longitude in 1714: 'AGRICULTURE has been totally neglected.'[78] In good measure, however, that was because there was so little call in England for such a policy, not least because of strong suspicions of centralised decision making and institutions. It is interesting to note here that the Board of Agriculture originated as an idea of Lord Kames and was delivered through the efforts of Sinclair, both Scots. It singularly failed to gain an enthusiastic reception from amongst most landowners (though that was somewhat due to Sinclair's misjudgment as to what the Board should do).[79]

This paper has explored the ways in which English landowners enthusiastically embraced statute making after the Glorious Revolution and what that meant in national terms. That then pointed to the distinctive national experiences of the English, Irish and Scottish landed interests in the parliamentary context, to the extent that the British landed interest did not clearly emerge in this period. But it has also shown that in the context of making acts English landowners were less absolute than is often supposed. They often turned their will into acts, but not always. No less importantly, because so many among the landed were unenthusiastic about a powerful state at home and because they worshiped a rhetoric of liberty and property they had, howsoever reluctantly, to compromise and, sometimes, retreat when confronted by other forms of property. They legislated abundantly, but somewhat disconnectedly. Crucially, they lacked those points of common cause which would have allowed them to band together. Consequently, significant divisions within the landed interest existed: between county and country, corn and horn, tenant and landlord, spiritual and secular, large and small. As Adam Smith noted, though he approached the issue from another direction altogether, the landed interest rarely understood clearly what its interest was.[80] Finally, the interconnections between agricultural raw materials, manufacture and trade were so clear and strong that the landed interest might be cut in half by, say, the woollen or the leather interests. All told, and to paraphrase Greene, if it might be said that the landed were powerful their authority was certainly negotiated.[81] Consequently, though the landed interest often claimed to represent and embody the national interest, it was so riddled by variety, tensions and contradictions that this rarely had either force or effect.

Notes

1 Some of the research for this paper stems from a project funded by the Leverhulme Trust, with the British Academy providing some supporting funding. I am very grateful for this.

2 *British public policy, 1776–1939: an economic, social and political perspective* (Cambridge, 1983), 12.

3 'Property, authority and the criminal law' in D. Hay, P. Linebaugh, J. G. Rule, E. P. Thompson and C. Winslow, *Albion's fatal tree: crime and society in eighteenth-century England* (Harmondsworth, 1977), 18.

4 *An humble address and earnest appeal to those most respectable personages in Great-Britain and Ireland . . .* (Gloucester, 1775), 19.

5 This definition of the landed interest is slightly narrower than that of G. E. Mingay, for whom it was 'the combined body of landowners and farmers': *English landed society in the eighteenth century* (1963), 4. I do not consider crown or church lands.

6 Notably J. Cannon, *Aristocratic century: the peerage of eighteenth-century England* (Cambridge, 1984), though it is concerned with only a small fraction of landed society.

7 L. Colley, *Britons: forging the nation, 1707–1837* (1992), 61.

8 [W. Wagstaffe], *The state and condition of our taxes, considered; or, a proposal for a tax upon funds: shewing, the justice, usefulness, and necessity, of such a tax, in respect to our trading and landed interest* (2nd edn, 1714), 19; G. Holmes, *British politics in the age of Anne* (revised edn, 1987), ch. 4.

9 P. G. M. Dickson, *The financial revolution in England: a study in the development of public credit, 1688–1756* (1967), ch. 2; D. Armitage, *The ideological origins of the British empire* (Cambridge, 2000), ch. 4.

10 D. Hayton, 'The country interest and the party system, 1689–c. 1720' in C. Jones (ed.), *Party and management in parliament, 1660–1784* (1984), 37–85.

11 *Considerations upon publick credit* (1720), 6.

12 W. Wood, *A survey of trade* (1718), 8–9. Generally see J. M. Rosenheim, *The emergence of a ruling order: English landed society, 1650–1750* (Harlow, 1998), chs. 4 and 5.

13 For 'interests' after 1780 see S. H. Beer, 'The representation of interests in British government: historical background', *American Political Science Review*, li (1957), 613–50 and D. Wahrman, *Imagining the middle class: the political representation of class in Britain, c. 1780–1840* (Cambridge, 1995), 90–6.

14 But see H. J. Habakkuk, 'The rise and fall of English landed families, 1600–1800: II', *Transactions of the Royal Historical Society*, 5th series, xxx (1980), 199–221; S. Lambert, *Bills and acts: legislative procedure in eighteenth-century England* (Cambridge, 1971), ch. 6; M. Bond, 'Estate acts of parliament', *History*, xlix (1964), 325–8.

15 The subject categories are listed in J. Hoppit (ed.), *Failed legislation, 1660–1800: extracted from the Commons and Lords Journals* (1997), 30–2. This statistic is the sum

of the sub-categories for Wealth, Status, the Land and Agriculture (codes 00, 01, 70 and 71 – though excluding fisheries (714) from the last). Table 5.1 is a count of codes 000 and 700 only.

16 L. Bonfield, *Marriage settlements, 1601–1740: the adoption of strict settlement* (Cambridge, 1983); J. Habakkuk, *Marriage, debt and the estates system: English landownership, 1650–1950* (Oxford, 1994).

17 Figures based on analysis of estate acts in four sessions: 1664–5, 1698, 1703–4, 1772.

18 B. English and J. Saville, *Strict settlement: a guide for historians* (Hull, 1983), 50.

19 Because sessions varied in length and periodicity this is unsatisfactory for precise analysis.

20 J. Hoppit, 'Patterns of parliamentary legislation, 1660–1800', *Historical Journal*, xxxix (1996), 112–16.

21 *The parliamentary diary of Narcissus Luttrell 1691–1693*, ed. H. Horwitz (Oxford, 1972), 189, 323.

22 *LJ*, xviii, 105–6.

23 J. Thirsk, 'Agricultural policy: public debate and legislation' in Thirsk (ed.), *The agrarian history of England and Wales, V (ii): 1640–1750, agrarian change* (Cambridge, 1985), 318.

24 L. Meager, *The mystery of husbandry* (1697), 139.

25 *CJ*, xxxviii, 232, 288.

26 Based on a detailed analysis of both Commons and Lords *Journals* for nine sessions: 1660, 1674, 1694–95, 1708–9, 1724–25, 1740–41, 1753, 1772–73 and 1795–96.

27 M. Turner and T. Wray, 'A survey of sources for parliamentary enclosure: the *House of Commons' Journal* and commissioners' working papers', *Archives*, xix (1991), 261. On related issues see Lambert, *Bills and acts*, ch. 7; W. E. Tate, 'Members of Parliament and their personal relations to enclosure: a study with reference to Oxfordshire enclosures, 1757–1843', *Agricultural History*, xxiii (1949), 213–20.

28 *The making of the English working class* (Harmondsworth, 1968), 237–8.

29 J. M. Neeson, *Commoners: common right and enclosure in England, 1700–1820* (Cambridge, 1993).

30 E. P. Thompson, *Whigs and hunters: the origin of the Black act* (Harmondsworth, 1977), 263.

31 E. C. K. Gonner, *Common land and enclosure* (2nd edn, 1966), 56–8.

32 29 George II *c.* 36, 13 George III *c.* 81, 41 George III *c.* 109; R. Mitchison, *Agricultural Sir John: the life of Sir John Sinclair of Ulbster 1754–1835* (1962), 156–8, 170–2.

33 6 and 7 William IV *c.* 115.

34 15 Charles II *c.* 17; 2 and 3 Anne *c.* 4 (amended by 5 Anne *c.* 18); 6 Anne *c.* 35; 7 Anne *c.* 20; 8 George II *c.* 6.

35 Quoted in D. Veall, *The popular movement for law reform, 1640–1660* (Oxford, 1970), 212.

36 [W. Carter], *England's interest asserted, in the improvement of its native commodities* (1669), 32.

37 J. Thirsk and J. P. Cooper (eds), *Seventeenth-century economic documents* (Oxford, 1972), 76–7, 79, 96; J. Locke, *Political essays*, ed. M. Goldie (Cambridge, 1997), 169.

38 *England's improvement by sea and land* (1677), 12. The late-seventeenth century discussion of land registries is outlined in R. M. Garnier, *History of the English landed interest: its customs, laws and agriculture*, 2 vols (2nd edn, 1908), i, 96–109.

39 *Two tracts on the benefit of registering deeds in England. I The draught of an act for a county register by . . . Whitlock and Lisle . . . II A treatise shewing how useful, safe,*

reasonable and beneficial the inrolling and registering all conveyances of lands may be to the inhabitants of this kingdom. By Sir Matthew Hale (1754), 33.

40 W. Blackstone, *Commentaries on the laws of England*, 4 vols (1765–69), ii, 343.

41 *Diary and correspondence of John Evelyn*, ed. W. Bray, 4 vols (1850–52), iii, 357.

42 J. S. Stewart-Wallace, 'Registration of title to land', *Journal of the Insitute of Bankers*, lix (1938), 21.

43 *CJ*, xiv, 248; F. Sheppard and V. Belcher, 'The deeds registries of Yorkshire and Middlesex', *Journal of the Society of Archivists*, vi (1980), 274–86.

44 *LJ*, xxv, 408, 483. The clerks of enrolment in Chancery again petitioned against the 1739 bill, making the point that a well-ordered office in Chancery Lane was already available for enrolling deeds. House of Lords Record Office, Main Papers, 10 May to December 1739, 1157, v: 22 May 1739. The 1740 bill failed in the Commons when put to the question 'Whether the Clerks of the Peace should be the Registers . . . As this Question was carried in the Negative, the Bill was dropped by the great Favourites of it, it being a Job only.' *Tory and Whig: the parliamentary papers of Edward Harley, 3rd earl of Oxford, and William Hay, MP for Seaford, 1716–1753*, ed. S. Taylor and C. Jones (Woodbridge, 1998), 38 and 48.

45 *CJ*, xvi, 291 and 293.

46 P. Langford, *Public life and the propertied Englishman, 1689–1798* (Oxford, 1991), 582 and generally 176–86.

47 M. Turner and D. Mills (eds), *Land and property: the English land tax, 1692–1832* (1986).

48 A further possibility is that the demand for registries also declined with the fall in litigation which has been observed in the late seventeenth and early eighteenth centuries. See C. W. Brooks, 'Interpersonal conflict and social tension: civil litigation in England, 1640–1830' in A. L. Beier, D. Cannadine and J. M. Rosenheim (eds), *The first modern society: essays in English history in honour of Lawrence Stone* (Cambridge, 1989), 357–99; H. Horwitz and P. Polden, 'Continuity or change in the court of Chancery in the seventeenth and eighteenth centuries', *Journal of British Studies*, xxxv (1996), 24–57.

49 Irish acts, 6 Anne *c.* 2.

50 P. Roebuck, 'The Irish registry of deeds: a comparative study', *Irish Historical Studies*, xviii (1972–3), 61–73.

51 J. G. Simms, *The Williamite confiscations in Ireland, 1690–1703* (1956), 195.

52 J. L. McCracken, *The Irish parliament in the eighteenth century* (Dundalk, 1971), 23. In this context it is worth noting 1 George I, session 2, *c.* 55 passed at Westminster: 'An act to oblige papists to register their names and real estates.'

53 F. G. James, *The Lords of the Ascendancy: the Irish House of Lords and its members, 1600–1800* (Blackrock, 1995), 12; T. Barnard, 'Protestantism, ethnicity and Irish identities, 1660–1760', in T. Claydon and I. McBride (eds), *Protestantism and national identity: Britain and Ireland, c. 1650–1850* (Cambridge, 1998), 206–35.

54 Differences in numbers of acts passed by the three parliaments need to be related to the frequency with which they met – after 1688 Westminster was usually annual and Dublin biennial – as well as their political, economic, demographic and geographic 'jurisdictions' and the availability of other sources of legal authority.

55 M. Turner, *Enclosures in Britain, 1750–1830* (1984), 21.

56 A good regional analysis is M. W. Dowling, *Tenant right and agrarian society in Ulster, 1600–1870* (Dublin, 1999).

57 G. E. Christianson, 'Landlords and land tenure in Ireland, 1790–1830', *Éire-Ireland*, ix (1974), 33. Defining and measuring absenteeism is fraught with difficulty, and levels may have been significant in both England and Scotland. See A. P. W. Malcolmson, 'Absenteeism in eighteenth-century Ireland', *Irish Economic and Social History*, i (1974), 15–35; P. Roebuck, 'Absentee landownership in the late seventeenth and early eighteenth centuries: a neglected factor in English agrarian history', *Agricultural History Review*, xxi (1973), 1–21.

58 P. Roebuck, 'The economic situation and functions of substantial landowners 1600–1815: Ulster and Lowland Scotland compared', in R. Mitchison and Roebuck (eds), *Economy and society in Scotland and Ireland* (Edinburgh, 1988), 81–92; T. C. Smout, 'Landowners in Scotland, Ireland and Denmark in the age of improvement', *Scandinavian Journal of History*, xii (1987), 79–97.

59 K. Whelan, 'An underground gentry? Catholic middlemen in eighteenth-century Ireland', *Eighteenth-Century Ireland*, x (1995), 8. The interplay between national, economic and religious identities in Ireland in the period is obviously highly complex and the summary here is very crude. For different views see S. J. Connolly, *Religion, law and power: the making of Protestant Ireland, 1660–1760* (Oxford, 1992), chs. 2 and 4; T. Bartlett, 'The rise and fall of the Protestant nation, 1690–1800', *Éire-Ireland*, xxvi (1991), 7–18.

60 I. and K. Whyte, *The changing Scottish landscape 1500–1800* (1991), 132.

61 Other general enabling legislation passed since 1660 included the 1661 'Act for planting and incloseing of ground' (c. 284), the 1669 'Act anent incloseing of ground' (c. 38) and the 1685 'Act in favours of planters and inclosers of ground' (c. 49).

62 T. M. Devine, 'Social responses to agrarian "improvement", the Highland and Lowland clearances in Scotland', in R. A. Houston and I. D. Whyte (eds), *Scottish society, 1500–1800* (Cambridge, 1989), 151. See also T. M. Devine, *The transformation of rural Scotland: social change and the agrarian economy, 1660–1815* (Edinburgh, 1994), 1, 51–2, 63–4.

63 A major exception was 10 George III c. 51, 'An act to encourage the improvement of lands, tenements, and hereditaments, in . . . Scotland, held under settlements of strict entail'; J. W. Cairns, 'Scottish law, Scottish lawyers and the status of the Union', in J. Robertson (ed.), *A union for empire: political thought and the Union of 1707* (Cambridge, 1995), 243–68.

64 *Commentaries*, i, 95. Kames provides a notable example of an attempt to bridge the divide. See D. Lieberman, *The province of legislation determined: legal theory in eighteenth-century Britain* (Cambridge, 1989), ch. 7.

65 T. C. Smout, 'Scottish landowners and economic growth, 1650–1850', *Scottish Journal of Political Economy*, xi (1964), 218.

66 L. Timperley, 'The pattern of landholding in eighteenth-century Scotland', in M. L. Parry and T. R. Slater (eds), *The making of the Scottish countryside* (1980), 138.

67 R. H. Campbell, 'The Scottish improvers and the course of agrarian change in the eighteenth century', in L. M. Cullen and T. C. Smout (eds), *Comparative aspects of Scottish and Irish economic and social history 1600–1900* (Edinburgh, 1977), 204–15; E. J. Hobsbawm, 'Scottish reformers of the eighteenth century and capitalist agriculture', in Hobsbawm, W. Kula, A. Mitra, K. N. Raj and I. Sachs (eds), *Peasants in history: essays in honour of Daniel Thorner* (Calcutta, 1980), 3–29.

68 [W. Mackie], *An address to the landed interest of Great Britain, on the present state of the distillery, by the farmers in Scotland* (Edinburgh, 1786), 17. On this affair see

V. E. Dietz, 'The politics of whisky: Scottish distillers, the excise, and the Pittite state', *Journal of British Studies*, xxxvi (1997), 35–69.

69 [Mackie], *An address*, 39, 51; *Resolutions of the landed interest of Scotland respecting the distillery; with reasons why the duty upon British spirits should be levied by an annual license upon the still* (Edinburgh, 1786), xiii.

70 *Resolutions of the landed interest of Scotland*, 80. Such language was also often used in comparisons between Irish and English landowners. See Bartlett, 'Rise and fall'.

71 [Mackie], *An address*, 33, note. The reference to Melchizedek presumably alludes to tithes: Genesis, 14, 20.

72 C. A. Edie, 'The Irish cattle bills: a study in Restoration politics', *Transactions of the American Philosophical Society*, new series, lx, part 2 (1970); P. Kelly, 'The Irish woollen export prohibition act of 1699: Kearney re-visited', *Irish Economic and Social History*, vii (1980), 22–44.

73 Stimulating analyses of lobbying and interest groups include J. Brewer, *The sinews of power: war, money and the English state, 1688–1783* (1989), 231–49; V. E. Dietz, 'Before the age of capital: manufacturing interests and the British state, 1780–1800' (Princeton University PhD thesis, 1991), ch. 1; S. Handley, 'Provincial influence on general legislation: the case of Lancashire, 1689–1731', *Parliamentary History*, xvi (1997), 171–84.

74 D. G. Barnes, *A history of the English corn laws from 1660–1846* (1930), 23–7, 59.

75 W. R. Ward, *The English land tax in the eighteenth century* (Oxford, 1953); C. Brooks, 'Public finance and political stability: the administration of the land tax, 1688–1720', *Historical Journal*, xvii (1974), 281–300.

76 Thirsk and Cooper (eds), *Seventeenth-century economic documents*, 800–11; J. V. Beckett, 'Land tax or excise: the levying of taxation in seventeenth and eighteenth-century England', *English Historical Review*, c (1985), 301; W. R. Ward, 'The land tax in Scotland, 1707–1798', *Bulletin of the John Rylands Library*, xxxvii (1954–5), 288–308. Langford, *Public life*, 342, valuably points out that the burdens of the land tax were clearly felt in towns, so potentially providing a common cause between the landed and commercial interests.

77 Quoted in J. Sinclair, *Account of the origin of the Board of Agriculture, and its progress for three years after its establishment* (1796), 8.

78 Sinclair, *Account*, 1, 5.

79 R. Mitchison, 'The old Board of Agriculture (1793–1822)', *English Historical Review*, lxxiv (1959), 41–69.

80 *An inquiry into the nature and causes of the wealth of nations*, ed. R. H. Campbell and A. S. Skinner, 2 vols (Indianapolis, 1981), i, 265. The paucity of physiocratic economic analysis in England and Scotland is worth noting.

81 J. P. Greene, *Negotiated authorities: essays in colonial political and constitutional history* (Charlottesville, 1994).

6

Patriots and legislators: Irishmen and their parliaments, c. 1689–c. 1740

David Hayton

Given that legislative autonomy was a major preoccupation of 'patriot' pamphleteers and politicians in eighteenth-century Ireland, we may naturally assume that the possession of a separate national parliament was closely bound up with notions of national identity. Moreover, the steady progress of the Irish parliament from its precarious re-establishment in the aftermath of the Williamite victory to a settled position at the heart of government seems to have run in parallel with the maturing of a sense of 'Irishness' among the Protestant propertied elite.[1] This close connection between parliamentary constitutionalism and the development of a distinctive Irish identity is particularly marked in the speeches and actions of opposition politicians, who seized upon issues of 'national' significance in order to achieve popularity and embarrass ministers; identifying themselves as 'patriots' and their cause as that of 'the nation'.[2] Although, as Joep Leerssen has observed, the term 'patriot', in an eighteenth-century context, need not have had any strong 'national' connotations,[3] the fact that these successive agitations were forged in a context of actual or assumed English misrule shaped their rhetoric into an elevated form of anti-Englishness: at the very least an awareness that the inhabitants of Ireland possessed essential interests separate from, and sometimes in conflict with, those of England. At the same time, 'patriotism' did not always express itself in the language of strident protest. Less well known to historians, though just as significant to contemporaries, was the emergence in the first half of the eighteenth century of a form of 'patriotism' inspired not by fear or envy of England, but by a positive vision of what Ireland might become if subjected to a sustained campaign of social and economic 'improvement'. Here too, as we shall see, the Irish parliament occupied a central role.

Throughout this essay, attention will be focused on parliamentary processes rather than the constitutional theories underpinning them. This emphasis should not conceal the importance to developing notions of Irish 'national identity' of the historical pedigree of the Irish parliament. One of the arguments used by 'patriots' to justify claims to legislative autonomy was that eighteenth-century Irishmen were the heirs to a distinct and venerable parliamentary tradition, originating with the establishment of the lordship of Ireland under Henry II. The most famous (and most often reprinted) 'patriot' ideologue, William Molyneux, introduced his *Case of Ireland* in 1698 with a lengthy historical discourse, while the arguments in favour of maintaining the appellate jurisdiction of the Irish House of Lords, in the recurring disputes of the period 1697–1720, almost always depended on the recitation of precedents.[4] A sense that they had inherited a continuous parliamentary tradition going back six centuries might well have encouraged Irish Protestants to think of themselves as Irishmen. However, the picture is complicated; first by the fact that 'patriots' were also capable of taking a Lockeian view of their natural rights to representative institutions, an interpretation which would have placed their parliament on a similar level to transatlantic colonial assemblies;[5] and second, by the willingness of Irish MPs to look to Westminster as a guide to procedure, which would suggest that they did not feel constrained by precedent. The members of the first Irish House of Commons to meet after the Revolution, in 1692, most of whom were parliamentary novices, established committees to search their own records in order to discover how their predecessors had gone about their business, but also followed English practice, inevitably perhaps, given the links between the political classes in the two kingdoms and the fact that a significant minority of Irish MPs were also MPs at Westminster.[6] In money matters for example, the Irish House of Commons went into committees of the whole on supply and ways and means in order to prepare supply bills, just as the English did. More generally, sessions after 1692 saw an increasing resort to committees of the whole house (frequently ordered to discuss 'the state of the nation') rather than 'grand' committees to investigate grievances. Even when Irish practice came eventually to differ sharply from English, most obviously in the scrutiny of government accounts through a standing committee rather than a parliamentary commission, this was not a case of inventing something new but of retaining an English tradition that had been abandoned at Westminster.

When the Irish parliament had reassembled in 1692 it was after a lapse of 26 years. (James II's parliament of 1689 was ostentatiously discounted as a 'pretended parliament' and its works rendered null and void.) The long period of non-parliamentary government following the dissolution of 1666 had been the product of political anxiety and financial security. On the one hand Charles II had feared an angry response from Irish Protestants to English mercantilist legislation, and also a pre-emptive strike against his plans for Catholic relief; on the other, the Restoration parliament had added to the King's 'hereditary revenue' by voting him 'additional taxes' for life, and the subsequent improvement in Irish public finances as a result of commercial expansion liberated government from monetary pressures. By 1692 the situation was reversed. King William's first viceroy, Lord Sydney, was obliged to call parliament not only to complete the settlement of the country, but because of the weakness of the Irish treasury – seriously in arrears with payments and with scarcely any cash available from a kingdom still recovering from a ruinous civil war. At the same time it would have been reasonable to expect that Irish Protestants, grateful for their recent 'deliverance', would vote a generous supply.[7] He was to suffer a rude awakening. The Commons declined to make adequate financial provision until they could make good their newly discovered claim to a 'sole right' to initiate supply bills; and investigations into official corruption reached dangerously close to the viceroy. Thoroughly alarmed, Sydney prorogued and then dissolved parliament.[8] Needless to say, the parlous state of the Irish treasury did not improve for want of funds, and three years later his successor, Henry Capel, was obliged to call new elections.

The political settlement negotiated by Capel was a landmark in Irish parliamentary history.[9] In deciding to convene another parliament English ministers had deliberately forsworn their trump card, the possibility of taxing Ireland directly from Westminster, presumably because they were afraid of political repercussions at home. Obliging Capel to recall parliament left the lord deputy with little alternative but to negotiate with the opposition of three years before. Effectively he acknowledged the Commons' claim to a 'sole right', though without abandoning what was perceived as the royal prerogative in this matter. For their part, however, Irish MPs were careful not to repeat the mistake of their predecessors in the 1660s and give more money than was necessary. Despite proclaiming loyalty, successive parliaments not only voted the government less funds than it required, but restricted the term of the 'additional' duties to two years at the most.

The re-established parliament endured a chequered history until the Hanoverian succession. Nearly five years was allowed to elapse between the final prorogation of King's William's second Irish parliament and the opening of Queen Anne's first, in 1703, because English ministers feared (unnecessarily, as it turned out) an eruption of Irish Protestant rage at the English parliament's interference with the Irish woollen manufacture and resumption of Irish forfeited estates. In 1707 and again in 1709 the Commons refused to give 'additional' supply for two years, offering a year and three-quarters and a twelvemonth respectively, in order to ensure more frequent sittings. Finally, the short-lived parliament of November–December 1713 was hastily prorogued, after a collapse of viceregal political management, and then dissolved without any grant of supply beyond Christmas of that year, so that for nearly two years government had to manage without any 'additional' taxes at all.[10] That the Irish treasury was not bankrupted was owing to a temporary increase in hereditary customs duties, as Dublin merchants took advantage of the expiry of other duties to stockpile imported goods. In the long run, however, this display of entrepreneurial opportunism worked against the interests of government. When George I's first Irish parliament met in the winter of 1715–16 MPs calculated ways and means on the basis of pre-1713 returns, but merchants did not maintain imports at previous levels, so that the yield fell below expectations. By the next session, in 1717, the Irish treasury was running a deficit, which continued, and indeed increased, over the next twenty years.[11] It thus became almost impossible for ministers even to contemplate dispensing with parliament. When Lord Sunderland thought long and hard on this subject in 1720, following another crisis in Anglo-Irish relations, he floated a number of desperate expedients, including a return to tax-farming, and the stripping of the Irish military establishment; but eventually he and his colleagues decided to take the risk of another attempt at parliamentary management, which happily paid off.[12]

By 1720 the Irish parliament had settled into a pattern of biennial sessions. Not only did the frequency and regularity of sessions increase, so too did their length. A decade-by-decade analysis demonstrates this steady advance: from 1692 to 1700 the Irish parliament was in session for a total of 259 days; from 1701 to 1710 for 324 days; and after a slight fall in the next decade (to 306 days from 1711 to 1720) the figure rose again in the 1720s, to 415, and in the 1730s to 452. The very fact of meeting more often encouraged members to improve the way in which parliament worked. This quiet 'constitutional revolution' was marked by, among other things, a proliferation of legislative activity and by a significant development in the power of the Commons to scrutinise government expenditure, its standing committee of accounts operating through various specialist sub-committees. In a development of the principle, abandoned in England, that supply should not be voted until grievances had been discussed, it was firmly established that until the committee of accounts had reported at the beginning of each session no significant progress would be made on supply.

Despite these advances, the parliament still laboured under a number of serious limitations to its authority. Potentially its greatest weakness was the claim of the Westminster parliament to be able to legislate in Irish affairs. This had been repeatedly asserted and exercised before being enshrined in the British 'Declaratory Act' of 1720. Occasionally Westminster legislated on issues of real political contention between the two kingdoms, but for the most part these English bills were routine and uncontroversial: implementing constitutional changes to bring Ireland into line with the other dominions of the crown at times when no parliament was sitting in Dublin (the transfer of the crown in 1689 and the consequent amending of the oaths of allegiance and supremacy, and the imposition of the abjuration act in 1703); carrying out administrative business which affected the two kingdoms equally (quarantine regulations, for example, or the emergency statute of 1714 to prevent French army agents from recruiting within Queen Anne's realms); and above all private bills. Only rarely did Westminster intervene directly in public affairs that were purely of Irish domestic concern: one notorious example would be the extension to Ireland in 1714 (again, it must be said, while the Irish parliament was prorogued) of the British Schism Act, intended to suppress Nonconformist academies, and this was at the instigation of Irish political interests.[13] Yet even the uncontentious statutes that were passed on Irish matters made quite breathtaking assumptions about the authority of the Westminster parliament: the bill of 1711, for example, which permitted the Dublin banker Sir Alexander Cairnes to purchase fee farms on the Ormond estates, specifically stated that this facility was granted 'notwithstanding' an Irish statute of the previous year; while, even more radically, a petition in February 1708 by the guardian of an Irish minor, John Hackett, requested a British bill for the specific purpose of amending two acts of the Irish parliament. In the event, Hackett's bill was not introduced, but the reason given was a practical one, not any admission that it was unconstitutional to amend an Irish statute.[14]

It may seem surprising, given the tendency of Irish 'patriots' to become indignant over English interference, that this most basic of constitutional grievances excited little emotion. True, Molyneux's *Case of Ireland* caused a furore when it was published in 1698, in the midst of conflict over the jurisdictional authority of the Irish House of Lords and proposed English legislation against Irish woollen exports. Many English observers, including Queen Anne, were persuaded that the Irish 'had a mind to be independent'.[15] In fact, nothing could have been further from the truth. Molyneux's pamphlet was disavowed by Irish politicians and pamphleteers, most of whom went out of their way to reject notions of 'independency'.[16] Few items of English/British legislation were protested against in Ireland; even the Declaratory Act, for all the apprehensions of Sunderland and his ministerial colleagues in 1720, aroused not a murmur of resentment in the Irish parliament.[17] The reasons for this restraint were partly practical – the balance of advantages accruing to Irishmen from these constitutional arrangements – and partly a reflection of the ambivalence characteristic of Irish Protestant attitudes towards the English connection.

On some issues, of course, a vigorous response was guaranteed. The most important was trade, in many respects the crux of all difficulties in relationships between the constituent kingdoms of the British crown. Much of the pamphlet debate over the Union between England and Scotland concerned the question of whether the Scots would benefit from a closer connection with their more powerful neighbour, while those Irishmen who urged Ireland's inclusion in these new arrangements based their arguments largely on economics. For an Irish audience, they claimed that union would kick-start the struggling Irish economy; when addressing the English they were keen to contradict the prevailing assumption that any gain for Ireland must represent a corresponding loss to England.[18] The assumption that Englishmen would think in this way helps to explain Irish reactions to such provocations as the Woollen Act of 1699, which effectively banned the export of Irish woollens. It was taken as axiomatic that when the English perceived their own and Irish interests to be in conflict they would act ruthlessly to secure their position at Ireland's expense. Thus Irish parliamentary 'patriots' naturally focused their attention on Anglo-Irish economic relationships, and were particularly alert for any evidence of imbalance. Their resentment erupted most spectacularly over Wood's Halfpence in 1722–25, when a careless and corrupt English administration appeared to threaten the foundation of Ireland's economy, its currency. The idea of Irish treasure being drawn away to England was a powerful one, and recurred in a number of 'patriotic' back-bench campaigns thereafter: over further proposals to reform the coinage; over the chronic problem of absenteeism, by English placemen and pensioners on the Irish establishment, and even by Anglo-Irish landlords; and in the 1750s over the disposition of surplus income from taxation remaining in the Irish treasury.[19]

The only other issue capable of arousing such emotion was landholding. This was what made the jurisdictional dispute between the Irish House of Lords and its Westminster counterpart so emotive. The claim by the English Lords to an appellate jurisdiction over civil cases in Ireland, which came to an explosive climax in the case of *Annesley* v. *Sherlock* in 1717–19, took decisions over Irish property rights out of Ireland and placed them in the hands of a 'foreign' legislature.[20] The first clause of the Declaratory Act of 1720, which dealt as shortly and decisively with the claims of the Irish House of Lords as the second clause pronounced the legislative superiority of Westminster, was the insult against which most Irish resentment was directed.[21] Although the dispute was couched in terms of constitutional rights, it was authority over the title to land which was fundamentally at stake. Curiously, this never became an issue in relation to private bill legislation at Westminster, even those bills which abrogated existing Irish legislation. Presumably the option of securing a private act at Westminster was simply too convenient. But anxiety over property rights was what made the forfeitures resumption of 1699/1700 so unpopular in Ireland and provoked an unprecedented, and unrepeated, campaign of political agitation, with petitions to the king from most counties and several major cities in Ireland, organised in the form of a 'national remonstrance'.[22]

In other respects, however, Irishmen were conscious of the ways in which they themselves might profit from the existence of an alternative means of securing legislative redress of grievances or advancement of their interests. This was most obviously the case in relation to private bill legislation. Throughout the first half of the eighteenth century there was a steady trickle of Irish estate bills on to the English statute book. In the early 1700s this briefly swelled to a flood, as a result of the forfeitures resumption, which prompted a large number of amending and explanatory bills, so much so that standing orders were amended several times in an effort to stem the flow.[23] This was exceptional; by the 1720s and 1730s there were customarily only a handful of Irish private bills per session, of which one or two would pass. Not only was this facility never challenged by Irish 'patriots', one of the most vociferous defenders of Irish constitutional rights, Archbishop King of Dublin, even made use of it himself.[24] The reasons were obvious. Since the Irish parliament met only every other year, the opportunities to secure a private Irish act were limited; it might be even more expensive to do so than to obtain a British act, given the cumbersome nature of the Irish legislative process and the need to employ an English as well as an Irish agent to ease the bill through the two Privy Councils;[25] and there was always the possibility that an Irish statute might be overridden or repealed by a British act.

It was not merely in the specialised area of private bill legislation that Irishmen, even determined 'patriots', would welcome English interference. There was no high-minded constitutional opposition to the inclusion of Ireland in the

British quarantine acts, nor, *a fortiori*, to those measures introduced at Westminster to encourage, rather than constrain, Irish trade. The political and economic difficulties arising from the implementation of the Woollen Act gave rise to several ameliorative measures. First, English ministers attempted a crude compensation by promoting linen manufacture in Ireland, an English act of 1705 permitting the export of Irish linens to the colonies. But despite these efforts the main wool-producing areas, especially in Munster, did not change over to linen production and instead substituted for the legal export trade that had been denied them a profitable illegal trade to the continent.[26] In response to the howls of complaint from English clothing interests Walpole's administration made several attempts in the 1730s to dissuade the Irish from smuggling woollens to France. Among the incentives offered were bills to remove the prohibitive English duties on imported woollen yarn and friezes, to repeal part of the navigation acts so as to allow direct importation to Ireland of some colonial produce, and even a major modification of the Cattle Act of 1667 to re-open the English market to Irish beef. To Walpole's surprise, most of these measures encountered opposition in Ireland and smuggling continued unabated. However, the opposition was not based on the presumption of the British parliament in legislating unilaterally for Anglo-Irish trade, but in each case something more specific and practical: Walpole's insistence on including in the yarn bill a scheme for the registration of Irish woollen exports, which would flood Ireland with excisemen; or the fact that Irish farming had adapted so well to the restrictions of the Cattle Acts that to reopen English markets to Irish livestock would damage the lucrative trade in beef and butter.[27] Where no such complications arose, as with the act of 1731 to permit the importation of colonial goods, there were no Irish objections.

The occasional effectiveness of the Irish 'lobby' at Westminster offered further encouragement. The Irish landowning elite enjoyed a variety of close connections with England. Many planter families of recent vintage had retained their English ancestral estates; other, grander families like the Boyles or Annesleys had even purchased more English property; others still had married into English landed families. These were the genuinely 'Anglo-Irish', as Barnard has redefined that over-used term, with interests on both sides of the Irish Sea.[28] A small number held seats themselves in the British parliament, or could command English parliamentary dependants, and formed the core of an 'Irish lobby' at Westminster, which would sometimes be bolstered by Irish office-holders and followers of the lord lieutenant.[29] Clearly the Irish lobby stood little chance of success when it was in conflict with powerful vested interests in England, notably the woollen manufacturers of Yorkshire, East Anglia and the over-represented west country, or fell foul of one or other of the English political parties (as happened over the resumption of forfeited estates in 1700, which was a specifically Tory project[30]). But at other times, especially when the ministry was keen to conciliate Irish interests, it enjoyed some success. One episode in particular not only provides a useful illustration of the strength of the Irish voice at Westminster, when supported by government, but also points up the advantages to the Irish in this respect of maintaining their own parliament: the conflict between Scottish and Irish 'lobbies' in 1711 over a bill imposing restrictions on the export of flax and linen yarn to Ireland, in order to protect Scottish manufactures from Irish competition.[31] At this time it was in the ministry's interest to ensure that Irish sensibilities were not outraged, for fear of putting at risk Irish parliamentary management. The recent Irish parliamentary session had been so difficult that Lord Treasurer Oxford was already thinking of replacing the duke of Ormond as viceroy, to avoid a complete breakdown in management when parliament met again.[32] By contrast the Scots were in no position to assist the Court significantly in either house of the Westminster parliament. Oxford therefore did nothing to prevent the Court interest following Ormond in successfully opposing the Scots' proposals.

Thus the limitations of Irish Protestant 'patriotism' reflected the way in which the legislative system functioned to the general advantage as well as to the occasional detriment of the Irish. When the Westminster parliament legislated on Irish affairs it sometimes offended Irish sensibilities, but at other times it produced outcomes which were to the benefit of Irishmen, and answered needs which could not be met by the Irish parliament. Irish Protestants in general welcomed legislation to confirm the change of monarch in 1689 and to settle the succession in 1701; the inclusion of Ireland in quarantine regulations; and the prohibition on French military recruiting. Irish Tory interests welcomed the imposition of the schism act of 1714; Whigs its repeal in 1719. Ulster Presbyterians urged the English ministry in 1720 to make use of the powers claimed in the declaratory act to pass relief measures at Westminster that could not be pushed through the parliament in Dublin.[33] That there was a strong element of pragmatism in Irish political thought in the early eighteenth century has recently been emphasised, in the context of discussions of the legitimacy of the Glorious Revolution.[34] It is equally apparent in attitudes to Irish constitutional subordination to Westminster: if Irish Protestants stood to gain, they would not merely accept but might actively solicit English legislation on Irish affairs.

The capacity to calculate immediate advantage against constitutional principle also reflects ambivalence over national loyalties. The Irish parliament was a Protestant institution, representing a Protestant electorate, and the maintenance of the Protestant establishment in Ireland depended in the last resort on the English connection. Even ardent patriots like Molyneux or Archbishop King expressed their ultimate preference for an incorporating union with England at the same time as they extolled the historical rights of the independent Irish parliament, while some more enthusiastic advocates envisaged such a union as a reunion of kindred peoples: the English of England and the English of Ireland.[35] An exemplar of this limited constitutional 'patriotism' was Alan Brodrick, Lord Midleton, himself the son of a Cromwellian planter, who early in his career took a prominent part in pressing the Commons' 'sole right' in supply legislation, and the importance of granting 'additional taxes' for limited periods, but who refused to join in the denunciation of the British House of Lords' claim to appellate

Table 6.1 Numbers and fortunes of bills of the Irish parliament, 1692–1740

	bills transmitted to England	bills engrossed and returned	percentage of bills engrossed and returned
1695–1705	142	75	53
1707–17	133	94	71
1719–28	121	84	69
1729–40	130	105	81
Total	526	358	68

jurisdiction.[36] Brodrick was an Irish patriot, but also a determined upholder of Protestant ascendancy who realised the danger in advancing pretensions to an untenable constitutional independence.

The second major restriction on the powers and independence of the Irish parliament, until the constitutional reforms of 1782, stemmed from the continuing operation of Poynings' law, which confined the legislative powers of the Irish parliament under the supervision of the Irish and English Privy Councils. Technically Irish bills could only originate in the Irish Council, which would transmit them to London, where they were inspected and could be suppressed or altered. When engrossed and returned to Dublin, bills were presented to the Irish parliament for acceptance or rejection, without any possibility of amendment. The power thus conferred on the English (after 1708 British) Privy Council was one that ministers were more than willing to exploit, as the Table 6.1 makes clear.[37] Taking the period 1692 to 1740, and ignoring the Irish parliamentary sessions of 1692 and 1713, both of which were foreshortened by tactical prorogations, we can see that of the bills transmitted by the viceroy as many as a third were 'respited', that is to say suppressed, in Whitehall and never returned to Ireland. Of the rest, preliminary research into the Privy Council papers at Kew[38] indicates that a good many, perhaps even the majority, were returned with significant amendment.

The crude statistical evidence might suggest that over time conciliar supervision relaxed, to the extent that the British Privy Council grew less inclined to 'respite' bills. On the other hand, the work of James Kelly on the operation of Poynings' law in the 1760s suggests that scrutiny of Irish legislation was still rigorous then, with a high level of emendation.[39]

The intervention of the British Privy Council on particular cases could well give rise to political problems when the engrossed bills were presented to the Irish parliament. Interference with a supply bill caused acute embarrassment to the Whig Lord Wharton in 1709 and threatened its passage. Pembroke lost a popular anti-Catholic bill in 1707 because it had been diluted in England.[40] Perhaps the most bitter controversy arose in 1704 over the 'tacking' by the Council to the bill 'to prevent the growth of popery' of a clause imposing on all crown and municipal office-holders in Ireland the obligation to take holy communion once a year in the established church. This was a blow aimed by English High Tory interests against Irish dissenters, in particular the presbyterian community in Ulster, whose concentration in a few boroughs and aversion to 'occasional conformity' made their political influence vulnerable to the imposition of a religious test.[41] The fact that it was attached to an anti-Catholic measure enabled Irish Whigs to swallow it, albeit with a bad grace, and once imposed it proved very difficult to remove. But this did not stop presbyterian interests from continuing to agitate against it, and to rail at the underhand manner in which it had been introduced.

Incidents of this kind focused public attention in Ireland on the irritations and injustices, large and small, perpetrated through conciliar interference in legislation, and from time to time voices were raised against the idea of submitting bills to government for approval. Interference with the tillage bill of 1711, for example, provoked some MPs to denounce Poynings' law in the Irish House of Commons and lament 'a mangled and torn constitution', and in the next parliamentary session, in 1713, efforts were made to introduce heads of a bill which would have modified legislative procedure so as to diminish conciliar powers significantly.[42] There was a strong element of political shadow-boxing about the resort to this kind of tactic, however. It was more often threatened than put into effect, and never attracted enough support to pass a resolution protesting against the prevailing constitutional arrangements. The truth was that for most of the time the system worked well. The British Privy Council, and the subcommittee of senior law officers to whom the examination of Irish legislation was entrusted, was not just concerned to safeguard English interests, but to make sure that bills properly answered the ends for which they had been drawn up.[43] Thus, although popular measures might sometimes be lost, transmission to England also meant that Irish bills would be subjected to scrutiny by men whose experience and expertise might repair the inadequacies of Irish draftsmanship, an important consideration since in this period no class of parliamentary draftsmen emerged in Dublin to iron out the anomalies in the legislation that Irish parliamentarians had devised for themselves.

Poynings' law was not, however, executed to the letter. In fact, most bills originated in the Irish parliament rather than the Council. By the seventeenth century the Irish parliament had found a way to circumvent the technical requirements of Poynings' law by the device of producing 'heads of bills', identical in every way to bills themselves except for their preamble, which would be presented and considered in one of the two houses before being sent to the viceroy and Council to be embodied into bills. A new parliament required that bills be prepared in advance by the Council, though these became fewer in number as the century wore on and the legislative process settled into a regular pattern: thus there were twelve in the session of 1692, and fourteen in 1695, but five in 1703, two in 1713, and three each in 1715 and 1727. Money bills were particularly contentious, because of the controversy over the 'sole right', but after the compromise negotiated by Capel the Commons seemed willing to collude in the

Table 6.2 Origins of bills in the Irish parliament, 1692–1740

	Irish Privy Council	Commons 'heads'	Lords 'heads'	Percentage as 'heads'
1692–1705	58	92	35	69
1707–17	25	94	31	83
1719–28	12	84	30	90
1729–40	8	94	25	94
Total	103	364	116	82

technicality of preserving the royal prerogative. Otherwise, the statistical evidence shows that the vast proportion of bills originated as 'heads', in the Commons rather than the Lords; and increasingly so as time went by.

In other respects, Irish MPs evidently did not regard the legislative process as immutable, for there were various experiments with parliamentary conventions: for example, it was tacitly agreed in one session that all 'heads' of private bills would be introduced in the Lords, only for the following session to see a reversion to the norm; on another occasion the Commons issued an order to limit the number of 'heads', insisting that no more be introduced until existing committee proceedings were completed, but again reversed this policy within a few years; while in the 1733–4 session the Commons briefly tried out the expedient of discussing 'heads' in both houses rather than one, in a conscious effort to bring their proceedings more closely into line with Westminster, before voting to return to the old method.[44] Although this willingness to experiment may be taken as testimony to the flexibility of the eighteenth-century constitution, and to the fact that members were not hidebound by precedent (or indeed by English example), it also suggests a degree of dissatisfaction with the way the legislative system was operating.

In fact, the most serious impediment deriving from Poynings' law was not the obvious one – the opportunities given to the executive to interfere in legislation – but the delays imposed by the elaborate method of proceeding by 'heads', and the necessity of a mid-sessional adjournment in order that 'heads' could be transmitted to London. It was impossible to secure the Royal Assent to any 'heads' introduced after the recess (where this was done, the purpose seems to have been to lay down a marker for a subsequent attempt). For practical purposes Irish MPs only had half a session in which to work.[45] Their productivity rate, in terms of acts passed, was thus much inferior to the Westminster parliament, although the comparison is not entirely fair, given that Ireland's smaller population and less developed economy, and the limited administrative competence of the Irish government, required far less legislation.

In statistical terms, the Irish parliament could pride itself on a higher success rate than that achieved at Westminster, but this is only further evidence of the

Table 6.3 The frequency of sittings and volume of enactments at Westminster and Dublin, 1690–1740[46]

	Days sitting			Acts passed		
	Westminster	Dublin	Dublin as %	Westminster	Dublin	Dublin as %
1690–1700	1,333	259	19.4	681	76	11.2
1701–10	1,056	324	30.7	738	114	15.4
1711–20	1,201	306	25.0	584	87	14.9
1721–30	1,096	415	37.9	619	111	17.9
1731–40	854	452	52.9	639	124	19.4

Note: 'Dublin as %' expresses the numbers of Dublin days sitting and acts passed as a percentage of the Westminster totals.

cumbersome nature of the Irish legislative process, which effectively discouraged members from introducing new measures, and even deterred interested parties from petitioning for 'heads' when there was so little time to complete the process of hearing the petition, securing an order, introducing the 'heads', having them read twice, heard in committee, reported, engrossed and transmitted to the viceroy for consideration by the two Privy Councils. The disparity in the proportion of private to public legislation between Westminster and Dublin is striking: whereas 45 per cent of acts passed by the British parliament in the reigns of the first two Georges were private, the figure for the Irish parliament would be under 19 per cent. This may be explained by differences in the subject-matter of private bill legislation in the two parliaments, most notably the almost complete absence of enclosure acts from the Irish statute book, but the practical difficulties facing sponsors of private bills in Ireland, and the additional expense, must also have been a factor.

Despite the development of the powers and functions of the Irish parliament, it was thus by no means a perfect legislative instrument, and some Protestant Irishmen declared their wish for incorporation into a united parliament if this could be accomplished. In recent years much has been written about the 'proto-unionism' of the early eighteenth century, and some historians would have us believe that there was a strong current of opinion in Ireland in favour of the idea.[47] Certainly various proposals were circulated, both in manuscript and in print, and there were occasional addresses from Commons and Lords asking for Ireland's inclusion in any incorporating schemes, especially while the Anglo-Scottish union was under active consideration between 1703 and 1707. How seriously we should take these manifestations of opinion, and whether they can be said to have amounted to a unionist 'discourse' is open to question. On closer inspection the parliamentary addresses, and indeed some examples of ostensibly pro-unionist pamphleteering, can be shown to have arisen from particular political circumstances and to have been motivated by narrower, tactical aims:

embarrassing a viceroy, for instance, or anticipating some popular scheme.[48] Because the English had no need to take these Irish requests seriously, the unionist discourse, if that is indeed what it was, took place within a vacuum. But at least the existence of these expressions of opinion, and a number of favourable references in private correspondence, would support the conclusion that in the immediate aftermath of the Revolution there was a consensus among the political classes in Ireland that, given the choice, union was preferable to continuing with their own parliament.

While arguments in favour of union addressed deep anxieties about the security of the Protestant establishment and the economic welfare of the country, the existing restrictions on the autonomy of the Irish parliament may also have been a persuasive consideration. In purely parliamentary terms, however, it is not easy to see that the interests of Irish Protestants would have been served by submerging their own legislature in a united parliament. The proponents of union did not bother to think through the implications of their proposals: none of the pamphlets advocating union, for example, was willing to face the thorny question of equality of taxation in a united kingdom; and the *bienpensant* optimism with which unionists assumed English goodwill towards Irish economic interests in a parliament in which the Irish contingent would be a small minority was remarkable. Practical experience demonstrated the value of having access to two parliaments rather than being confined in one corner of a united assembly. Had Ireland been already included in the British union in the 1730s, for example, the Walpole ministry would have been able to intervene directly against Irish wool smuggling, instead of offering a series of legislative inducements to persuade the Irish parliament to take action.

The value to Irishmen of having their own parliament was most apparent in the use made of statutory powers to encourage economic development. In this respect there was a strong contrast with Scotland, where, as John Shaw and others have demonstrated, 'improvement' was fostered through non-parliamentary institutions like the Convention of Royal Burghs, the Royal Bank and the Board of Trustees for Fisheries and Manufacture.[49] In Ireland parliament itself remained the focus. Of possible alternatives, the authority of the Irish Privy Council to act by proclamation in such matters as regulating the coinage or laying temporary embargoes on exports afforded it a minor role in economic regulation, and although attempts to establish a national bank in Ireland failed, there were parallels to the Scottish Fisheries Trustees in such institutions as the Linen Board (1711) and Tillage Commission (1730). However, both the Linen Board and the Tillage Commission were established and controlled by act of parliament. They formed part of a broader strategy of priming economic growth through parliamentary means, with public funds directed to support various projects, and legislation to regulate commerce, encourage manufactures, and facilitate the construction of harbours, roads and canals.

During the first half of the eighteenth century the Irish parliament developed various methods of assigning public expenditure. Recent research by Eoin

Magennis has done much to explain the peculiarly Irish practice of funding projects and projectors through parliamentary grants, appropriations and bounties, which in due course commentators like Arthur Young would condemn as corruption.[50] Its origins lay partly in the ramshackle nature of the Irish administration, in which no responsible local official had authority to issue payments from the Irish treasury; and partly in the recovery of the Irish public revenue in the 1730s, which saw the appearance of surpluses that MPs were anxious to dispose of themselves. The inclusion in supply bills of clauses making specific grants of money to named persons arose from the absence of any Irish equivalent to the English Treasury Board, where government creditors might apply for settlement of their debts. The first beneficiaries were a former clerk to the Commons and the family of a former Speaker; but the method was extended to comprehend prospective as well as retrospective awards, with a sum granted in 1722 to the Linen Board. By 1740 nearly £9,000 p.a. was being disbursed in this way. Appropriations of revenue began in 1711, again with the Linen Board as the first beneficiary.[51] Here the most important step was the passage of the Inland Navigation Act of 1730, which established commissioners to promote the use of tillage and improvements in navigation, funded by the produce of specific duties.[52] Finally there were the bounties included in bills to promote particular kinds of trading activity, which were designed to swallow up surplus revenue before it could be siphoned off to England. Once more the linen industry was the first to benefit, in 1707, from a bounty on the import of flax seed.

A little under a third of all Irish statutes passed between 1692 and 1760 covered subjects of broadly 'social' and 'economic' concern (including acts to improve transport and communications), that is to say 220 out of a total of 730.[53] More specifically, during the 1720s and 1730s, a period in which the 'improvement' of Ireland was canvassed widely in the press, and embodied in the formation of the Dublin Society and the founding of the Charter Schools,[54] a substantial and increasing proportion of public bills were designed to encourage economic activity, in the exploitation of land and other natural resources, the development of industrial enterprises, commerce, and financial services, transport and communications, and the renewal of the urban fabric: nearly a third in 1721–30 (45 out of 145) and two-thirds in 1731–40 (109 out of 166). The success rate for this kind of legislation was a little below average, but not much: in all 25 per cent of the public acts passed in the 1720s were designed for economic 'improvement' (22 out of 88), and in the next decade 58 per cent (64 out of 109).

A detailed breakdown of these statistics in terms of the subject-matter of bills points to a particular increase in the number concerned with the development of transport and communication links. Much of this is to be explained by what can only be described as a craze for road-building, which erupted in 1731–32 and reached a peak in 1733–36 before quietening down, though not subsiding completely, thereafter. The 1729–30 session had seen the passage of two such acts, for the repair of existing highways out of Dublin. In the next session there

Table 6.4   Irish legislation for social and economic 'improvement', 1721–40,
by session

	Agriculture		Industry and trade		Commerce		Infrastructure	
	heads of bills	acts	heads of bills	acts	heads of bills	acts	heads of bills	acts
1721–2	2	1	2	0	3	2	1	0
1723–4	3	1	4	1	0	0	0	0
1725–6	4	2	5	2	0	0	2	1
1727–8	3	1	2	1	0	0	3	2
1729–30	2	1	2	1	2	1	5	5
Subtotal	14	6	15	5	5	3	11	8
1731–2	1	1	4	2	1	1	9	8
1733–4	2	2	6	3	1	1	11	10
1735–6	6	1	4	2	2	0	12	11
1737–8	2	1	3	1	0	0	4	3
1739–40	0	0	2	1	0	0	5	5
Subtotal	11	5	19	9	4	2	41	38
Total	25	11	34	14	9	5	52	46

Note: 'Agriculture' includes fisheries, land use and mining; 'Industry and trade' includes
poor law; 'Commerce' includes banking; 'Infrastructure' relates to roads, canals, harbours
and urban development.

were eight, all involving the construction of new roads, and only two beginning
in the capital. Further new roads, and bills to amend the existing acts, followed:
nine in 1733–34, ten in 1735–36, extending the road network deep into the
south-west and linking urban centres in the north-east with the ports of Belfast
and Newry.[55] Though the impetus slackened after 1736, highway bills remained
a significant element in Irish legislation throughout the middle decades of the
century. At the same time, it would be wrong to suggest that MPs' interest in
'improvement' was concentrated on this one issue, for legislation covered a range
of problems and projects. Among the subjects which recurred in parliamentary
debate were the encouragement of agricultural innovation by the extension of
tillage or afforestation, the development of fisheries, the linen manufacture, the
employment of the poor, and various lighting, water, and paving schemes for
Dublin and other major urban centres.

This kind of activity was associated with a certain type of parliamentary 'patriot'.
Identifying individuals or interest-groups responsible for legislative initiatives
in the Irish parliament can be difficult, since there are no connected accounts
of debates until the last quarter of the century, but some use can be made of the
evidence of the *Journals*, in relation to tellerships or nomination to committees,
not necessarily conclusive proof of interest in a particular measure but certainly
suggestive. Research of this kind by Dr Neal Garnham on the criminal law suggests

that, in contrast to Westminster, there was considerable input from government officials.[56] But their participation does not seem to have extended to legislation on economic and social affairs. Instead, we find a number of back-bench members, all committed to the ideal of 'improvement', who were primarily responsible for drafting heads of bills to promote economic growth: men like the economic writer David Bindon, Arthur Dobbs, the future governor of North Carolina, David Chaigneau, the Dublin Huguenot merchant, and the County Down landowners Arthur Hill, Sir John Rawdon and Michael Ward.[57] These were the kind of constructive, non-secessionist, 'patriots' of whom Gerard McCoy and Patrick Kelly have written; concerned to advance the interests of Ireland within the existing constitutional framework.[58] There was also a powerful strain of evangelical piety underlying their drive for 'improvement', which identified prosperity with civility, Protestant virtues, and ultimately Protestantism itself, an explicitly religious motivation that would help to explain their commitment to the maintenance of the English connection, as the final guarantor of the Protestant establishment.

Historians of eighteenth-century Ireland are accustomed to characterise parliamentary 'patriotism' as a 'reactive' phenomenon, manifested in angry responses to incidents of English 'oppression', actual or anticipated: the Woollen Act of 1699, the Forfeitures Resumption of 1700, the *Annesley* v. *Sherlock* case, the Declaratory Act, Wood's Halfpence, and eventually the Money Bill crisis of 1753–55. Contemporaries, especially those on the ministerial side, could only see the windy rhetoric of self-interested or self-important troublemakers, who would 'patriotise' for hours over non-existent grievances.[59] Yet on closer inspection the real patriotism of the Protestant propertied elite in Ireland seems to reside instead in an intensely pragmatic attitude to Anglo-Irish political relationships. Irish Protestants in this period may have lamented the weaknesses of the Irish parliamentary constitution, but they were prepared to work within its limitations, for their own personal benefit and for the benefit of 'the nation'. The advantages of having access to Westminster as well as their own parliament compensated for the difficulties created by the procedures imposed by Poynings' law and the potential threat embodied in the Declaratory Act. There was no prospect of fundamental constitutional reform: continuing political uncertainty and the abiding memory of the Jacobite regime made separatism unthinkable; and while proposals for union attracted interest within Ireland, there was never any likelihood that the English would take them seriously. In these circumstances it made sense to exploit the opportunities that were available to deal with Ireland's economic and social problems by legislative means.

There are, of course, serious objections to seeing the early eighteenth-century Irish parliament as the cradle of a genuinely inclusive and constructive 'patriotism', even though indications of this kind of political outlook may be detected in the legislative activity of back-bench 'improvers' in the 1720s and 1730s. For one thing, parliament was a vehicle for the pursuit of local or sectional as well as national interests, and these local or sectional interests might well be in conflict with each other: the surviving remnants of the woollen industry (mainly in the south-west) against the emerging interest of linen manufacturers (mainly in the north-east), for example; and in a rather different way the conflict between supporters of Protestant Dissenters, hoping to abolish restrictive legislation, and High Church Anglicans, determined to keep it in place. Furthermore, the parliament was far from being a truly representative institution, not even of the Protestant minority. The operation of the sacramental test effectively excluded Dissenters from borough representation, and the drift into conformity of the Presbyterian gentry of Ulster deprived Dissenting freeholders in counties of candidates of their own persuasion.[60] 'Virtual representation' was assured to Anglicans in both town and country by the over-representation of boroughs in the Irish electoral system – a legacy of the constitutional gerrymandering that had followed successive schemes of plantation in the sixteenth and seventeenth centuries – but it was effectively denied to Presbyterians, and *a fortiori* to Catholics, as the maintenance, and indeed repeated reinforcement, of penal legislation made abundantly clear.

None the less, for a time semi-independence was perceived to work to Ireland's advantage. Arguably, Irishmen achieved more in this period from the retention of their separate parliament than did the Scots from an incorporating union. However, there was always a fundamental weakness in the Irish parliament as a legislative machine; a weakness deriving from the operation of Poynings' law, although not from the enforcement of English superiority. Most of the bills that were respited, or amended out of existence, were simply bad bills whose loss did no great harm. But the cumbersome method necessary to circumvent Poynings' law placed a premium on the time available for legislating and restricted the number of bills that could be debated and passed. This is precisely what seems to have happened during the middle decades of the century. Just as Irishmen perceived the need to broaden the scope of legislation, to provide more support for their expanding economy, they ran up against the inadequacies of the parliamentary system, with political instability restricting still further the time that parliament was in session. Productivity declined perceptibly, certainly in comparison with Westminster. During the 1730s the Irish parliament had passed a fifth of the number of acts of its British counterpart; between 1751 and 1770 this figure went down to around 8.5 per cent. There was a slight improvement in the 1770s, but not enough to quell the growing sense of frustration felt by Irish MPs and by the public at large. The more assertive 'patriots' of the later eighteenth century saw only the imperfections of their parliamentary constitution, and came increasingly to think of it as a half-grown parliament, requiring to be forcibly matured into full independence. For an earlier generation of Irish Protestants, sufficiently fearful for their own security to cherish their dependence on England, semi-independence was acceptable, and much could be made from it. Ultimately, however, the Irish parliamentary constitution proved inadequate to answer the weight the Irish political nation wished to place upon it.

Notes

1 D. W. Hayton, 'Anglo-Irish attitudes: changing perceptions of national identity among the Protestant Ascendancy in Ireland, c. 1690–1750', *Studies in Eighteenth-Century Culture*, xvii (1987), 145–57; C. Kidd, *British identities before nationalism: ethnicity and nationhood in the Atlantic world, 1600–1800* (Cambridge, 1999), ch. 7.

2 See, for example, British Library [BL] Add. MSS. 21122, fos. 88–9, 21123, fos. 1–4: Marmaduke Coghill to Edward Southwell, snr, 23 Oct. 1729, 18 Apr. 1730.

3 J. Th. Leerssen, 'Anglo-Irish patriotism and its European context: notes towards a reassessment', *Eighteenth-Century Ireland*, iii (1998), 7–24.

4 I. L. Victory, 'Colonial nationalism in Ireland, 1692–1725: from common law to natural right' (Trinity College, Dublin, Ph.D. thesis, 1985); J. G. Simms, *William Molyneux of Dublin, 1656–1698*, ed. P. H. Kelly (Blackrock, 1982), ch. 8.

5 P. Kelly, 'Perceptions of Locke in eighteenth-century Ireland', *Proceedings of the Royal Irish Academy*, lxxxix (1989), sect. C, 17–35; compare J. G. McCoy, 'Court ideology in mid-eighteenth-century Ireland' (St Patrick's College, Maynooth, MA thesis, 1990), 29–34.

6 J. I. McGuire, 'The Irish parliament of 1692', in T. Bartlett and D. W. Hayton (eds), *Penal era and golden age: essays in Irish history, 1690–1800* (Belfast, 1979), 11–15.

7 McGuire, 'Parliament of 1692', 2–8; C. I. McGrath, *The making of the eighteenth-century Irish constitution* (Dublin, 2000), 49–60, 74–7.

8 McGuire, 'Parliament of 1692', 11–23; W. Troost, *William III and the Treaty of Limerick (1691–1697): a study of his Irish policy* (Leiden, 1983), 55–67; McGrath, *Irish constitution*, 79–90.

9 D. W. Hayton, 'The beginnings of the "undertaker system"' in Bartlett and Hayton (eds), *Penal era and golden age*, 40–1; Troost, *William III*, 96–139; McGrath, *Irish constitution*, 90–117.

10 D. W. Hayton, 'The crisis in Ireland and the disintegration of Queen Anne's last ministry', *Irish Historical Studies*, xxii (1980–1), 193–215; McGrath, *Irish constitution*, chs. 5–7.

11 D. W. Hayton, 'Ireland and the English ministers, 1707–16' (University of Oxford, D. Phil. thesis, 1975), 91–3; McGrath, *Irish constitution*, 284–5.

12 D. W. Hayton, 'British Whig ministers and the Irish question 1714–1725' in S. Taylor, R. Connors and C. Jones (eds), *Hanoverian Britain and empire: essays in memory of Philip Lawson* (Woodbridge, 1998), 54–60.

13 G. V. Bennett, *The Tory crisis in Church and state 1688–1730: the career of Francis Atterbury bishop of Rochester* (Oxford, 1975), 178; Hayton, 'Crisis in Ireland', 212.

14 Historical Manuscripts Commission, *The manuscripts of the House of Lords [1710–1712]*, new series, ix (1949), 125; *CJ*, xv, 543.

15 *The private diary of William, first Earl Cowper*, ed. E. C. Hawtrey (Eton, 1833), 37.

16 *A letter from a soldier, being some remarks upon a late scandalous pamphlet; entituled, An address of some Irish-folks to the House of Commons* (1702), 5; *Some few remarks upon a pamphlet intitul'd, A letter from a soldier to the Commons of England* . . . (n.d.), 3; *London Gazette*, 6–9 Apr., 30 Apr.–4 May 1702; *An essay upon an union of Ireland with England* . . . (Dublin, 1704), 3; *Considerations concerning Ireland, in relation to England, and particularly in respect of an union* (n.d.), unpaginated; *Journals of the [Irish] House of Lords*, 5 vols (Dublin, 1779–86), ii, 91.

17 BL Add. MS. 74049 (unfol.): Horatio Walpole to Lord Sunderland, [1720]; P. McNally, *Parties, patriots and undertakers: parliamentary politics in early Hanoverian Ireland* (Dublin, 1997), 184–5; R. E. Burns, *Irish parliamentary politics in the eighteenth century*, 2 vols (Washington, DC, 1989–90), i, 113–32; compare Victory, 'Colonial Nationalism', 162–3, 182–7.

18 See, for example, *Considerations concerning Ireland, in relation to England . . . ; Some thoughts humbly offer'd towards an union between Great-Britain and Ireland* (1708), 28–9.

19 Burns, *Irish parliamentary politics*, i, 253–4; ii, 120–83; McNally, *Parties*, 191–5; D. O'Donovan, 'The Money Bill dispute of 1753' in Bartlett and Hayton (eds), *Penal era and golden age*, 55–87.

20 I. Victory, 'The Making of the 1720 Declaratory Act' in G. O'Brien (ed.), *Parliament, politics and people: essays in eighteenth-century Irish history* (Blackrock, 1989), 8–21; F. G. James, *Lords of the Ascendancy: the Irish House of Lords and its members, 1600–1800* (Blackrock, 1995), 68–72; P. O'Regan, *Archbishop William King of Dublin (1650–1729) and the constitution in Church and state* (Dublin, 2000), 98–111, 261–86.

21 BL Add. MS. 47029, fos. 16–18: Lord Abercorn to Lord Perceval, 18 Feb. 1719/20; Christ Church, Oxford, Wake MSS, Arch W. Epist. xiii, no. 159: Bishop Nicolson to Archbishop Wake, 3 Apr. 1720.

22 *CJ*, xiii, 718, 743–6; J. G. Simms, *The Williamite confiscation in Ireland, 1690–1703* (1956), 124–5.

23 *CJ*, xv, 530.

24 Trinity College, Dublin, MS. 1995–2008/1181 (Lyons (King) collection), Archbishop King to Robert King, [1705]; Sir Charles S. King (ed.), *A great archbishop of Dublin: William King . . .* (1906), 135–6; O'Regan, *Archbishop King*, chs 4–5, 8, and esp. 137.

25 Trinity College, Dublin: MS. 3821/109 (Crosbie papers), Maurice Fitzgerald to [David Crosbie], 4 July 1709; MS. 1995–2008/1185, Mary, Lady Dun to [Archbishop King], 22 Dec. 1705 and no. 1207, Francis Annesley to same, 30 Apr. 1706; F. G. James, *Ireland in the empire, 1688–1770* (Cambridge, Mass., 1973), 56, 58, 60–2, 64, 155–6.

26 L. M. Cullen, 'The smuggling trade in Ireland in the eighteenth century', *Proceedings of the Royal Irish Academy*, lxvii (1969), sect. C, 149–75.

27 BL Add. MS. 38015, fos. 27–8: Lord Carteret to Edward Southwell, snr, 16 Mar. 1729/30; Historical Manuscripts Commission, *Manuscripts of the Earl of Egmont. Diary of Viscount Perceval*, vol. 1 (1922), 173; James, *Ireland in the empire*, 156–7.

28 T. C. Barnard, 'Crises of identity among Irish Protestants, 1641–1685', *Past and Present*, 127 (1990), 39–83.

29 F. G. James, 'The Irish lobby in the early eighteenth century', *English Historical Review*, lxxxi (1966), 543–57; R. Sedgwick (ed.), *The history of parliament: the House of Commons, 1715–1754*, 2 vols (1970), i, 156–8.

30 D. W. Hayton 'The "country" interest and the party system, 1689–*c.* 1720' in C. Jones (ed.), *Party and management in parliament, 1660–1784* (Leicester, 1984), 60–3.

31 *The Lockhart Papers . . .* , ed. A. Aufrere, 2 vols (1817) i, 328, 535; D. Szechi, *Jacobitism and Tory politics, 1710–14* (Edinburgh, 1984), 85.

32 Hayton, 'Crisis in Ireland', 199–201.

33 Public Record Office of Northern Ireland, T/2929/2/48 (Rossmore papers), John Henderson to Sir Alexander Cairnes, 31 Oct. 1719.

34 S. J. Connolly, 'The Glorious Revolution in Irish Protestant political thinking' in S. J. Connolly (ed.), *Political ideas in eighteenth-century Ireland* (Dublin, 2000), 27–63.

35 J. Smyth, '"No remedy more proper": Anglo-Irish unionism before 1707', in B. Bradshaw and P. Roberts (eds), *British consciousness and identity: the making of Britain, 1533–1707* (Cambridge, 1998), 314–20. Compare D. W. Hayton, 'Ideas of union in Anglo-Irish political discourse, 1692–1720: meaning and use', in D. G. Boyce, R. Eccleshall and V. Geoghegan (eds), *Political discourse in seventeenth- and eighteenth-century Ireland* (Basingstoke, 2001), 151–4.

36 S. J. Connolly, *Religion, law and power: the making of Protestant Ireland, 1660–1760* (Oxford, 1992), 75, 89–92, 272.

37 These and other statistics on Irish legislative output are my own calculations, based on the evidence of the Irish Lords' and Commons' *Journals*.

38 By Mr John Bergin of University College Dublin, whose forthcoming Ph.D. thesis will illuminate this neglected area of Irish parliamentary history.

39 J. Kelly, 'Monitoring the constitution: the operation of Poynings' law in the 1760s', *Parliamentary History*, xx (2001), 87–106.

40 D. W. Hayton, 'Divisions in the Whig junto in 1709: some Irish evidence', *Bulletin of the Institute of Historical Research*, lv (1982), 212–14; Historical Manuscripts Commission, *Calendar of the manuscripts of the Marquess of Ormonde*, new series, vol. viii (1920), 311, 313; BL Add. MS. 9715, fo. 199: [Anderson Saunders] to Edward South-well, snr, 14 Oct. 1707. For a similar example some twenty years on, see BL Add. MS. 21122, fo. 103: Marmaduke Coghill to Edward Southwell, snr, 3 Jan. 1729[/30].

41 J. G. Simms, 'The making of a penal law (2 Anne, c. 6), 1703–4', *Irish Historical Studies*, xii (1960–61), 105–18.

42 D. W. Hayton (ed.), 'An Irish parliamentary diary from the reign of Queen Anne', *Analecta Hibernica*, xxx (1980), 111, 128.

43 For examples of the kind of detailed amendments made by the Privy Council's committee on Irish bills, in this case from the Irish parliamentary session of 1723–24 see BL Add. MS. 21134, fos. 14–26: committee minutes, 3, 6, 13 Jan. 1723[/4].

44 D. W. Hayton, 'Introduction: the long apprenticeship', *Parliamentary History*, xx (2001), 13. Compare BL Add. MS. 21123, fos. 11–15: Marmaduke Coghill to Edward Southwell, jnr, 4 Dec. 1732.

45 For contemporary observation of this very point, see BL Add. MS. 47032, fos. 107–9: Marmaduke Coghill to Lord Perceval, 5 Apr. 1729; Add. MS. 38016, fos. 9–10: Lord Carteret to Edward Southwell, snr, 30 Nov. 1729.

46 For these and other statistics relating to the legislative output of the Westminster parliament I am greatly obliged to the kindness of Julian Hoppit.

47 J. Kelly, 'The origins of the Act of Union: an examination of unionist opinion in Britain and Ireland, 1650–1800', *Irish Historical Studies*, xxv (1986–7), 240–4 and 'Public and political opinion in Ireland and the idea of an Anglo-Irish union, 1650–1800' in Boyce, Eccleshall and Geoghegan (eds), *Political discourse*, 113–21; Smyth, '"No Remedy More Proper"'.

48 Hayton, 'Ideas of union', 142–68.

49 J. S. Shaw, *The management of Scottish society, 1707–1764* (Edinburgh, 1983), ch. 6; Bob Harris, below, 132–9.

50 E. Magennis, 'Coal, corn and canals: the dispersal of public moneys, 1695–1772', *Parliamentary History*, xx (2001), 71–86.

51 H. D. Gribbon, 'The Irish Linen Board, 1711–1828' in M. Cohen (ed.), *The warp of Ulster's past: interdisciplinary studies on the linen industry* (Basingstoke, 1997), 71–91.

52 During its passage it was described by the viceroy, Lord Carteret, as the parliament's 'favourite bill'; 'all our chief concern', he wrote, 'is for that one bill': BL Add. MS. 38016, fos. 19, 23: Carteret to Edward Southwell, snr, 8 Jan., 9 Feb. 1729/30.

53 This proportion was roughly comparable with the situation in the British parliament, but of course the overall numbers of acts passed were very much greater at Westminster, where some 1,496 statutes out of a total of 5,301 in 1689–1760 covered 'social' and 'economic' issues.

54 D. Clarke, *Thomas Prior, 1681–1751: founder of the Royal Dublin Society* (Dublin, 1951); T. de Vere White, *The story of the Royal Dublin Society* (Tralee, 1955); K. Milne, *The Irish charter schools, 1730–1830* (Dublin, 1997).

55 J. H. Andrews, 'Land and people, *c.* 1780' in T. W. Moody and W. E. Vaughan (eds), *A new history of Ireland, IV: eighteenth-century Ireland, 1691–1800* (Oxford, 1986), 254–5; D. Broderick, 'The Irish turnpike road system' (Trinity College, Dublin, Ph.D. thesis, 1998).

56 N. Garnham, 'Criminal legislation in the Irish parliament, 1692–1760', *Parliamentary History*, xx (2001), 55–70 and his 'The criminal law 1692–1760: England and Ireland compared' in S. J. Connolly (ed.), *Kingdoms united? Great Britain and Ireland since 1500: integration and diversity* (Dublin, 1999), 215–24.

57 D. Clarke, *Arthur Dobbs esquire 1689–1765* . . . (Chapel Hill, 1957); P. Kelly, 'The politics of political economy in mid-eighteenth-century Ireland' in Connolly (ed.), *Political ideas in eighteenth-century Ireland*, 112–22; R. A. Richey, 'Landed society in mid-eighteenth-century County Down' (Queen's University, Belfast, Ph.D. thesis, 2000), chs 6–8.

58 G. McCoy, 'Local political culture in the Hanoverian empire: the case of the Anglo-Irish' (University of Oxford, DPhil. thesis, 1994); P. Kelly, 'Politics of political economy'. See also C. Robbins, *The eighteenth-century commonwealthman: studies in the transmission, development and circumstance of English liberal thought from the Restoration of Charles II until the war with the thirteen colonies* (Cambridge, Mass., 1959), ch. 5.

59 BL Add. MS. 20105, fos. 118–20: John Wainwright to Mrs Charlotte Clayton, 19 Nov. 1733.

60 D. W. Hayton 'Exclusion, conformity and parliamentary representation: the impact of the sacramental test on Irish dissenting politics', in K. Herlihy (ed.), *The politics of Irish Dissent, 1650–1800* (Dublin, 1997), 52–73.

7

The Scots, the Westminster parliament, and the British state in the eighteenth century[1]

Bob Harris

Union with England in 1707 presented the Scots with a series of opportunities, but it also created risks, as Devine has recently re-emphasised.[2] One such risk was political in nature, but appeared at the time potentially to have much broader repercussions. It is simply stated: how could Scotland ensure that its interests were properly represented in the new 'British' parliament which the Treaty of Union would bring into existence.

This question hung over the Union negotiations and the Treaty's subsequent ratification in the Scottish parliament.[3] How could Scots be certain that the new parliament, in which the English would be numerically hugely predominant, would not simply ignore the Treaty of Union and the protections for Scottish interests painstakingly inserted within it? The question had other, equally pressing ramifications. Would the new parliament, dominated by Anglicans, respect the Kirk's monopoly of jurisdiction on its own affairs enshrined in the acts of security passed by the English and Scottish parliaments in 1706? Andrew Fletcher argued that the new parliament would favour English economic interests at the expense of Scottish ones, just as English MPs had done in relation to the Irish woollen industry in 1699.[4] Partly because of this, the prospect of prosperity which many pro-Unionists were holding out was a delusion, or so Fletcher argued.

In one sense, of course, Fletcher was to be proved entirely wrong, for the Scottish economy began to grow and develop very rapidly from the later 1730s. With economic progress came changing attitudes towards the Union; by the later eighteenth century few dissenters can be found from the idea that the Union, the sovereignty of the Westminster parliament, and prosperity were causally linked.[5] Yet this hardly disposes of the issue of how Scottish interests fared at Westminster. Existing historical literature provides only limited help here, something which might be surprising, but for several important facts. Firstly, comment on Scottish parliamentary and indeed political history in the eighteenth century has been, for the most part, denigratory and frequently brief.[6] Secondly, the inclination to examine the impact of parliament and the state on eighteenth-century Scottish economic life has not been a strong one, particularly in recent years.

Nationalist feelings probably provide only part of the explanation for this, and even then not a very large one. Most economic historians have, until recently, looked elsewhere for the sources of eighteenth-century Scottish economic dynamism, to factors such as religion, the existence of a dynamic mercantile class, and the early commitment of its landed classes and political elites to commerce and the pursuit of profit.[7]

Of the few historians who have seriously examined the role of the Scots in the eighteenth-century Westminster parliament, their conclusions differ, although they were looking at different periods. Patrick Riley noted of the years 1707–27, 'regardless of English cross currents, any threat to what were thought to be Scottish interests at once united the Scottish members [of parliament]'.[8] He also drew attention to how quickly the Convention of Royal Burghs assumed a lobbying role in relation to Westminster, a role which involved the appointment of an MP as their official agent in 1709 and of ad hoc agents for particular lobbying campaigns. Riley also noted the strength of feeling in the early 1710s that Scottish interests were being ignored at Westminster. One response to this was Robert Harley's creation of the Commission of Chamberlainry and Trade in November 1711, although this body never became an effective institution of government. Looking at the following two decades, John Shaw's verdict was a sharply negative one.[9] Shaw emphasised the subordination of Scottish politics in this period, together with the apathy and often hostility felt in England towards Scotland. Between 1727 and 1745, he noted that only nine acts of parliament were passed which dealt solely with Scottish problems or issues. The picture he created was one of inconsequentiality: 'If Scotland's MPs were so ineffectual, their friends in Scotland were bound to be weaker still: they could not hope to dictate to the English political and commercial lobbies.' He also saw significance in the fact that the Commons would not receive petitions on revenue questions, concluding: 'Since the main schemes for Scottish improvement, then as now, depended on expenditure of public funds, this was sure to cut off most Scottish social initiatives at root.'[10] Alexander Murdoch, meanwhile, examining the political management of Scotland in the 1750s and early 1760s, reached a slightly more favourable judgment.[11] Where Shaw emphasised subordination and lack of initiative, Murdoch portrayed the third Duke of Argyll and his allies as reasonably successful in defending Scottish interests against English intrusion. Faced with a determined and stable English ministry and vengeful English majority in the Commons, such as existed after the '45, little could be done. English influence in Scottish administration was, however, successfully resisted when political conditions were more favourable, as occurred following the death of Henry Pelham (in 1754). Argyll and his allies were also successful in pressurising Newcastle and parliament to restore what to the Scottish linen industry was a very important bounty on the export of coarse linen, which had ceased in 1754, but which was re-imposed in 1756.

The purpose of this chapter is not principally to quarrel with any of these views. Nevertheless, Scotland's relations to parliament in the first seventy years of the Union, and also to other central institutions of the British state, do merit

fresh examination. Our knowledge of parliament and its role in English government in this period has developed considerably in recent years, but such work
has as yet prompted no reconsideration of the role of Westminster in Scottish
government and society.[12] Secondly, recent debates about the integration of Scotland into the British state in the eighteenth century have tended to focus heavily
on ideology and on the external aspects of state power – the expansion of empire
and the role of the military – but said rather less about what role parliament or
the domestic faces of the state may have played in the process.[13] If the domestic
role of the state is discussed in this context it is usually in primarily negative
terms, in terms of how far Scotland maintained a position of semi-autonomy
within the Union. One of the ways, therefore, in which the imposition of the new
fiscal apparatus of the British state was made less disruptive than it might have
been was limited intrusion into local administration by the central state.[14] At
least one recent account of eighteenth-century Scotland has sought, nevertheless,
to highlight the positive influences of the state in crucial areas of economic life
in the first fifty years or so of the Union.[15] Anna Gambles, writing about the
promotion of the fisheries in the later eighteenth and early nineteenth centuries,
has also directed our attention more strongly to fiscal policy as a means of
strengthening the British state.[16] The eighteenth-century invention of North Britain
may have been as much as achievement of political economy as of ideology, but,
if so, it is a process historians have done surprisingly little to recover.

The chapter explores Scottish relations with the Westminster parliament
from two overlapping perspectives: the place of a Scottish 'national interest' at
Westminster; and Scottish lobbying of Westminster and central departments
of the state, especially the Treasury. The account which follows is far from comprehensive; nor is it based on an exhaustive analysis of all relevant legislation.[17]
The aim instead is to capture the basic characteristics of Scottish relations with
Westminster in this period.

Eighteenth-century Scottish MPs and representative peers tended to attract
very negative views at the time, and subsequent judgments by historians have not
been much better. There were some MPs who were by temperament and conviction independents – for the final third of the century, George Dempster of
Dunnichen readily comes to mind – but the majority were not, and were typical
of a Scottish political class who travelled southwards for, in Michael Fry's words,
'the sake of the spoils they could bring home'.[18] Although between 1707 and
the death of George II, cross-currents of English and Scottish factional politics
disrupted too neat a pattern, Scottish MPs and representative peers provided
ministers with generally reliable support.[19]

This much is well known. The pervasive influence of patronage in Scottish
politics and society in this period is similarly not worth disputing. What does,
however, deserve greater recognition is that, alongside the evident hunger for
office and official favour amongst the Scottish political classes, there existed a
clear sense of a Scottish 'national interest'. The fact that this interest often tended
to coincide with self interest scarcely detracts from this point. In any society, the

'national interest' tends to be what the politically powerful succeed in defining it to be; what is important is the processes, accommodations, and discourses through which specific interests manage to identify themselves as the national interest at any given time and place. As Patrick Riley has emphasised, and as was referred to above, Scottish MPs and politicians quickly learnt from 1707 to act collectively and in defence of a perceived national interest (or interests) at Westminster. This reflected in part a natural tendency to look to fellow Scots for support in pursuing Scottish legislative objectives. More importantly, however, it was a role forced upon them by the frequently clumsy interventions of English ministers and parliament in Scottish matters in the years which immediately followed the Union. By 1713, the growing, cumulative sense that Scottish interests were being disregarded or undermined by ministers and parliament culminated in Lord Findlater's famous motion in the Lords to dissolve the Union. The motion – which was supported by all Scottish peers and which was only defeated by four proxy votes – was the outcome of joint conferences held in London between the peers and commoners, and reflected a deep national disenchantment with the early political fruits of Union.[20]

This early crisis in Anglo-Scots political relations was quickly overtaken by the Hanoverian succession and the '15 Jacobite Rebellion. Scottish politicians and MPs continued, however, to defend the Scottish national interest at Westminster against measures perceived to be hostile or damaging to it. Two important episodes from the 1720s serve to illustrate this role very clearly. The first of these concerns the linen industry, the fortunes of which were crucial to early eighteenth-century Scotland in terms of its actual and potential economic, social and political importance.[21] The Union had provided no immediate stimulus to linen manufacturing; if anything the short-term effects were negative. 1711 saw the imposition of a new excise duty on stamped and stained linen produced in Scotland, which placed a significant added burden on the industry. In 1719, it faced a new threat when English woollen and silk manufacturers mounted a campaign for further parliamentary support in the form of prohibition on using or wearing alternative printed or dyed foreign and domestic textiles, notably calicoes and linen.[22] The response from Scotland and the Scottish linen interest was to flood parliament with petitions calling for Scotland's linen industry to be excluded from the provisions of any legislation to support English woollen manufactures.[23] The petitioners emphasised the role of the linen industry as a major source of employment. Just as the woollen industry sought to portray itself as England's national interest, so the linen industry was presented in many of these petitions as Scotland's national interest. The barons and heritors of Perthshire declared that were such a measure to be enacted, it would ruin

many hundreds of thousands of poor People, dispersed through every Village, Town and County, in all Scotland, who are employed in the Manufacture of Linen Cloth; and being made wholly of the Product of their native Country, ought to be equally preserved, and encouraged, with the Woollen Manufacture of England ...[24]

Much emphasis was also placed on the disadvantages under which the industry already lay as a result of the imposition of the earlier duty. A total of forty petitions was submitted to the Commons in defence of the Scottish linen industry between December 1719 and the end of the following month.[25] Most came, unsurprisingly, from important centres of the industry. Thus, Perth, Forfar, and Fife were all well represented. Perthshire produced nine petitions, while the magistrates of five burghs in Fife submitted a joint petition. The City of Aberdeen produced two petitions, one from the magistrates, burgh council, and local merchants and traders in linen cloth, and a second from the incorporation of weavers. Several weavers incorporations issued petitions, as did those employed in linen manufacturing in one parish in Perthshire. Other petitioners included the Convention of Royal Burghs, and merchants and traders in linen cloth in London. The campaign embraced, therefore, burgh and county elites, merchants, and those employed in linen manufacturing. The Duke of Roxburghe, then secretary of state for Scotland, impressed upon ministers the potentially catastrophic political and economic effects of any prohibition on the access of Scottish linen to the English market.[26] The petitions were referred to a committee of the whole house, originally appointed to consider the petitions from the woollen industry. This committee heard evidence on behalf of the royal burghs and on behalf of merchants, traders and factors in London representing themselves and linen manufacturers in Scotland.[27] The committee's resolutions were reported on 12 February 1720. They included the stipulation that any resultant legislation to ban the use and wearing of printed, stained or dyed calicoes and linens should except linens which were produced in Great Britain and Ireland. Three Scots were named as members of the committee appointed to prepare legislation embodying the resolutions.[28] The result was the famous Calico Act (1721). In this instance, the Scots had secured their objective – to retain a crucial market for Scottish linens – and a potentially severe blow to the struggling Scottish economy had been averted.

The significance of such an outcome should not be underestimated. Economic legislation readily formed a focus for anti-Union feeling north of the border in the decades immediately following the Union.[29] For pro-Unionists, the linkage between industry, prosperity and loyalty was axiomatic in early-Hanoverian Scotland and Britain, and promoting trade and manufacturing were to become crucial aspects of a patriotism which was both Scottish and British at the same time.[30] In the mid-1720s, the linen industry was to be identified as the main hope for attempting to prove that loyalty followed industry, as Walpole and other English ministers (and their Scots allies) formulated plans for public support for Scottish economic development. The result was the formation of the Board of Trustees for the Promotion of Manufacturers and Fisheries, a concerted attempt to demonstrate the benefits of Union to an uneasy, restive Scottish population struggling with the twin pressures of political and economic integration into the British state and economic modernisation.[31]

Our second episode is better known, at least in certain respects, and had, on the face of it, a less satisfactory outcome for the Scots. It also begins to demonstrate the tight political constraints under which the Scots often operated at Westminster in this period. The episode was the imposition of the malt tax on Scotland in 1725. The consequences of this measure were, in the first place, widespread resistance to and protests against the tax across Lowland Scotland.[32] It was the role of Roxburghe in encouraging the protests which was to lead to his dismissal as Scottish secretary, and the beginnings of the Argathelian supremacy in early Hanoverian Scottish political life. It was also the related upsurge of anti-Union sentiment which was to provide the immediate stimulus to the foundation of the Board of Trustees, referred to above.[33]

The immediate motive for raising the issue of Scottish non-payment of the tax in the early 1720s may have been factional, although it also reflected strong anti-Scots feeling in the Commons. It is significant that the issue first came up in the context of parliamentary inquiries into customs frauds in the Scottish tobacco industry. The opening shots were fired on 29 January 1723, during a meeting of a committee of the whole, which had been appointed to prepare the heads of a bill for preventing 'Frauds and Abuses in the tobacco trade'. In the course of debate, Thomas Broderick, independent Whig MP for Guildford, suggested that the committee also investigate low yields of malt duty in Scotland. It was a call subsequently taken up on 8 February by another independent Whig, John Trenchard, but rebuffed on that occasion by Sir Robert Walpole.[34] The matter was not let drop, however. On 24 January 1724 a motion was passed in the Commons calling for an account of the malt tax collected in Scotland in the previous seven years. The proposer of the motion was Broderick. Seconded by the Tory John Hungerford, Broderick also kept up the pressure in several debates on supply during early February.[35] Walpole again wanted to deflect this manoeuvre, but appears to have come to the conclusion that he needed an alternative proposal. A committee of four Scots MPs – Daniel Campbell of Shawfield, Sir Gilbert Elliot, James St Clair, and Robert Dundas, the Lord Advocate – was formed to wait on Walpole.[36] Although no counter proposals appear to have been forthcoming at this stage, the pressure for action was maintained in the following parliamentary session. On 7 December, Treasury secretary John Scrope, moving the duty on malt in a committee of ways and means, hinted that an equivalent would be found if the Scots would or could not pay their share of the duty. It was Walpole who then proposed a 6d additional excise on a barrel of beer, and the removal of the bounty and drawbacks on the export of corn. That this proposal had been devised without consultation with Scottish members is suggested by their united opposition to it in a further debate on the question two days later.[37] Their opposition was, in the short term, completely unavailing. On 10 December 1724 a committee of the whole House passed resolutions which proposed that in lieu of the malt tax, an additional duty on beer should be laid on Scotland, and that as a further equivalent the bounty on the export of grain would not be paid in Scotland for one year after 23 June 1725. One Scottish MP, William Fraser, MP for Elgin burghs, in the heart of a grain exporting district, declared openly that the proposals represented a breach of the Union.[38]

The declaration accurately reflected reactions in Scotland. Scots felt that the burden of taxation was already sufficiently high, and that further taxation would only deepen poverty and hardship. The view was also expressed that deficiencies in receipts of the malt tax had been already made good by new taxes levied on other items. Grain exports had been one of relatively few areas of growth in the economy on the east coast after the Union; the bounties payable on them also lined the pockets of the politically powerful in Scotland – the landed classes. At the same time that the malt tax protests were getting underway, landed opinion in some eastern counties was agitating about illegal imports of Irish grain and victuals. Scots MPs appear to have been inundated with letters, remonstrances, and instructions calling on them to do their utmost to defeat these resolutions, which were seen as contravening articles 6 and 7 of the Treaty of Union.[39] Archibald Grant, MP for Aberdeenshire, received a letter from Edinburgh written just five days after the resolutions were passed, which informed him:

> It's impossible to describe the consternation with which every body here is struck with this dreadful Resolution of the house of Commons – the worst we thought could befal us was the imposition, (I mean effectual) of the Malt tax itself – yet the people have hop'd that somewhat less [. . . ?] than the tax itself, but never dreamt of having a thing far more heavy and grievous imposed on them, a thing not only burdensome in itself and ruinous to the greatest part of the country but a direct and violent infraction of several Articles in the solemn Treaty of Union – where is all the Parliamentary faith and English honesty now –[40]

Later in the same month, the 'gentleman of Aberdeen' sent a letter to Grant advising him that if the resolution should pass into law, then he should retire from parliament as they would consider the Union 'to be dissolved by such a procedure'.[41] The MPs were in frequent communication, via letters, with their constituents. Grant was writing every two or three days, and his letters were being passed round all gentlemen of the county then in Edinburgh. Robert Dundas, MP for Midlothian, was corresponding regularly with Sir John Clerk of Penicuick, president of a committee formed at the time of his election (in 1722) and with which he was instructed to maintain regular communication on matters relevant to the interests of the county in parliament.[42] Meanwhile, in London, Scots MPs quickly met as a group to consider how best to proceed. Walpole was still disposed to compromise, and a committee was formed from the MPs to negotiate with him. Walpole agreed to meet this committee in his capacity as a fellow MP.[43] Thus was born the proposal that Scotland would have levied on it a malt tax at 3d per bushel but that any deficiency from the sum of £20,000 would be made good through the malt tax in the following year.

In one sense, the intervention of the MPs had been a failure; they could not shield Scotland from an English parliamentary majority insistent that Scotland pay a share of the malt tax. One contemporary summed up things thus: it was the 'best of a bad bargain in this hard case'.[44] Equally interesting, in the present context, however, is the way in which the MPs had sought to operate as a national interest group. During the crisis, they had formed from their number a committee to negotiate with Walpole; this committee had met daily; it had also referred important matters back to the Scots MPs as a whole; the MPs had also corresponded regularly with contacts in Scotland in their efforts to find a compromise and to assess how this would be met in Scotland.

Ministers were also genuinely alarmed by depth and violence of opposition to the tax in Scotland, and Walpole was to emerge in the mid 1720s as a powerful spokesman in the Commons for the notion of a British interest which transcended English national interest. The Convention of Royal Burghs, along with the elites in several counties, continued to press parliament and ministers for relief from the tax in 1725–26.[45] The means to future tranquillity was to be the creation of the Board of Trustees and provision to pay over to it funds for economic improvement, some of which were owing from the Equivalent agreed at the time of the Union, and by further legislation of 1718 and 1724 on compensation due to the Scots for losses incurred at the Union. Another source of funding was any surplus over and above £20,000 raised by the malt tax. This last proposal was made to the Commons in March 1726 by the Lord Advocate, Duncan Forbes. The reaction from some English MPs was strongly negative, claiming that such a provision was unfair to England. Some English MPs also took delight in pointing out a supposed contradiction between such a provision and Scottish complaints that the tax was too heavy and also unequal. Robert Dundas who, like Roxburghe, had been dismissed in the course of the malt tax protests, and who remained opposed to the measure, reported that the issue had led to 'no small dispute and made us a long Day'.[46] It was Walpole who decided to give the Commons a lesson in political realities, arguing that even the £20,000 was more than a fair share of the tax for Scots to pay, and that there was no point in seeking more if that meant having to maintain 6,000 troops in Scotland to maintain the peace. He also urged that Scottish prosperity was in British interests. In Dundas's opinion, Walpole had spoken 'exceeding strong and just as well as handsome'. George Drummond described the speech as the 'finest I ever heard in that house'.[47] Drummond had been sent to London in early 1726 as the agent of the Royal Burghs to petition for a total exemption from the tax, a move which apparently angered some Scots MPs who felt that he was intervening in what was their sphere of responsibility. The new proposal, and Walpole's speech, appear to have begun the process of winning Drummond over, and he was to go on to play a key role in ensuring that the Convention of Royal Burghs played a full part in the establishment of the Board of Trustees and in the formulation of its policies.[48]

The emergence of the Argathelian interest to a position of dominance in Scottish politics after 1725 imposed greater stability on Anglo-Scots relations. The presence of a Scottish national interest in London and at Westminster was, nevertheless, maintained, even if there was before the later 1740s less occasion for it to become active. On some issues, it also came very close to being in reality the interest of the 2nd Duke of Argyll and his allies. In 1737, Argyll organised strong opposition to punitive legislation against the city of Edinburgh and its council, a response to perceived shortcomings in its role in the Porteous riot. Edinburgh Council was an Argathelian stronghold, and the legislation was a direct attack on the duke's political interest. Walpole deleted several clauses from the bill, but this was insufficient to undermine Argyll's opposition.[49] In 1747, the 3rd Duke of Argyll, better known as the Earl of Ilay – his title before assuming the dukedom on his brother's death in 1743 – made clear his opposition, albeit in a somewhat indirect fashion, to the abolition of heritable jurisdictions, part of a programme of measures designed to eradicate once and for all political disaffection in Scotland after the 1745 Jacobite Rebellion. These jurisdictions had been protected explicitly by the Treaty of Union, but perhaps equally relevant was the fact that Argyll was the possessor of the largest of these in Scotland.[50]

A Scottish political interest at Westminster can also, however, be glimpsed in slightly more constructive mode in these years in respect of Scottish economic interests, and in this we can perhaps begin to detect the beginnings of an important shift in the character of its role. In 1737, a bill was introduced into parliament to take off drawbacks on foreign linen exported to British plantations. This was the first of a series of initiatives on linen concerted between various elements of the Scottish, Irish and English linen industries. A letter reporting a meeting held in early February between merchants and representatives of Scotland, Ireland and England, noted: 'The Duke of Argyll and all the Scotch gentlemen are very zealous on this affair.'[51] The campaign failed, partly because of fears about the potential repercussions in German markets for wool and metal goods, but also because parliament was unconvinced that the domestic industries were yet in a position to supply the needs of the plantations.[52] Five years later (in 1742), Scottish lobbying was successful when bounties were granted on the export of coarse linens.[53] In 1744, it was Scottish MPs, acting in support of the linen industry, who helped hand out a rare Commons defeat to Henry Pelham on fiscal matters, although they were in this instance stage extras in a drama pitting Pelham against the West India interest. Pelham had proposed an additional duty on sugar to fund the interest on new public borrowing for that year. The plans to defeat it included proposing an alternative which, in the words of one Pelham supporter, 'captivated the Scotch members'.[54] The alternative was an additional duty on foreign linen imports. Two months later, in July, the Convention recommended that the Lord Provost of Edinburgh write to all Scottish MPs 'requesting them zealously and unanimously to countenance and support every measure that may have a tendency to promote and enlarge the linen manufacture of Great Britain and Ireland'. The letter was also to urge an additional duty on foreign linen as 'by far the most eligible and conducive to the interest of this country'.[55] In 1745, the hand of the Scots can again be detected in the payment of additional bounties on linen exports.[56] Between 1754 and 1756, as referred to at the beginning of this paper, Argyll and his allies organised a successful lobbying effort to restore the bounties on coarse linen exports, which, owing to opposition from English fancy linen manufacturers, had ceased in 1754. As Murdoch has demonstrated, the outcome did not please all Scottish linen manufacturers, and it certainly favoured Argyll's own interest in coarse linen production. But, as Murdoch also emphasises (and as we will see further below), it is also hard not to acknowledge that Scottish interests were well served thereby.[57] In the later eighteenth century, Scottish politicians were to be involved in several other major parliamentary lobbying campaigns on behalf of the linen industry, although none were as important as the one of the mid 1750s.[58]

Scottish MPs in the early Hanoverian period also helped expedite the progress through parliament of a steady trickle of private, local or non-ministerial legislation relating to or affecting Scotland. It was a role the MPs had played since 1707, albeit with fluctuating intensity.[59] Some of the legislation was uncontroversial and originated in Scotland, and such legislation continued to be forthcoming in subsequent decades. 1741, for example, saw the passage of an act to make effective an act of the Scottish parliament of 1703 which had provided for the import of grain and food from Ireland when prices reached a certain level. This was necessary because of the abolition of the Scottish privy council in 1708, which rendered the existing law inoperative. It was also a response to the dearth and high food prices of the winter of 1740–41.[60] There was also legislation which was designed to expedite commercial and economic progress, consistent with Scotland's ongoing re-creation as a commercial society. Before 1760, this included the Scottish Fisheries Act (1756), as well as an unsuccessful attempt in 1753 to secure new legislation on bankruptcy.[61] The quantity of this sort of legislation was to grow in the later eighteenth century, as commercial and economic development accelerated.[62] Scottish burghs looked to parliament for authority to levy a local tax on beer and ale to finance improvements; before 1707 this had come from the Scottish parliament.[63] In the later eighteenth century, burghs would also begin to seek more specific legislation to facilitate improvements of various kinds, while landed and commercial interests would seek statutory authority to form commissions to manage the construction of turnpikes and canals and to commute to cash payment labour service on road repair. Before 1760, only Edinburgh applied to parliament for an improvement act, in 1754. The most substantial growth in these different types of legislation was to occur in the early nineteenth century.[64]

At one level, the fact that Scottish MPs and politicians saw themselves as representatives of a national interest at Westminster is unsurprising. As has already been emphasised, the Scottish political classes possessed and nurtured a clear sense of national purpose in this period, one which was not diminished by the strong Anglicising tendencies at work in Scottish culture and politics. Societies such as the Select Society, the Linen Society, and later in the century the Highland Society, ad hoc administrative bodies such as the Board of Trustees and the Commissioners for the Annexed Estates – membership of which was frequently overlapping – gave strengthening institutional form and support to this commitment. (These bodies also sponsored particular pieces of legislation.) The Convention of Royal Burghs looked to MPs from member burghs and, on occasion, county representatives to defend or expedite Scottish interests at

Westminster. The Scottish press which began to strengthen quite significantly as a force in Scottish society in the central decades of the century also helped increasingly to reflect and reinforce similar expectations of Scottish MPs.[65] From this period, Scottish newspapers frequently contained letters from correspondents in London which gave news of the parliamentary activities of the nation's MPs.[66] This was one facet of developing public sphere in Scotland in the second half of the century, partly focused on parliament and legislation.[67]

So far, the focus has been mainly on Scottish MPs and politicians and their role at Westminster during the reigns of the first two Georges. The following section looks briefly at the matter of Scottish lobbying techniques in the decades after 1707. The *Commons Journals* contain plenty of evidence of the readiness of Scottish commercial and other interests to petition the Westminster parliament in the years which followed the Union. From a national and indeed British perspective, a prominent feature of this type of activity is the important and unique role which the Convention of Royal Burghs regularly played. It was, in many ways, the natural institution to speak for and represent the commercial interests of Scotland, or certainly some of these. On paper at least, the burghs had a monopoly of overseas trade; the Convention had also played a similar role with regard to the Scottish parliament.

What range of interests did the Convention actually represent? Like other Scottish political and administrative bodies, it was susceptible to close political control, from the 1720s by the Argathelian interest. A crucial aspect of its management was control of Edinburgh city council. Edinburgh contributed distinctly the largest proportion of the cess tax raised by the Convention, and, as a consequence, sent the largest number of delegates to it. The annual meeting of the Convention was always held in Edinburgh, and the Lord Provost of Edinburgh was normally elected president.[68] To this extent, the views it represented tended to be those of, or supported by, the Edinburgh political classes. Glasgow commercial interests could, as a consequence, find themselves less well represented by the Convention. Because of this, the MP for Glasgow burghs may have had a vital role to play in ensuring these interests were properly supported in London. In 1722, the burden of representing the views of Glasgow tobacco merchants in Treasury inquiries into customs frauds in the tobacco trade appears to have fallen solely on the shoulders of the local MP, Daniel Campbell of Shawfield. In the later 1740s, when this topic was again the subject of Treasury activity, it was not the Convention, but the Lord Provost of Glasgow who forwarded petitions from Glasgow merchants to the Treasury Secretary.[69] Some other important commercial interests also fell outside the immediate interests of the burghs and thus the Convention. One such would be the landowner-led Forth coal producers, who successfully defended their monopoly, created at the time of Union, on the domestic (Scottish) market until 1793.[70] It was only in the 1780s that, as the formation of the Glasgow and Edinburgh Chambers of Commerce indicates, Scottish commercial bodies and manufacturers began to seek new ways of co-ordinating and organising lobbying activity.

The importance of the Convention as a parliamentary lobbying body reflected its usefulness as a vehicle for directing and co-ordinating the collection and dissemination of information and the formulation of tactics. The annual committee of the Convention, which met when the Convention itself was not in session, had as part of its brief communicating with the burghs' MPs on trade and other matters of relevance to the burghs' interests.[71] In London, another point of regular contact was the official agent of the Convention.[72] Agents, as Riley observed, were also periodically appointed on an ad hoc basis to conduct specific lobbying campaigns. John Cathcart, for example, was the Convention's agent in negotiations with the Treasury which led to the Scottish Fisheries Act of 1756. He also oversaw its drafting and passage through parliament.[73] The Convention used its contacts with the burghs and other economic bodies to collect information and produce memorials for submission to MPs and the Treasury; to co-ordinate petitioning campaigns; and to solicit the support of MPs in favour of its parliamentary campaigns. The Convention also regularly petitioned parliament in its own name.

Using the printed and unpublished records of the Convention, it would easily be possible to reconstruct the main lobbying campaigns it conducted or co-ordinated, although there is not space to pursue this here.[74] What is worth emphasising, however, is, firstly, the scale of some of the campaigns. These could last several years, such as the one in the mid 1750s which aimed at restoring bounties on coarse linen exports. This began in 1752, but was only successful in 1756. Because of their length, such campaigns could involve considerable expense. In 1756, the two ad hoc agents of the Convention on the linen affair, William Tod and George Drummond, were each paid £300, and a solicitor who acted on their behalf a further £331 5s 11d, which latter sum was one third of the expenses of obtaining the act restoring the bounty.[75] Typically the campaigns involved co-operation with other interested bodies in Scotland – for example, after 1727, the Board of Trustees. As mentioned earlier, in the case of the linen industry, a tradition of co-operation with the Irish linen lobby appears to have begun in the 1730s. Other features included the use of agents to make contact with linen manufacturers in England; liaison via these same agents with Scottish MPs; the arrangement of meetings with ministers in London, usually the Chancellor of the Exchequer. Tactics were co-ordinated from London, especially in regard to the timing of the submission of petitions to parliament. The goal was create as much consensus as possible around a particular demand or series of demands, and to secure ministerial backing for the introduction of such a demand into parliament. In the case of the linen bounty in the mid 1750s, this meant accepting that the drawback on exports of foreign linen could not be removed, a demand being made by Glasgow merchants, and combining the demand for restoration of bounties on exports of coarse linen with removal of the duty on imports of foreign yarn. The latter was strongly advocated by linen manufacturers in the north west of England, but was opposed by those involved in the Scottish fancy linen trade. Lord Dupplin was reflecting ministers' perceptions when he reported to Lord Deskford in 1755:

> Your L.p will easily imagine that in so complicated a question where there is so great a variety of contending interests, the Administration must be laid under great difficulties and perplexed not only with numberless sollicitations, but also with a contrariety of reasoning upon facts differently stated, and urged by all parties with equal vehemence.

He also noted that the Duke of Newcastle was keen to help the linen industry but 'with what shall be right for ye good of ye whole'.[76]

Much of the above has a familiarity from work on commercial lobbying in this period by other groups and lobbies within the British empire. Its effectiveness depended on several factors, but important before 1760 was the willingness of Scottish political managers to make personal representations to ministers, and through this to facilitate access for Scottish lobbyists to the Treasury. As the cases of the linen bounty in the mid 1750s and of the Scottish Fisheries Act of 1756 show, the evidence suggests that it was role the 3rd Duke of Argyll played with considerable assiduity.[77]

How, then, should we characterise Scottish relations with Westminster and the central state in the early decades of the Union? The case can be made that Scottish interests were reasonably well served by their politicians. When the 'national interest' was perceived to be under attack, Scottish MPs and peers worked hard, albeit with mixed results, to repel or to deflect such assaults. Only future work examining the parliamentary performance and diligence of individual MPs will reveal how well particular constituencies and interests were represented. This may well reveal a more uneven picture than the one I have been sketching here. It is worth noting that in a key division on the proposals for an equivalent for the malt tax in 1724, 41 were against, and of these one contemporary noted that there were 'about 10' English MPs. This leaves as many as around 15 Scottish MPs not present in the Commons on that occasion.[78]

Scottish influence in London and at Westminster in the eighteenth century, especially before 1760, was more often than not defensive and reactive. What leverage the Scots had in the early Hanoverian period was largely to impress on ministers and parliament the adverse political and economic consequences of taking measures which threatened important Scottish interests and by implication British interests. The Treaty of Union has a political significance in this general context which can be missed, and which could serve as a counterbalance to the deep-rooted anti-Scots opinion which intermittently bubbled up at Westminster. The clauses of the Treaty were periodically abrogated by parliament in the first half of the eighteenth century, especially where British political security was judged to be at issue. On other occasions and matters, however, ministers proved reluctant to support measures which contravened clauses in the Treaty. In 1751, to give one example, the Treasury resisted strong pressure from some English tobacco merchants and their supporters to take steps against customs frauds in the Scottish tobacco trade which would have involved unequal treatment of Scottish and English merchants.[79] Glasgow tobacco merchants had not been slow to lobby the Treasury against a proposed bill which included clauses which would have imposed additional regulations on the passage of tobacco overland from Scotland into England. The resulting legislation omitted these clauses.[80] Even as late as 1793, the Scottish saltmasters argued that the ending of the exemption from taxation of coal shipping within the Forth estuary was a violation of the Union; they also urged that they should be compensated for any losses incurred because of changes to the salt laws.[81] The force of inertia in eighteenth-century government and administration, the caution with regard to threatening vested and propertied interests, are well established. In the case of Scotland, the Treaty of Union gave added ideological force to this tendency, and furnished an additional layer of protection to important Scottish interests.

John Shaw has pointed out that before 1760 the power to initiate legislation in favour of Scottish interests which involved public expenditure did not rest with the Scots.[82] The formation of the Board of Trustees and the Commission for the Forfeited Estates were the result of policy determined by English ministers; the Scottish contribution only commenced when these measures were decided on. Some of the commercial legislation which most affected the Scots in the eighteenth century was also initiated by English politicians and commercial interests in London. This was true, for example, of bounties on whale and herring fishing granted in the later 1740s. These were respectively increased and introduced as part of a wider politics of reconstruction following the end of the War of the Austrian Succession, and were designed principally to boost British naval power and, secondarily, in the case of the fisheries to help integrate the Highlands into the British state and commercial society.[83] The Scottish role in these measures was one of enthusiastic support for them and their continuation. Even in the case of the linen industry, legislative support needs to be seen in terms of consistent parliamentary support for British textiles manufacturing, and for English and Irish linen manufactures before 1707.[84] In alliance with Irish and English linen interests, the Scots were, nevertheless, able to secure considerable and crucial state support for the linen industry in the eighteenth century. English mercantile and political opposition to such support was, it is true, limited. In the 1770s and early eighties, the Scottish linen interest called for new support in the form of higher duties on foreign linen imports. On this occasion, opposition from Hamburg merchants, who imported continental linens, was stronger. Against a background of depressed overseas trade, they also succeeded in raising fears in the English woollen industry of retaliatory action against woollen cloth and goods by foreign governments. The outcome was a parliamentary inquiry into the state of the linen industry in 1773, but no additional legislative support.[85]

Finally, what role did parliament play in the transformation of Scottish society in this period? Parliament was in general less important in Scottish government and society than south of the border. To this extent, Scotland cannot be readily incorporated into the notion of the 'reactive' parliamentary state which has been proposed for south of the border.[86] For several areas of policy in Scotland, judge-made law, in the form of the decisions of the Court of Session, was much more relevant and important. This was true of Scottish social policy, which barely detained MPs at Westminster for any length of time.[87] It was also true of labour relations and labour disputes. The readiness and ability of the Court of Session, the highest civil court in Scotland, to make law through its judgments which reflected the changing needs, real and perceived, of the powerful in Scottish society in this period was clearly another important factor which lessened the call on parliament for new legislation.[88] Parliament was to play no direct role in the transformation of the eighteenth-century Scottish rural economy in the final third of the eighteenth century. There was also, as alluded to earlier, relatively less private and local legislation passed relating to Scotland, even in the later eighteenth century. One partial explanation for this is the Highlands. Many of the major road improvements in eighteenth-century Scotland were funded by the Treasury or through the Commission for Forfeited Estates, either for military reasons or as part of state-supported economic development in the Highlands. So far as urban administration and improvement was concerned, the Convention of Royal Burghs was, in many respects, a more important authority than parliament. The Convention was a revenue raising body, and it provided regular financial support for urban improvement.[89]

Where, however, the influence of parliament was felt far more strongly was in economic life. In an underdeveloped economy such as Scotland's in this period, mercantilist regulations and legislation had relatively greater importance than in England. Here we need to note important continuities with the period before the Union, when the Scottish parliament had passed a barrage of measures aimed at promoting national economic development. These may have had strictly limited effect, but they signalled a clear recognition in Scotland that the state had a crucial role to play in economic development.[90] The Earl of Ilay and Lord Milton, his sous-ministre in Edinburgh, were firm believers in mercantilist support for manufactures, as were the rest of the Scottish ruling classes in the early-Hanoverian period.[91] The importance of the state as an influence on economic development was perhaps most evident in the linen industry, as referred to at several points in this paper, although it was also present in others. As the modern historian of the industry has demonstrated, the first main phase in expansion of the industry coincided with the provision, from 1742, of the bounties on exports of coarse linen.[92] As was referred to earlier, these bounties ceased temporarily in 1754, with severe effects on the industry. They were, as has also been noted, restored in 1756 and subsequently periodically renewed for the rest of the century. Each time they became due for renewal, Scottish lobbyists did not hesitate to remind MPs of the earlier disastrous effects of removing them. In 1753, William Tod had told one correspondent that if they were not restored 'the manufacture and industry of this country will receive a blow which cannot be recovered in our age.'[93] The industry received other forms of legislative support, notably through protection against foreign competition by raising duties on imports of foreign linen and through efforts to promote the raising of flax in Britain. Imports of foreign cambrics and lawns were also prohibited by parliament between 1748 and 1787. It was not just a question of raising the output of Scottish manufactures, but also of improving their quality, and in this area too the state was seen as having a vital role to play.[94] It is perhaps ironic, therefore, that it was to be the Scottish Enlightenment which would produce the eighteenth century's leading critic of mercantilism – Adam Smith. Parliament was a crucial site of influence in Britain's 'fiscal-military state' in the eighteenth century, along with the Treasury and the Board of Trade, and for this reason alone Scots fully recognised the importance of having their interests and views well represented there. In the first half of the eighteenth century, when the balance between achievement and failure in the Scottish economy was a precarious one, parliamentary decisions had a crucial influence on important sectors of the economy. That a Scottish national interest was firmly represented at Westminster, and was, from the 1720s, capable on occasion of shaping ministerial policy and parliamentary legislation should not, therefore, be overlooked as another factor which helped to facilitate Scotland's integration into the British state and its re-creation in the central decades of the eighteenth century as 'North Britain'.

Notes

1 I would like to thank my colleague, Professor C. A. Whatley, for the valuable comments he made on earlier drafts of this chapter. I learnt much from the typically acute comments of T. C. Smout at the Neale Colloquium, and from the comments of other contributors and discussants. I am also grateful to Joanna Innes for allowing me to read, prior to its delivery, a copy of her lecture, around which this volume is based.

2 T. M. Devine, *The Scottish nation* (London, 2000), especially ch. 3.

3 See especially J. Robertson, 'The Union debate in Scotland, 1698–1707' in Robertson (ed.), *A union for empire: political thought and the Union of 1707* (Cambridge, 1995), 198–227.

4 A. Fletcher, *An account of a conversation concerning the right regulation of governments for the common good of mankind. In a letter to the Marquiss of Montrose, the Earls of Rothes, Roxburgh and Haddington, from London the first day of December 1703* (Edinburgh, 1704).

5 See J. Brims, 'The Scottish Jacobins, Scottish nationalism and the British Union' in R. A. Mason (ed.), *Scotland and England, 1280–1815* (Edinburgh, 1987).

6 See e.g. T. C. Smout, *A history of the Scottish people, 1560–1830* (1972), 201. Comment in more recent general studies, for example, Devine's *The Scottish nation*, may be slightly less dismissive, but it is similarly sparse.

7 This is not true of all historians. See e.g. G. Jackson, 'Government bounties and the establishment of the Scottish whaling trade, 1750–1800' in J. Butt and J. T. Ward (eds), *Scottish themes* (Edinburgh, 1976), 46–66; C. A. Whatley, *The Scottish salt industry, 1570–1850* (Aberdeen, 1987) and his 'Salt, coal, and the Union of 1707: a revision article', *Scottish Historical Review*, lxvi (1987), 26–45. Two historians of an earlier generation who emphasised the importance of the economic role of the state are H. Hamilton in *An economic history of Scotland in the eighteenth century* (Oxford, 1963) and E. Hughes in *Studies in administration and finance, 1558–1825* (Manchester, 1934).

8 P. W. J. Riley, *The English ministers and Scotland, 1707–1727* (1964), 118–19.

9 J. S. Shaw, *The management of Scottish society, 1707–1764: power, nobles, lawyers, Edinburgh agents and English influences* (Edinburgh, 1983) and similarly in his *The political history of eighteenth-century Scotland* (1999).

10 Shaw, *Management of Scottish society*, 126.

11 A. Murdoch, *'The people above': politics and administration in mid-eighteenth-century Scotland* (Edinburgh, 1980). See also his 'Scottish sovereignty in the eighteenth century' in H. T. Dickinson and M. Lynch (eds), *The challenge to Westminster: sovereignty, devolution and independence* (East Linton, 2000), 42–9.

12 For the recent literature on the role of parliament in the English context, see the introduction to this volume.

13 A key text here has been L. Colley's *Britons: forging the nation, 1707–1837* (New Haven and London, 1992). But see also A. Murdoch, *British history 1660–1832: national identity and local culture* (1999); C. Kidd, 'North Britishness and the nature of eighteenth-century British patriotisms', *Historical Journal*, xlix (1996), 361–82; M. G. H. Pittock, *Celtic identity and the British image* (Manchester, 1999).

14 This was a point much emphasised by Riley in relation to Godolphin's stewardship of the Treasury in the years which immediately followed the Union: *The English Ministers and Scotland*. See also the extended discussion of office holding in Scottish revenue departments in R. Scott, 'The politics and administration of Scotland, 1725–1748' (University of Edinburgh Ph.D. thesis, 1981).

15 C. A. Whatley, *Scottish society 1707–1830: beyond Jacobitism, towards industrialisation* (Manchester, 2000), especially ch. 5.

16 A. Gambles, 'Free trade and state formation: the political economy of fisheries policy in Britain and the United Kingdom circa 1750–1850', *Journal of British Studies*, xlix (2000), 288–316.

17 Such an analysis is currently being developed by the present author and C. A. Whatley based on material extracted from the *Journals of the House of Commons* by Rhona Fiest.

18 M. Fry, *The Dundas despotism* (Edinburgh, 1992), 55. See also Shaw, *Eighteenth-century Scotland*; and for a typically trenchant treatment of this theme, B. Lenman, 'A client society: Scotland between the '15 and the '45' in J. Black (ed.), *Britain in the age of Walpole* (1984), 69–93.

19 See the disappointingly brief comment in R. Sedgwick (ed.), *The history of parliament: the House of Commons, 1715–1754*, 2 vols (1970), i, 159. The figures cited there do, however, show that, with the Scottish Tories eliminated as a political force by the '15 Jacobite Rebellion, a large majority of Scottish MPs supported the ministry. The main exceptions to this pattern occurred as a result of the 2nd Duke of Argyll going into opposition briefly between 1717 and 1719 and his resumption of opposition in the later 1730s. At the 1741 general election, Argyll joined forces with the Squadrone to return a significant number of MPs (26) in opposition to Walpole. See also Scott, 'Politics and administration', 301.

20 Riley, *English ministers and Scotland*, 243. Some of the factors behind the Scottish lack of success at Westminster in the years immediately after 1707 are identified in Hayton's contribution to this volume.

21 Linen's status as Scotland's main export earner by the later seventeenth century was confirmed by commercial data examined by the Edinburgh parliament in 1704. According to the estimates for 1704, linen goods accounted for almost 22 per cent of

exports by value. The next most important were woollen goods and sheepskins and herrings, both at around 14 per cent (R. Saville, *Bank of Scotland: a history, 1695–1995* (Edinburgh, 1996), 59–62).

22 P. K. O'Brien, T. Griffith and P. Hunt, 'Political components of the industrial revolution: parliament and the English cotton textile industry, 1660–1774', *Economic History Review*, xliv (1991), 406–9.

23 The case of the Scottish industry was also articulated in print. See *The answer of the Scots linnen manufacturers to the Report of the Lords Commissioners of Trade and Plantations* (1720–21); *The Case of the Convention of Royal Burghs, in relation to the linnen manufactory of that country* (1720–21).

24 *CJ*, xix, 212.

25 *CJ*, xix, 196–240.

26 Whatley, *Scottish society*, 193.

27 *CJ*, xix, 240, 244, 252.

28 They were: Sir James Campbell, MP for Argyllshire; Henry Cunningham, MP for Stirling Burghs; and Daniel Campbell of Shawfield, MP for Glasgow Burghs. (*CJ*, xix, 263.)

29 For contemporary comment on this, see e.g. National Archives of Scotland [NAS], Montrose Papers, GD 220/5/468/19: Charles to Jo. Cockburn, 9 July 1715.

30 See esp. Kidd, 'North Britishness'.

31 For recent comment on the 1720s, and the multiple problems of economic adjustment in this period, see C. A. Whatley, 'The Union of 1707, integration and the Scottish burghs: the case of the 1720 food riots', *Scottish Historical Review*, lxxviii (1999), 192–218.

32 The fullest discussion of the malt tax riots is contained in Scott, 'Politics and administration', ch. 9.

33 See especially Shaw, *Management of Scottish society*, 124–30.

34 *The parliamentary diary of Sir Edward Knatchbull, 1722–1730*, ed. A. N. Newman, Camden Society, third series, xciv (1963), 11–12.

35 *Knatchbull diary*, 26–7.

36 NAS, Clark of Penicuick Papers, GD 18/3194/13.

37 *Knatchbull diary*, 33–4.

38 *Knatchbull diary*, 35. Fraser was to be unseated on an election petition in 1725. His intervention appears to have directly reflected pressure on him from constituents.

39 See National Library of Scotland [NLS], Saltoun Papers, MS. 16,529, Lord Milton to the Earl of Ilay, 17 Dec. 1724. On 25 Dec. a letter to Archibald Grant referred to the 'Remonstrances, Instructions and Addresses from some of more southerly counties already made' (NAS, Grant of Monymusk Papers, GD 345/578). See also *A letter from a Fyfe gentleman, at present in Edinburgh, to the chief magistrate of a burgh in Fyfe, upon our present situation, with regard to the malt tax* (Edinburgh, 1725), especially 5–6. For the Midlothian heritors' instructions to Robert Dundas, issued on 19 Dec., see GD 4/15/2, vol. 2, 56. See also GD 6/1037: copy of a petition from the heritors and freeholders of the county of Haddington to parliament, 1724; copy of petition from the county of Perth to the House of Commons, 1724; the representation of the Barons and Freeholders of Midlothian, 1724. See also *Knatchbull diary*, 34–5.

40 NAS, GD 345/578, unfoliated letter, R. Gordon to Alexander Grant, MP, 15 Dec. 1724.

41 NAS, GD 345/578.

42 NAS, GD 345/578; GD 18/3194, 3197, 3199 and 3200.

43 The committee included Squadrone members such as Sir John Anstruther and Robert Dundas, as well as supporters of Argyll, for example, Daniel Campbell of Shawfield and his brother, John, at this time Lord Provost of Edinburgh.

44 NAS, GD 345/578, R. Gordon to Archibald Grant, 4 Feb. 1725.

45 Shaw, *Management of Scottish society*, 126. There were also petitions in early 1726 calling for relief from the tax from Morayshire, Midlothian, Renfrewshire, Banffshire, the burgh of Elgin, and Ayrshire (*CJ*, xix, 594–605). In early 1727, the Squadrone again sought to stir the issue of the malt tax through a petitioning campaign. See National Register of Archives, Strathmore Papers, Glamis, box 256, bundle 4, letter to the Earl of Strathmore, 8 Jan. 1727, which refers to two forms of petition to the crown against the malt tax, one for the counties and one for the burghs, sent by the Marquis of Tweeddale; also NAS, GD 22/3/798, instructions by the gentlemen freeholders of Stirling to their representatives in parliament, 1727.

46 NAS, GD 18/3194/4.

47 NAS, GD 18/3194/4; Edinburgh City Archives [ECA], Convention of Royal Burghs, Moses Collection, SL 30/242, Drummond to Annual Committee of the Convention of Royal Burghs, London, 19 Mar. 1726. Dundas was one of only two Scottish MPs who opposed the proposal; the other was another Squadrone supporter, Sir John Anstruther.

48 Shaw, *Management of Scottish society*, 126–7.

49 Scott, 'Politics and administration', 423; G. Menary, *The life and letters of Duncan Forbes of Culloden, Lord President of the Court of Session, 1685–1747* (1936), 105–21.

50 While Argyll gave passive support to the bill, his lack of enthusiasm was abundantly clear. He did not order his supporters to oppose the bill, but they did so anyway. As Scott has noted, Argyll believed that more active opposition would be futile: 'Politics and administration', 529. See also Kidd, 'North Britishness', 372–3.

51 Public Record Office of Northern Ireland, Castleward Papers, D 2092/1/5, fos. 49–50.

52 ECA, Convention of Royal Burghs, Moses Collection, SL 30/244, Letter, Alex Dundas, London, anent Duty on Foreign Linens Exported, 1 Dec. 1737; *CJ*, xxiv, 26–57, 189–333, 584–648, 770–891; *Extracts from the records of the Convention of Royal Burghs, 1711–38* (Edinburgh, 1885), 637–8. The campaign also produced a pamphlet [D. Bindon?], *A letter from a merchant who has left off trade, to a Member of Parliament, in which the case of the British and Irish manufacture of linen, threads and tapes, is fairly stated* (Belfast, 1738).

53 *Extracts from the records of the Convention of Royal Burghs, 1738–59* (Edinburgh, 1915), 88–90; *CJ*, xxiv, 24, 256. Advised by the Board of Trustees not to apply again for the removal of drawbacks on exports of foreign linen, the Convention put its weight behind a campaign to have duties removed on imports of soap and potashes used in preparation of yarn and bleaching.

54 *Tory and Whig: the parliamentary papers of Edward Harley, 3rd Earl of Oxford and William Hay, MP for Seaford, 1716–1753*, ed. C. Jones and S. Taylor (Woodbridge, 1998), 193.

55 *Records of the Convention of Royal Burghs, 1738–59*, 143, 159. The resolution was to be repeated in 1747.

56 *Records of the Convention of Royal Burghs, 1738–59*, 177, 178–9; *Memorial for the linen-manufacturers of Scotland* (1745). The agent of the Convention in this matter was Archibald Stuart, MP for Edinburgh. It is likely there was a strong connection between this application and the plans, then underway under the guidance of Lord

Milton, for the formation of the British Linen Company. Stewart was involved in the establishment of the company. A key element in the plan was export to the colonies across the Atlantic. To facilitate this, links were built with the West India interest. One of the founder directors of the company, when it was granted a royal charter in 1746, was William Beckford.

57 Murdoch, 'The people above', 68–73.

58 The main ones were in the later 1760s, when the Scottish linen interests successfully campaigned for state support for flax growing in Britain, and the early 1770s and 1780, when they looked for higher duties on imports of foreign linen.

59 In the case of one particularly active MP, George Yeaman, MP for Perth Burghs between 1708 and 1715, this activity can be traced in the Dundee and Perth burgh minutes.

60 *Records of the Convention of Royal Burghs, 1738–59*, 65, 66, 66–7, 68, 74. Regulating the bread market was an area in which the Convention periodically urged that Scotland be brought under English (or British) legislation on importing and exporting grain, engrossing, and the assize of bread. In 1763, the Scots obtained legislation on the bread assize. There were also new corn laws passed for Scotland in 1773, 1774, 1780, and 1792. There is no existing work on this topic.

61 *Records of the Convention of Royal Burghs, 1738–59*, 346, 365, 368, 376, 378, 381, 418, 445, 446. An act of bankruptcy was successfully steered through parliament in 1772.

62 See e.g. the famous acts on entail (1770) and on abolishing serfdom in the coal and salt industries (1775, 1799). There was also important new legislation on banking in 1765.

63 Between 1715 and 1727, acts were passed conferring this power on twelve burghs: Glasgow (1716); Edinburgh (1717, 1723); Dumfries (1717); Inverness (1719); Dunbar (1719); Montrose (1720); Pittenweem (1720); Burntisland (1720); Dundee (1721); Jedburgh (1721); Elgin (1722); Linlithgow (1723).

64 See the chapter by Joanna Innes above.

65 There is no satisfactory modern study of the Scottish press in this period, but see M. E. Craig, *The Scottish periodical press, 1750–1789* (Edinburgh, 1931). The *Scots Magazine*, which was founded in 1739, contains a substantial amount of material on commercial issues. See e.g. *Scots Magazine*, xv (1753), 606–10, for commentary on the need to renew the linen bounty.

66 For comment on this, see B. Harris, *Politics and the rise of the press: Britain and France, 1620–1800* (1996), 42–3.

67 This development has not been studied in any great detail, but was one of the more dynamic aspects of Scottish sovereignty in the later eighteenth century. Another crucial element to it was the emergence of county meetings as important forums for debate and government. For the latter, see A. E. Whetstone, *Scottish county government in the eighteenth and nineteenth centuries* (Edinburgh, 1981), 69–70.

68 One exception was 1746, when there was no Lord Provost. On this occasion, the Lord Provost of Glasgow was elected instead.

69 J. M. Price, 'Glasgow, the tobacco trade, and the Scottish customs, 1707–1730', *Scottish Historical Review*, lxiii (1984), 18; Public Record Office [PRO], Treasury Board Papers, T1/400/48, 49.

70 They also operated as a price cartel. See Whatley, 'Salt, coal and the Union'.

71 Its exact brief was to correspond with the burghs' MPs on trade and the state of the burghs, to give notice to the burghs so that they could write to their MPs on their own

behalf on such matters, and in case of an application to parliament to again give notice so that all members of the committee might attend the relevant meetings. For one example of the system in operation, see NAS, GD 124/1468, letter from the Annual Committee of the Convention to David Morison and David Sands, Dunfermline, 28 Feb. 1737.

72 The only years in which no such individual existed were 1749–54. In 1749, the Convention decided to cease employing an agent because delegates believed it would have less need for one in peacetime. In 1754, this decision was reversed, and George Ross, the Cromarty merchant and contractor, was appointed as agent in London.

73 B. Harris, 'Scotland's herring fisheries and the prosperity of the nation, c. 1660–1760', *Scottish Historical Review*, lxxix (2000), 57–8.

74 The unpublished records of the Convention are currently held in the ECA.

75 *Records of the Convention of Royal Burghs, 1738–59*, 518–19.

76 NAS, Seafield Papers, GD 248/562/55, fo.18. Deskford was a keen supporter of linen spinning in the Highlands and was, therefore, opposed to the eventual scheme for restoring the bounty arranged under Argyll's direction.

77 See NLS, Saltoun Papers, MS. 17,578, fos. 40–1: John Cathcart to Lord Milton, 21 Nov. 1752; Murdoch, *'The people above'*, 68–73.

78 *Knatchbull diary*, 34.

79 For a draft of the proposed bill, see PRO, T1/345/65.

80 PRO, T1/345/48, 49, 52. The Treasury had adopted a similar position in the early 1720s. Jacob Price has observed of this earlier episode, that Walpole was successful in 'deflecting' the strongly anti-Scots agitation to the extent that only one clause of the final bill was 'in any sense anti Scots'. The act was also to have much less effect on the Glasgow and Scottish tobacco traders than many feared, partly because of concessions on duties (Price, 'Tobacco trade', 27).

81 Whatley, *Scottish salt industry*, 85.

82 See above note 9.

83 See B. Harris, 'Patriotic commerce and national revival: the Free British Fishery Society and British politics, c. 1749–58', *English Historical Review*, cxiv (1999), 285–313.

84 T. Keirn, 'Parliament, legislation and the regulation of the English textile industries, 1689–1714' in L. Davison et al. (eds), *Stilling the grumbling hive: the response to social and economic problems in England, 1689–1750* (Stroud, 1992), 1–24; O'Brien, Griffith and Hunt, 'Political components'; N. B. Harte, 'The rise of protection and the English linen industry, 1690–1790' in Harte and K. G. Ponting (eds), *Textile history and economic history: essays in honour of Miss Julia de Lacy Mann* (Manchester, 1973), 74–112; R. L. Sickinger, 'Regulation or ruination: parliament's consistent pattern of mercantilist regulation of the English textile trade, 1660–1800', *Parliamentary History*, xix (2000), 211–32.

85 See NAS, RH 2/4/387, fos. 381–2: W. Sandeman, Perth, to Earl of Suffolk, 1 Jan. 1780.

86 The notion is advanced in the introduction to Davison et al. (eds), *Grumbling hive*.

87 R. Mitchison, *The old poor law in Scotland: the experience of poverty, 1574–1845* (Edinburgh, 2000).

88 For labour relations and the law, see W. H. Fraser, *Conflict and class: Scottish workers, 1700–1838* (Edinburgh, 1988). But see 24 Geo II, c. 31 and 22 Geo II, c. 27 for legislation on labour conditions in the linen and other textiles industries; see also the acts abolishing serfdom amongst colliers and salters.

89 The Convention's authority to change the constitutions or 'sets' of burghs was successfully challenged in the later eighteenth century. In 1777, the Court of Session gave a ruling against the reform of the set of Edinburgh, ruling that this could only be obtained by application to parliament.

90 Comparisons between the Scottish and Westminster parliaments need to bear this point strongly in mind. Much of what the Scottish parliament was doing was seeking to render effective previous legislation which had failed in its purpose.

91 Roger Emerson is currently at work on Ilay's economic ideas. For those of Milton, see Shaw, *Management of Scottish society*, 156–8.

92 A. J. Durie, *The Scottish linen industry in the eighteenth century* (Edinburgh, 1979).

93 *The British Linen Company, 1745–1776*, ed. Alistair J. Durie (Edinburgh, 1996), 54.

94 This was a major concern of the Board of Trustees. It was also the subject of several pieces of legislation.

8

Government, parliament and politics in Ireland, 1801–41[1]

Peter Jupp

In the planning of the British–Irish Union British ministers gave little, if any thought to the likely effect that a united parliament might have on national identities. Their view, in common with that of many Britons, was that parliament represented kingdoms rather than nations; and within kingdoms, the leading economic interests and the different types of local communities rather than mere numbers of people. This coincided with what by today's standards was a very limited view of parliament's role. In essence this consisted of raising sufficient money to pay for defence and administration, of providing legal frameworks for maintaining the peace and settling disputes between conflicting interests, and of redressing grievances. It is true that parliament had occasionally acted more positively in the eighteenth century – particularly on welfare issues – but this had not led to a wide-spread belief that this is what its role should be. It was for these reasons that Pitt was able to rest his case for the Union almost entirely on the greater security and material prosperity that it would provide by means of direct rule and the infusion of private capital. He certainly believed that the united parliament could promote greater harmony in Ireland by giving Catholics equal political rights with Protestants but the prospect of it being a promoter of a shared United Kingdom identity did not enter his mind.

In Ireland, on the other hand, the Irish parliament was much more closely connected to the question of identity because membership was restricted to a religious and largely ethnic minority. Thus although it had developed many of the investigative and legislative functions of the Westminster parliament in the course of the eighteenth century, the key issue by the 1790s was how far it could serve competing visions of a future Irish polity, each of which involved religious and ethnic considerations. Within the parliamentary classes, these were chiefly either a continuing Protestant 'ascendancy' or a gradual Protestant-led accommodation of the Catholic interest that stopped short of a Catholic 'ascendancy'. Outside the parliamentary classes, alternative formulations were considered such as Wolf Tone's republic in which representative institutions would compliment the objective of substituting 'the common name of Irishman in the place of the denominations of Protestant, Catholic and Dissenter . . .'.[2]

The Union therefore took place at a time when politicians in Britain and Ireland had different expectations of representative institutions. In Britain, the majority still regarded parliament as largely representative, either directly or indirectly, of the leading interests and communities and as only part of the total apparatus of government that included the quarter sessions and the civic corporations and commissions. The fact that most MPs were so firmly rooted in the much larger apparatus of local government is surely one of the reasons why they preferred to act in parliament as a court of last resort rather than economic, social or cultural engineers. In Ireland, on the other hand, the majority was chiefly concerned with how any representative institution would affect the balance between Protestant and Catholic in Ireland.

In the next forty years the prevailing views in Britain on the responsibilities of governments and parliament began to change. Governments intervened more in welfare and education. Parliamentary inquiry and legislation grew significantly and with it, the sponsorship of reform measures by independent MPs. The view that parliament should represent the dominant economic interests and different types of communities was put to the test by a greater consciousness of class loyalties and hostilities and the congregation of workers in areas straddling the conventional boundaries between county and town. It has also been argued that the war effort, 1793–1815, created a new expectation of parliament on the part of the public which led ultimately to the great reforms of 1828–33 and a 'redefinition' of citizenship and 'the nation'.[3]

But what happened to Ireland? How did governments and parliament deal with their new responsibility? How far did they seek to incorporate Ireland into a United Kingdom? To what extent did the Irish embrace their new representative institution? How far were they included in the redefinition of 'the nation'. These are large questions which this essay, although focusing predominantly on parliamentary business, might help to answer. The first section below deals with the framework of the government of Ireland; the second section with the role of Irish MPs; the third with legislation and other forms of parliamentary business; and the fourth with the impact of parliament on 'the public sphere'. Throughout, the principal question being addressed is the extent to which developments in each of these subjects promoted uniformity or separateness.

A survey of the basic evidence pertaining to the governing of Ireland in this period, first brought together by Professor McDowell nearly forty years ago, suggests that two processes were at work.[4] The first led to greater uniformity in government by absorbing or integrating Irish departments into the British equivalents, while the other emphasised separateness by establishing new administrative bodies that were designed to suit Irish needs. Both of these processes can be observed at the highest level of the Irish administration – that occupied in 1800 by the Lord Lieutenant and the Chief Secretary on behalf of the British cabinet and by the First Lord of the Irish Treasury and the Chancellor of the Irish Exchequer who were responsible to the Irish parliament. Immediately after the Union, serious consideration was given to curtailing severely the influence of the Lord Lieutenant or even abolishing the post, to investing the Home Secretary with direct responsibility for Irish matters, and to bringing the two Irish financial offices under the control of their British equivalents. Ireland would therefore have been brought directly under the aegis of the British government. This idea was rejected, however, one of the principal reasons being that the Lord Lieutenant's presence in Dublin with substantial patronage at his disposal was regarded as essential to the successful management of the various political interests within the Irish propertied elite. Yet as the Union evolved, three things happened. First, the Lord Lieutenancy was retained with much of its influence intact, despite spasmodic attempts to abolish the post. Second, the two Irish financial posts were abolished and their duties assumed by British ministers. And third, the Chief Secretary increasingly became a more influential political figure in London than the Lord Lieutenant as a result of his being the minister responsible for Irish matters in the Commons. The preservation of a separate head of the Irish administration in Ireland therefore co-existed with the development of greater ministerial control over policy through the abolition of senior Irish offices and the growing political influence of the Chief Secretary.

The process of bringing Irish administration under the direct control of the British departments of state was chiefly devoted to fiscal and military matters. On the fiscal side, the first major step was taken in 1816 when the Irish and British revenue departments were consolidated and the Irish Treasury absorbed into the British, albeit with seats provided for Irish representatives. Thereafter the process quickened. Between 1823 and 1827 the consolidation of the Irish and British customs, excise and stamp departments took place or got under way; and the responsibilities of the Irish department dealing with crown lands placed under the care of the Whitehall commissioners of the Royal Woods, Forests and Land Revenues. In 1831–32 the separate Irish Post Office disappeared and the remnants of the accounting offices were placed under the supervision of the British commissioners of Public Accounts. It is also worth noting that the Irish Poor Law established in 1838 was put under the supervision of the English Poor Law Commission – partly because it was a rating, and therefore a financial, matter. As for the military, the unification of the respective command and administrative systems had been decided upon soon after the Union and the process reached its conclusion in the 1820s with the abolition of the five remaining responsible Irish departments. Moreover it is significant that within a few years of the Union all the Irish departments mentioned above, as well as most of the others, were treated to the same doses of 'economical reform' that were applied in Britain. By the 1830s the Irish administration was therefore not only smaller – eighteen of the twenty-two departments of 1801 had disappeared – but leaner and fitter as a result of the disappearance of sinecures, the introduction of salaries and pensions for officials, and the establishment of more efficient working practices. However, although there were parallel developments in Britain, this was not a solely British initiative.[5] Some steps had been taken in this direction by the Irish parliament before the Union[6] and the impetus in this period came as much from Irish sources as from the British. Thus, John Foster and Sir John Newport were largely responsible for setting up the crucial inquiries into the revenue departments in 1804 and 1815 and there were Irish as well as English members of the commissions involved.

The process by which the fiscal and military responsibilities of the Irish administration were brought under the control of London-based departments, co-existed with another that moved in an opposite direction and was concerned chiefly with welfare, education, policing and economic development. It had three general features. The first was a recognition that Irish circumstances in these areas were different from those in Britain and therefore necessitated special treatment.[7] The second was the enhancement of the responsibilities of the Lord Lieutenant. And the third was the resort to a variety of methods to administer these responsibilities.

By far the most common method was the creation of a board or commission of (usually) unpaid commissioners that acted under the authority of the Lord Lieutenant. Two such boards – the Linen and Inland Navigation boards – had existed prior to the Union but in this period another ten were established. Five of this total of twelve dealt with economic development, including employment, although only two of these – the boards of Inland Navigation and Works – survived into the 1830s[8]; five dealt with public health, education and the associated matter of charitable bequests, all of which lasted until at least 1841; and two dealt with Public Records and the Church of Ireland (the Ecclesiastical Commission established by the Whig administration in the 1830s). In other areas, however, it was thought best to invest the Lord Lieutenant with direct responsibility. This was the case with the various experiments in policing in 1814, 1822 and 1836, but it also extended to local government where, for example, the Lord Lieutenant was given statutory powers to make arrangements for the auditing of county and borough accounts in 1836 and 1840.

The shaping of the post-Union governing of Ireland therefore took two different courses: the one drawing fiscal and military matters under British ministerial control; and the other placing new areas of administration in the hands of the Lord Lieutenant and his advisers. How far this was planned or merely the result of a series of ad hoc decisions is a difficult question to answer. The course taken with regard to fiscal and military policy was certainly envisaged at the time of the Union and was therefore to a certain degree premeditated, whereas the leaving of other matters in the hands of the Irish administration and the new boards and commissions seems much less so. However, parliament was clearly central to both courses. Thus all the measures adumbrated above were the result of acts of parliament and most of them drew extensively on commission or select committee inquiries and the accounts and papers requested of government departments. In the case of the reform of public offices, for example, a recent catalogue of parliamentary papers shows that in this period there were two select committee reports, fourteen reports from the Commission of Inquiry into Fees and Emoluments (1806–14) and thirty-seven different accounts and papers that informed policy and contributed to the drafting of the relevant bills.[9]

Although some Irish MPs initially found the differences between the Irish and British parliaments in terms of the physical setting of debate and the style of speaking difficult to adjust to, the majority adapted easily, both then and subsequently, to the dominant methods and assumptions of public rhetoric. The basic reason for this, as Brian Crowe points out in his important thesis on Irish MPs in the 1830s, was that virtually all the Irish MPs of this period, including the O'Connellites, shared a 'historical and political' culture with their British counterparts based on historic ties between the two countries, similar education, family connections and property ownership.[10] Most Irish MPs set their views in an historical context. In particular, they expressed admiration for the British constitution and regarded key events in its evolution – Magna Carta, the Bill of Rights, the Revolution settlement, the new 'constitution' of 1782, the Union, Catholic relief and the Reform acts of 1832 – as stages in a developing compact between the state and the people. Further, all sides frequently referred to a common litany of writers and politicians to provide philosophical and historical justification for their points of view, including Locke, Paley, Blackstone, De Lolme, Burke, Grattan, Pitt, Fox, Canning and Grey. In the debate on the Catholic question in 1813, for example, two Irish county members, Sir Frederick Flood and Robert Shapland Carew, each invoked five of the above luminaries to justify their support for concessions, adding for good measure Windham, Grenville and Sheridan.[11] Moreover as Crowe has shown in his study of the 1830s – a period when the land question came to prominence – there was as much agreement between all shades of Irish opinion on the object of civil society being the protection of landed property as there was amongst British MPs. The views of Irish MPs on the virtues of the British constitution and its underlying purpose therefore enabled them to integrate easily into the traditional forms and terms of parliamentary debate.

However, there were different views on the relative merits and implications of the 'stepping stones' of the constitution. All shades of opinion consistently regarded the Union as a contract or compact between the two kingdoms but agreement ended there. Conservatives saw it as a way of safeguarding Protestant property, the established religion and 'the rational system of liberty' that they believed to be enshrined in the constitution by the Revolution settlement.[12] It was from this perspective that they viewed the Catholic Relief Act of 1829 and parliamentary reform. Most might have been reconciled to the former, Crowe argues, if it had led to the cessation of agitation but the fact that it did not led them to condemn it as a failure. Similarly, they were prepared to accept parliamentary reform on the grounds that it continued to base representation on the principle of property, but like Peel said it should be a 'final' measure. Post-Union developments therefore served to underline the differences between Irish conservative hopes and the drift of the constitution towards a more inclusive and participatory state. In 1832 O'Connell felt there was a growing disillusionment amongst Irish conservative MPs with the results of Ireland's incorporation into an evolving UK constitution, remarking that although they sought 'ascendancy' they were 'after that Irish, often very very Irish' and might become repealers.[13]

Irish liberals and eventually the O'Connellites expressed a different view in their public statements. In the case of liberals, they initially saw the Union as a means by which Ireland could share fully in the virtues of the constitution and secure what they regarded as essential reforms. As Grattan said in support of Catholic Relief in 1813, Catholics had been responsible for Magna Carta and the liberties re-affirmed by the Declaration of Rights and that all that Irish Catholics now sought was equal citizenship under the protection of the constitution.[14] After the passage of the Relief Act, however, liberals began to abandon the whiggish constitutionalism of Grattan and to develop a more progressive ideology which envisaged a non-denominational Irish propertied elite securing a series of political and economic reforms from the British government and thereby reconciling the Catholic masses to that elite's leadership. Yet this form of Irish liberalism was severely tested in the late 1830s and early 1840s by both conservatism and O'Connellism with the result that some liberals sought Ireland's full assimilation with the British administrative and political systems while others began to toy with repeal.[15]

The O'Connellites also explored the advantages of repeal or full integration in their parliamentary rhetoric. Repeal was to the fore between 1831 and 1834 but following the failure of the campaign in parliament and the compact with the Whigs at Lichfield House, O'Connell spoke of his readiness to consent to the Union if steps were taken to produce 'an identity of laws, an identity of institutions, and an identity of liberties'. What he looked for, he said, was a new state in which there was no distinction between 'Yorkshire and Carlow'. This was a theme that was taken up by some of his colleagues who insisted that the Irish and English were fellow 'countrymen' in the empire and therefore deserved equal treatment in the way of reform. As O'Connell put it in 1839, 'what is union without identification?'[16] Later, of course, this dream also faded.

Thus although Irish MPs shared a common historical and political culture with their British counterparts and were to that extent integrated into the new expanded polity, their parliamentary rhetoric reveals a variety of views on Ireland's place within it. Some regarded the Union as a means of either maintaining a Protestant ascendancy or of creating a new form of non-denominational elite leadership within a part of the United Kingdom that would have its own distinctive political and administrative systems. Others favoured either complete integration or repeal, although there was a variety of views as to what the last might lead to – some favouring a federal structure and others separation.

With regard to the relationship between Irish MPs and party politics, there are some reasons for arguing that a considerable degree of integration took place.

Many, for example, had close personal ties with British MPs as a result of family connections or a common education. On occasion, large numbers voted on key British issues such as parliamentary reform. Some, such as Castlereagh, Croker, George Ponsonby, Sir Henry Parnell and Thomas Spring Rice, exercised considerable influence within their respective parties. However, the great mass of evidence points in a different direction and suggests that as a whole Irish MPs were never fully or even significantly engaged in the daily battles between the parties.

There were three main reasons for this. The first involved the distance between Ireland and London. The constant attendance of party activists meant lengthy absence from constituency and local government duties and the heavy expense of living near Westminster during parliamentary sessions. Only a minority could afford either the time or the money. Certainly the speaking and voting records of Irish MPs – at least in the first half of this period – are noticeably poor.[17] The second was the result of the fact that from the outset of the Union, one of the principal responsibilities of the Lord Lieutenant and the Chief Secretary was to use their patronage to secure the maximum number of supporters for the party in power. This not only had the effect of encouraging Irish MPs to think of themselves as a distinct species, it also militated against long-term party commitments.

The third reason arose from the nature of parties in this period. The fundamental point here is that especially until the 1830s, parties – that is committed and known activists – did not make up more than half the House of Commons. In other words, it was unnecessary for Irish MPs to become a member of a party in order to have a role to play. Indeed no party made much effort to recruit and retain new members. Furthermore the history of parties in this period must have made them as difficult for the majority of Irish MPs to engage with as they have been for historians to understand. Engagement would have been particularly difficult in the first twelve years of the Union during which Pitt's following dissolved into four or five competing personal groups, one of which joined Fox's Whig party. Between 1812 and 1830 a clearer line of demarcation emerged between a party of government (which involved only some designated 'Tory') and a Whig party of opposition, though even when added together these comprised only about half the members of the Commons. Moreover not only did these two parties dissolve into as many as five sub-divisions in response to the Catholic question, but all sides were involved in a tactical game that would have perplexed the average back-bencher.[18] Finally, although clearer, more comprehensive, and better organised lines of demarcation between two parties may have emerged after 1832, long-standing differences and traditional practices still persisted. Thus, as a number of historians have argued, the Whig-Liberal party of government and the Conservative party of opposition may have comprised the vast majority of the Commons, but they were nevertheless coalitions, sometimes as much at loggerheads with each other as with members on the other side of the House. Indeed, Peel, like the Whigs in the late 1820s, had sometimes taken the view that it was best to sustain the party opposite in power rather than seek its removal.[19]

Irish MPs as a whole must have found the complexities of party warfare confusing and off-putting. As mentioned earlier, the one consistent organising feature of their parliamentary conduct throughout this period was the determination of the party in power to distribute Irish patronage exclusively to its supporters. It is the evidence of how this was done together with contemporary estimates of political allegiance and voting records which provides the basis for the various assessments of those who were in support of the party in power and those who supported opposition groups.[20] However, such assessments, which usually include all Irish MPs at any given point in time, can give a very misleading impression of the number who were fully integrated into any of these parties. Before 1830 the number of wholly committed Pittites/Tories or Whigs was about only twenty to thirty out of the total of 100 Irish members, with the Irish Whigs possessing the greatest affinity with their British counterparts.[21] Crowe reaches a similar conclusion for the period after 1833, arguing that although the Irish Conservatives and Liberals usually acted with their British counterparts, they saw themselves as only loosely attached and tended to regard parties as transient phenomena. He also makes the point that although the O'Connellites regarded themselves as an independent group, they held a variety of views on the issues of the day and can hardly be regarded as a homogeneous party.[22]

Thus the prevailing modes of party politics did not encourage much integration of Irish MPs into that aspect of parliamentary life. Parties were very much Westminster-based institutions, whose inner workings were a mystery to those who were unable to commit themselves to constant attendance and to not a little socialising. Loose attachment to them was relatively easy but full membership far more difficult. This, when considered together with the point made earlier on the subject of debate, suggests that once again it is a case of Ireland being both incorporated and separate.

The Union took place during a period when there was a rapid increase in all forms of parliamentary business. The average number of public, local and private bills considered at Westminster every year, for example, rose from just over 200 in the 1780s and nineties to about 360 during the next thirty years. Over the same period there was a near three-fold increase in the number of accounts and papers produced and printed at the request of members.[23] Irish business obviously contributed to that increase and it is to the ways that it was handled and their effects on the relationship between the two countries that we now turn.

One element of this new business was the annual grants of money for 'Irish Miscellaneous Services'. These consisted of the costs of Irish civil and judicial administration, together with those of a number of educational and charitable institutions that had been met by the Irish parliament and which the UK parliament agreed to continue. The history of these two kinds of 'Services' has a bearing on our subject. In the case of the costs of the Irish administration, these amounted to an average of £138,000 during the last seven years of the Irish parliament and rose to £158,000 in 1840, by which time, of course, the number of departments and personnel had been significantly reduced. Nevertheless this part of the 'Services' rarely led to much controversy in debate. This was not the case with the other grants. Prior to the Union they had averaged about £47,000 per year, but reached £159,000 in 1840 when grants were made to seven hospitals; five schools and colleges, including Maynooth, a general educational fund, sundry non-conformist and dissenting ministers, and various boards and commissions responsible for improvement schemes. Controversy focused, at least until the 1830s, on whether such grants concentrated too much on administratively top-heavy Dublin charities and whether, in general, they were still appropriate in a UK context. The details of this need not concern us here; the important point is that successive governments chose to honour the commitments made by the Irish parliament and to preserve their distinctiveness within the UK.[24]

As Innes has pointed out, a similar approach can be detected in the legislation that applied to Ireland during this period.[25] In view of the fact that I am dealing with a longer post-Union period than she does, there is some overlap between her statistics on this matter and those presented here. However, this is a large and complex subject and it may be useful to the reader to compare two slightly different approaches. In this case, we will proceed in stages, comparing the numbers of Public and General acts that dealt specifically with Ireland with those for the UK as a whole. These were as follows:

Table 8.1 Irish and UK public and general acts, 1801–41

	Total Irish acts	Av. no. Irish acts per annum	Total UK acts	Av. no. UK acts per annum	Total all acts	Av. no. all acts per annum
1801–15	511	34	320	21	2,163	144
1816–30	303	20	650	43	1,632	109
1831–41	185	17	438	39	1,109	101

Sources: *Acts passed 1800–1833* (PP 1834, XLVIII), 281 and *Number of acts of parliament . . . 1834–42* (PP 1843, XLIV), 151.

Four particular conclusions can be drawn from Table 8.1. First, there was a steady decline in the overall volume of Public and General legislation in this period. Second, the proportion of all legislation that applied to Ireland (Irish and UK acts) rose from 42 per cent in 1801–15 to a plateau of about 56 per cent thereafter. Third, the proportion of specifically Irish legislation fell from about 24 per cent at the beginning of the period to 17 per cent at the end; and the proportion of UK legislation rose from about 15 per cent to 39 per cent. In this respect session-by session figures show that the critical period of change was

1813–17. And fourth, despite this trend, it was still thought necessary to legislate separately for Ireland in 1841. So, although parliament increasingly legislated as though the United Kingdom was one, it continued to recognise the special needs of its component parts.

What, then, was the subject matter of Irish legislation and to what extent did it change over time? Here I have dealt with specifically Irish 'Publick General' legislation only: partly to reduce the task to manageable proportions and partly on the assumption that this would inevitably reveal subjects that became matters for UK legislation over the course of time. Obviously categorising legislation is extremely problematic: many acts, such as those allocating money for public works, could be said to fall into more than one category – in that case government finance and welfare. Moreover, the overall figures for different categories of acts can obscure the fact that some repealed or amended earlier Irish acts, others continued earlier acts, and that many were of very modest importance while other, single, acts had an immense impact. That said, the table below presents the results of a personal (and manual) attempt to categorise Irish legislation for the three specific periods chosen earlier, the subjects included in each of the categories being placed in the endnotes.[26]

As most of this legislation was promoted by the ministers responsible for Ireland, Table 8.2 adds substance to points made earlier about the history of the Irish administration and the growth of UK legislation applicable to Ireland. The principal topics of legislation during the Napoleonic wars were government finance, regulating commerce and industry, recruiting and paying the militia and yeomanry, and the law, particularly that involving the suppression of purportedly politically inspired disturbances. In the post-war period there was an inevitable reduction in the number of measures relating to the Irish military and a much more dramatic decline in financial and commercial legislation as a result of the amalgamation of the Irish and British treasuries and revenue services. On the other hand there was a substantial increase in legal measures, many of which were of an assimilative kind, and equally notable increases in changes to local administration and the provision of various kinds of welfare. These trends continued into the 1830s, especially respecting the decline of finance legislation and the importance of that dealing with the law, local government and welfare.

If these calculations have confirmed the point that Ireland was legislated for as both an integral *and* distinct part of the United Kingdom, the question arises of who the authors of Irish legislation were. If ministers were the principal authors of both UK *and* Irish legislation, this might suggest that the distinction is meaningless and that all legislation served purely British interests. If, on the other hand, there was a significant Irish input into legislation dealing specifically with Ireland, this would strengthen the case for there having been a dual approach.

Innes has shown that there was a small number of independent Irish MPs who promoted legislation in the first twenty or so years of the Union.[27] The details of

Table 8.2 Categories of Irish acts, 1801–41

	1801–15	1816–30	1831–41	Total
Irish government	33	13	14	60
Government finance	221	68	7	296
Trade and commerce	45	25	14	84
Agriculture	18	1	0	19
Land	6	12	11	29
Transport	26	12	19	57
Military	52	15	1	68
Law	27	66	50	143
Order	19	18	14	51
Religion	12	16	10	38
Elections	8	6	2	16
Local government	3	21	20	44
Welfare	21	32	21	74
Education	4	1	0	5
Savings	1	4	2	7
Total	496	310	185	991

Sources: as for Table 8.1.

Note: The subjects included in each category are: *Irish Government* – public offices and officials, the census and management of crown lands; *Government Finance* – servicing the Irish debt, government borrowing, the Bank of Ireland, assessed taxes, customs and excise; *Trade and commerce* – regulation and encouragement of trade, commerce and industry, drawbacks and bounties; *Agriculture* – regulation and encouragement of agriculture, including distilling; *Land* – drainage, management of Church of Ireland land, including tithes; *Transport* – harbours, shipping, lighthouses, roads, coaches, paving and lighting of towns; *Military* – yeomanry, militia (including pay); *Law* – changes to all branches of the law (except special measures to deal with disturbances), including all officers and personnel of the law; *Order* – special measures to deal with disturbances such as the suspension of Habeas Corpus; *Religion* – Church of Ireland and other sects, including the building of churches and chapels; *Elections* – qualifications of MPs and elections; *Local government* – counties, corporations and the officers, grand juries, sheriffs and magistrates, local taxes; *Welfare* – hospitals, asylums, poverty, public works; *Education* – schools; *Savings* – savings banks, loan societies.

what happened in the period before 1828 remains unclear but two points might be made. Firstly, there was clearly a much greater input by Irish officials and MPs into fiscal and military legislation before amalgamation took effect in 1817 than there was subsequently. Secondly, and more conjecturally, after due allowance is made for the effects of amalgamation there is no particular reason for thinking that the pattern after 1828 would have been much different to that beforehand.

If this conjecture is regarded as justifiable, studies by myself and Crowe for the years after 1828 suggest that the following points might apply for the period as a whole. First, Irish ministers *and* independent Irish MPs were the principal promoters of Irish legislation. Second, the ratio of ministerial to private member bills was approximately 70:30 prior to 1828 and 60:40 in the 1830s.[28] Third, ministerial bills mainly dealt with economic regulation and law and order, whereas private member bills dealt pretty evenly with all categories. And fourth, there was a disproportionate success rate for both petitions for bills and for bills themselves with ministers being far more successful than independent members. In the case of bills that became law the success rates for 1828–30 are 78 per cent for ministerial bills and 14 per cent for private members' bills. The figures for 1833–41 are 73 per cent and 31 per cent respectively.[29]

Ministerial bills were therefore not only far more numerous than private member bills but also far more successful. However, on some issues there was considerable co-operation between government and independent members. In the case of the 1828–30 period, for example, two government bills to restrict the over-issue of banknotes and to regulate the butter trade involved collaboration with two prominent Irish MPs who were associated with the Whig opposition. The Wellington government's Irish arm also gave approval to six private member bills dealing with county rates and the drainage of bog-lands.[30] Moreover, Crowe has identified twenty-three bills between 1833 and 1841 which he classifies as being jointly sponsored by the government and independent members;[31] and in a detailed analysis of fifteen private member bills dealing with the sale of spirits, land tenure and improvement and the reform of the civil bill courts, he shows how government co-operation was critical to their success or failure. In particular, he draws attention to the government's readiness to make parliamentary time available not only to bills that it favoured but also to those it did not. This he says was due to the government's concern to enable minority positions to receive a hearing and to ensure 'impartiality in proceedings, and to generally allow for the progress of bills for discussion without actually supporting them'.[32] Clearly the distinction between government and private member bills should not be drawn too sharply; there was considerable collaboration between the front and the back-benches on both sides of the House.

Did the authors of Irish legislation consult the broad mass of Irish MPs and the public at large on the framing of bills? This question brings into focus the particular authors of independent member legislation and the roles of lobbies and interest groups and for particular consideration here, of select committees and petitioning. In the case of authorship, the proportion of Irish independent members responsible for bills rose after 1828. Between 1828 and 1830 seven Irish MPs were responsible for twenty-two private member bills – a figure that, bearing in mind Innes's suggestion, is likely to have been the norm beforehand.[33] In the period after 1833, however, Crowe identifies some fifty who were responsible for 88 private member bills.[34] However, in both periods there were select groups of Irish MPs who were particularly zealous in producing bills. In the 1828–30 period, two MPs were responsible for three bills each and one was responsible for five;[35]after 1833, twenty three Irish MPs sponsored between two and five bills and nine sponsored six or more.[36] Taken as a whole these figures suggest that although sponsorship was an activity of only a small proportion of Irish MPs, the numbers grew in significance.

With regard to the participation of Irish MPs as a whole and their influence on legislation, one way of assessing it is to examine the role of select committees. On this issue some preliminary points need to be made. First, the number of Commons select committees appointed each session on all subjects increased after the Union to reach an average of about twenty from 1810–30, before rising to nearer thirty in the 1830s.[37] Second, although small numbers of Irish MPs were often but not always represented on committees dealing with mainland matters, they were always represented on those that dealt with UK issues. Third, committees on Irish matters throughout this period were a small percentage of the total: about 8 per cent in the period before 1830 and even less thereafter. This suggests that governments were reluctant to concede committees on Irish issues. And fourth, on the assumption that the practice before 1828 was the same as that afterwards, parliament and governments were content to see a majority of Irish members on committees dealing with relatively unimportant Irish matters but a substantial but not a majority presence on ones that were controversial or might involve the British taxpayer. Thus in the cases of the 1828 select committee on Irish Education and the 1830 committee on the Irish poor, the number of Irish MPs and Irishmen or ministers was ten out of twenty-one and seventeen out of thirty-six respectively. This contrasts with twenty-four out of twenty-nine members of the 1830 committee on the much less controversial issue of Irish Tolls and Customs.[38] These are conclusions also reached by Crowe for the much longer 1833–41 period.[39]

But what influence did this comparatively small number of committees have on legislation? In the case of government bills it is very difficult to say, not least because there was often a time-lag between the emergence of a committee report and legislation. However, the evidence suggests that a modest number of government bills drew on select committee work. In the 1828–30 period, for example, three such bills drew on select committee investigations.[40] As for private member bills, we have more extensive evidence. Crowe shows that seventeen of twenty select committees appointed on Irish matters from 1833–41 were requested by independent members and that of the twenty reports, seven preceded legislation, although in only two cases did this prove to be in complete accordance with the committees' recommendations.[41]

In the case of the input from the public at large, the most basic way of taking soundings was by publicising bills in the press and by the circulation of printed versions to interested parties. So far little research has been devoted to either method but the evidence for the 1828–30 period suggests that both were a normal part of the legislative process. In the case of circulation, for example, we have firm evidence of four bills being sent around the country, one of which was amended and recommitted twice in the light of comment.[42] Indeed it seems probable that many acts were the result of bills that had been introduced and re-introduced in various forms following consultation with relevant members of the public.

Finally, there is the issue of petitioning. As is well known, the number of petitions to parliament and the number of different subjects that they addressed grew substantially in the 1820s and throughout the 1830s. Furthermore, recent research has shown that most petitioning was related to legislation before the House or recently passed by it, as opposed to issues of purely extra-parliamentary concern.[43] Petitioning may therefore have been generated as much by MPs for their own particular purposes as by concerned members of the public. Further, the extent to which petitioning initiated bills, influenced their content and determined their success or failure are very difficult matters to assess. In the case of the initiation and content of bills there is some evidence of petitioning playing a role. For example, a petitioning campaign against the 1826 Sub-Letting Act (7 George IV c. 29) which had evidently driven large numbers of poor from the land, led in 1830 to an amending government bill which was itself supported by a separate campaign. In the end, the government withdrew the measure, possibly because it did not go far enough to satisfy the original petitioners.[44] However, evidence of this kind is too slim for any conclusive judgment on the matter.

The question of how far petitioning influenced the success or failure of bills is equally problematic. That most petitioning was devoted to these ends is clear enough. Thus Crowe demonstrates that of more than 10,000 Irish petitions presented between 1833 and 1841 containing, collectively, millions of signatures, some 73 per cent dealt with legislation before the House.[45] Of course, even major petitioning campaigns might fail, as in those to support the Church of Ireland in 1833–35, to stop the Coercion Bill in 1833 and to influence municipal reform in 1836–37.[46]

Overall, this survey of parliamentary business has underlined, and provided additional evidence for, the duality of the approach of governments and parliament to their new responsibilities in Ireland. In the first years of the Union virtually all Irish legislation was generated locally by a combination of ministers, Irish officials and Irish MPs. After 1817, however, fiscal and military matters became a matter of UK legislation, leaving most other matters to flow from ministerial or other sources in Ireland. Most of these matters were legislated for by ministers representing the party in power, but a growing proportion was the result of private member initiative or of collaboration between ministers and private members. How far legislation generated in Ireland was the result of consultation with, or pressure from, the public is a very difficult question to answer in the current state of knowledge. That some consultation did take place and that some pressure had an effect seems incontrovertible, but it seems unlikely that it was extensive. Much more likely is a scenario in which the chief sponsors of Irish legislation were a small group of ministers and private member zealots. In this respect it is worth noting that Irish local, personal and private bill legislation was a minuscule proportion (3 per cent) of the total number for the UK and two and a half times less than that for Scotland. This suggests a much lower level of interest in the sponsorship of legislation at a local level than was the case elsewhere.[47]

The final subject to be addressed is the relationship between parliament and the Irish public. In this respect a broader definition of Habermas's concept of the 'public sphere' can be a useful way of understanding the movement of public opinion in a country where urbanisation was limited. Thus if we define the 'public sphere' as meaning the places at which, and the means by which, the public discussed political issues and the non-violent and constitutional action to be taken upon them, the evidence suggests that it expanded considerably in Ireland during this period. This is not the place to go into any great detail, but a sketch of developments is needed in order to provide a context for an assessment of the impact of parliament upon them.

One key development was the growth of the print media: books, pamphlets, periodicals and newspapers. Ireland had not been particularly poorly served by any of these before the Union, but there was undoubted growth in periodicals and newspapers subsequently. Thus some twenty magazines were founded between 1807 and 1836 and the number of newspapers rose from about twenty at the time of the Union to 64 in 1830 and 83 in 1839 – the majority being provincial papers.[48] Admittedly some caution has to be exercised about these figures. For example, only five of the twenty new periodicals survived for more than a few years and total sales of newspapers may have fallen prior to 1818, following Peel's crackdown on the independent press.[49] On the other hand, total newspaper readership and listenership certainly increased substantially thereafter – a factor of particular relevance given that virtually all newspapers devoted considerable space to the parliamentary debates.[50]

The growth in the number of newspapers was, of course, partly a reaction to the growth of the population, particularly to that in the leading towns and cities – a natural habitat of the 'public sphere'. Although this growth was modest by comparison with that of the rural population or the scale of urbanisation elsewhere, it seems to have stimulated an increase in the number of civic institutions that could or did have a political role. Thus, leaving aside the exceptional case of Dublin, note can be made of: an increase in the number of new (and usually elected) bodies established to deal with various aspects of civic improvement and expansion such as that established in Sligo in 1803 to improve harbour facilities;[51] the establishment of new Chambers of Commerce such as those in Limerick, Waterford and Cork; the foundation of Mechanics Institutes in the 1820s in, for example, Cork, Belfast, Armagh, Limerick, Waterford and Clonmel; and an increase in the number of more elite societies such as the Literary Society (1801), the Historic Society (1811) and Natural History Society (1821) in Belfast or the Society of Arts (1815), the Scientific and Literary Society (1834) and the Horticultural Society (1835) in Cork.[52] In addition, there were clubs and societies that represented specific political and/or religious viewpoints. These were far too numerous to catalogue here – Belfast, for example, with a population of about

20,000 by the end of the first decade of the Union, had Pitt and Nelson clubs, several dining groups, as well as at least seven religious societies[53] – but one particular development might serve as an example of a general trend. Thus in virtually all of the thirty or so leading towns and cities there developed political interest groups usually consisting of liberal Protestants and Catholics with links to local trades guilds and chambers of commerce which opposed the prevailing electoral oligarchies and by the 1820s supported various degrees of parliamentary, religious, economic and civic reform.[54]

However, as one might expect in a largely rural country, civic institutions formed only one part of the 'public sphere'. Initially it is likely that county meetings, such as those that led to many of the anti- and pro-Catholic petitions presented to parliament in 1813, continued to be the principal means of organising rural opinion for a particular cause. In due course, however, these gentry-sponsored events gave way in scale and significance to other means. In the case of Protestant opinion, key developments were the continued growth of the Orange Order and evangelical Protestantism, particularly in the north. These were matched by the evolution of the elite Catholic Board into the popular Catholic Association, an increase in the number of Catholic chapels, particularly in the midlands and the south, and the emergence of a confident clerical generation that had never known the penal laws. As a result popular rural opinion became organised on a much larger scale through the medium of clerics and priests, churches and chapels, and local branches of Dublin-based national organisations.[55] The scale of the change overall is indicated by reference to the less well-known Protestant side of the equation: namely, that in 1824 there were 144 Orange lodges in Co. Down alone.

The role that parliament played in the increasing politicisation of Ireland and what impact it had on perceptions of identity are extremely difficult issues to assess. Parliamentary elections clearly played an important part until the disfranchisement of the forties freeholders in 1829. The crucial factors here were the predominance given to the county and county-borough constituencies by the terms of the Union; the massive increase in the number of Catholic voters; and the eventual predominance of those voters in the majority of electorates. These enabled O'Connell to threaten the system by sheer weight of numbers and so achieve the Catholic Relief Act. Thereafter the steps taken in 1829 and 1832 to produce an Irish electoral system that possessed a more even balance between Protestant and Catholic and between property and numbers reduced the importance of elections – which is presumably the reason why O'Connell eventually resorted to mass meetings.

Parliamentary debate must also have had some impact. As has been mentioned earlier, most of the increasing number of newspapers carried extracts from the debates and most were provincial in origin. The space devoted to the debates can probably be accounted for to some extent by the fact that they provided syndicated, and therefore cheap, copy but it seems likely that editors had an eye to material of interest to their customers. In the first thirty years or so of the Union, the government itself was a major 'customer' to key Dublin papers by way of subsidies but this can only mean that it regarded their copy as influential. This was probably the case with the greater number of unsubsidised editors. Perhaps O'Connell's actions and thoughts are instructive in this respect. Thus he not only began his parliamentary career by using his position to extract information from government departments and put it into the public domain, he also became increasingly concerned that accurate reports of his numerous speeches reached the Irish public.[56]

O'Connell's persistence with regard to requests for accounts and papers from government departments leads us to another way in which parliament had an impact. As mentioned earlier, the number of reports from select committees, from various types of commissions, and the number of accounts and papers rose steeply in the first forty years of the Union, many of them relating specifically to Ireland. Little research has been carried out on how much seeped into public debate through the press but it seems very unlikely that it failed to do so. Indeed, it is likely that dissemination was extensive. In March 1830 Thomas Spring Rice, with the support of government, moved successfully for a select committee on the state of the poor in Ireland and the means of improving their condition. In July the committee produced a report with three volumes of evidence and made a series of recommendations incorporated into the heads of nineteen draft bills, one of which was the establishment of a compulsory system of poor relief.[57] The report immediately added to an ongoing newspaper and pamphlet debate on the poor. In Dublin that year Michael Staunton, an ally of O'Connell, published *Hints for Hardinge* (the Chief Secretary) with an appendix containing comment on the report.[58] This coincided with the publication of at least two other pamphlets on the subject – one in Dublin and another in Belfast. In the following year, by which time the contents of the report would have been more fully digested, at least nine pamphlets were published in Dublin and Cork on the state of the poor and two of these were specifically concerned with the recommendations of the Spring Rice committee.[59]

Finally, there is the question of petitioning. The scale of the increase in the numbers of petitions and signatures to them in the latter part of this period in both Britain and Ireland has been seriously under-estimated by historians. In the case of the UK as a whole a conservative estimate suggests a twelve–fold increase from 1810 to 1840 with as many as 13,661 petitions on a substantial number of different subjects receiving over 4.5 million signatures in 1839.[60] In the case of Ireland, where the Union dramatically diminished the ability of members of the public to put direct pressure on MPs prior to debates and divisions, petitioning may have increasingly seemed the only alternative.[61] However, as Table 8.3 illustrates, the practice, following a slow start, increased spectacularly.[62]

Several points need to be made about Table 8.3. The first is that it excludes petitions to the Lords where, if the petitioning on the Catholic Question in 1829 is anything to go by, many petitions hostile to reform were traditionally sent.[63] The second is that they conceal extraordinarily high numbers of petitions and

Table 8.3 Public petitions presented in the House of Commons, 1818–40, with estimates of the number of subjects of petitions and the number of signatures to them

	Petitions	Subjects	Signatures
1818	38		
1828	1,600		
1833	1,089		
1834	1,364	10+	607,434+
1835	664		
1836	1,299	16+	750,019+
1837	1,152	14+	650,676+
1837–38	831	10+	199,275+
1839	1,422	13+	828,039+
1840	1,746		

Source: see note 62.

signatures on particular issues. For example (and in each case the figures quoted are a minimum), 462 petitions with 538,978 signatures for the repeal of the Union in 1834; 547 petitions with 438,580 signatures against Lords' amendments to the Irish Municipal Corporations Bill in 1836; and 716 petitions with 554,834 signatures in support of the Government of Ireland in 1839. These were petitioning campaigns that not only involved very considerable numbers of people – possibly one in four or five of the *adult* population – but they also necessitated a substantial degree of organisation. Taken in conjunction with the overall figures for petitioning, these points suggest that parliament occupied an increasingly important role in the public's political consciousness.

But how was petitioning organised, particularly on the scale indicated above? The evidence suggests that there was a major change during this period. Initially, it seems, petitions were organised by specific economic interest groups and by leading Protestant or Catholic gentry and freeholders following properly authorised county or civic meetings summonsed for that purpose. The three petitions against the duties on bark presented by the tanners of Dublin, Bandon and Cork in 1818 are typical of the first category; and the 91 pro-Catholic petitions presented in the following year typical of the second. In due course, however, it seems that because an increasing proportion of petitioning was organised through the agency of the churches, huge increases in the numbers of petitions and signatures took place. However, although this can be deduced from the lists of places from which petitions were sent that were entered in the *Journals*, our knowledge of the organisation involved is scanty. That it must have been substantial is obvious enough and the following sketch of how the Dublin Brunswick Club organised anti-Catholic petitions from Drumcree, Co. Armagh early in 1829, is probably a fair indication of the amount involved. The leading Brunswick institution in Co. Armagh was the Portadown Brunswick Club and its leading light, the Rev. Charles Irwin of Drumcree parish church. The immediate vicinity was divided for petitioning purposes into at least 16 different kinds of administrative units such as Church of Ireland parishes, specific manors and towns, and the various Presbyterian and Methodist congregations. On 6 January 1829, Irwin was in Dublin and sent a colleague in Portadown the Drumcree petition 'engrossed for both houses [of parliament]' and appended a parchment with columns of a suitable width for 'the *fist* that some country fellows write' to accommodate 264 names. Two weeks later he heard that the petition was pretty full but advised his colleague to obtain two more 'whole skins' of parchment for it from Armagh City.[64] In due course the petition was completed and presented to parliament, along with others from Armagh. The single Drumcree parish petition therefore involved a degree of central planning in Dublin, some local planning by the Portadown branch of the Club, the organisational skills of the Drumcree parish clergyman, some money for skins, the input of local 'leaders' to collect the signatures, and, we may suppose, at least 200 willing signatories.

This evidence suggests two principal conclusions. First, that the growth of the 'public sphere' which had taken place in the eighteenth century continued at a more rapid and expansive rate in this period. And second, that within that context, the business of the Westminster parliament became increasingly well known and parliament itself became an increasingly important focal point for the expression of opinion on an expanding range of political issues by an increasing number of people. The key questions for our purposes, then, are whether this led to a popular identification with parliament (and the Union) or whether it fostered a greater sense of separateness. Here only conjecture is possible but the material presented earlier on other aspects of Irish politics may serve as a guide. Thus the central argument with regard to the governing of Ireland, the behaviour of Irish MPs and the conduct of Irish parliamentary business is that trends encouraging incorporation and assimilation co-existed with those emphasising Ireland's distinctiveness. It is probable that the same was true of the impact of parliament on non-elite opinion. Thus although there seems little doubt that public knowledge of parliamentary business and popular engagement with it increased, there are few signs that parliament was seen as more than an institution whose purposes were to arbitrate between conflicting interests, to have its decisions given the force of law and most of all, to redress grievances. Parliament was therefore seen more as a court than an institution which could adequately represent national interests.

Notes

1 I am very grateful to Allan Blackstock, Sean Connolly, Brian Crowe, David Hayton, Julian Hoppit, Joanna Innes and Anthony Malcomson for their comments and suggestions on an earlier draft of this paper. The usual disclaimers apply.

2 Quoted in M. Elliott, *Wolfe Tone: prophet of Irish independence* (1989), 312.

3 L. Colley, *Britons: forging the nation, 1707–1837* (1992), ch. 8, particularly p. 324, from which the quotations are taken.

4 R. B. McDowell, *The Irish administration, 1801–1914* (1964), *passim*, but particularly, 21–6, 32, 65–8, 86–95, 109, 113–14, 136, 164–5, 167–8, 171–6, 194–204, 230, 230–6, 242–3. I have also drawn on the chapters by S. J. Connolly and O. MacDonagh in W. E. Vaughan (ed.) *Ireland under the Union, 1801–1870* (Oxford, 1989).

5 P. Harling, *The waning of 'Old Corruption': the politics of economical reform in Britain, 1779–1846* (Oxford, 1996) deals comprehensively with developments in Britain but does not comment on those in Ireland.

6 I am indebted to Professor Connolly for drawing my attention to this point and to an article on the subject by D. Kennedy, 'The Irish Whigs, administrative reform and responsible government, 1782–1800', *Éire-Ireland*, viii (1973), 55–69.

7 For a discussion of this by Oliver MacDonagh, see *Ireland under the Union*, 204–7.

8 These boards were criticised for favouritism with regard to the allocation of funds. It was on these grounds, for example, that the Linen Board was abolished in 1828, the government preferring to stimulate manufacture by even-handed regulation rather than by subsidy. See, McDowell, *Irish administration*, 195–98; *Mirror of Parliament*, (1828), ii, 807.

9 P. Cockton, *Subject catalogue of the House of Commons parliamentary papers, 1801–1900*, 5 vols (Cambridge, 1988), iv, 133–41 under 'Public Offices (Ireland)'.

10 B. D. Crowe, 'The parliamentary experience of the Irish members of the House of Commons, 1833–41' (The Queen's University of Belfast Ph.D. thesis, 1995), chs 6–7. Much of this section on debate is drawn from these chapters. The quotation is taken from p. 239.

11 *Cobbett's Parliamentary Debates*, xxiv, cols. 877, 999–1002.

12 The quotation is from a speech in 1834 by Thomas Lefroy, MP for Trinity College, Dublin and referred to by Crowe, 'Irish MPs', 168.

13 J. Ridden, '"Making good citizens": national identity, religion, and liberalism among the Irish elite, *c.* 1800–1850' (University of London Ph.D. thesis, 1988), 192 for the quotation. A revised version of this thesis should be published soon.

14 *Cobbett's Parliamentary Debates*, xxiv, cols. 750–5.

15 Ridden, '"Making good citizens"', 193–200; Crowe, 'Irish MPs', 168–70 in particular.

16 Crowe, 'Irish MPs', 166, 169–70 for the quotations.

17 P. J. Jupp, 'Irish MPs at Westminster in the early nineteenth century', *Historical Studies* vii (1969), 76–8.

18 See ch. 7 of my *British politics on the eve of reform* (Basingstoke, 1998).

19 Ian Newbould has argued this case forcibly in a number of publications, for example: 'The emergence of a two-party system in England from 1830 to 1841: roll call and reconsideration', *Parliaments, Estates and Representation*, v (1985), 25–31; 'Whiggery and the growth of party 1830–41: organisation and the challenge of reform', *Parliamentary History*, iv (1985), 137–56.

20 The following figures are taken from R. Thorne (ed.), *The history of parliament: the House of Commons, 1790–1820*, 5 vols (1986), i, 107 and for 1828–30, Jupp, *Reform*, 312–19. For the 1830s, I have relied on Crowe, 'Irish MPs', 44 and B. M. Walker (ed.), *Parliamentary election results in Ireland, 1801–1922* (Dublin, 1978). I have followed Crowe in designating Walker's 'Liberal (Repealers)' as 'O'Connellites' but have used Walker's general election results and the details of those returned after petition to arrive at the numbers for each party. Crowe, 'Irish MPs', 17, shows that after 1835 the term 'Repealer' was rarely used, MPs preferring to see themselves as followers of 'O'Connell.

	Prime Minister	Pro	Con	Independent
1802	Addington	73	17	10
1804	Pitt	79	18	2
Dec. 1806	Grenville	77	14	9
1807	Portland	58	34	8
1812	Liverpool	67	29	4
1818	Liverpool	71	28	1
1828–30	Wellington	66	24	10
General election	Liberals	Conservative		O'Connellites
1832	36	31		38
1835	34	38		33
1837	40	34		31

Note: there was one vacant seat in 1804.

21 Jupp, 'Irish MPs at Westminster', 78–9.

22 This is the gist of ch. 1 of Crowe's 'Irish MPs'.

23 I made these points in 'The landed elite and political authority in Britain, ca. 1760–1850', *Journal of British Studies*, xxix (1990), 68 and fns. 57–60.

24 *Account of sums granted for Charitable and Literary Institutions . . . and Miscellaneous Services of Ireland* (PP 1828, XVII), 475; *Mirror of Parliament* 1828, iii, 1875ff (9 June 1828); *CJ*, xcv, under 'Irish miscellaneous services' in the index.

25 See Joanna Innes' essay above.

26 These findings should be compared with those of Innes, above, 31. The clerks who calculated the numbers all types of acts of parliament since 1800, see sources to Table 8.1 above, arrived at a figure of 999 Irish acts for the 1801–41 period. My own calculations are based on analysis of the statutes session by session and these suggest that the clerks found it difficult to classify Irish acts in the first years of the Union. My figures and their figures for the period *c.* 1801–10 therefore differ, though my total of 991 is only eight less than their own.

27 Innes, above, 32–3.

28 I have defined 'ministerial' bills as those promoted by office-holders, and 'private member bills' as those promoted by those without office and therefore 'independent' of government. Crowe calculates that of bills originating in the Commons 1833–41, 55 per cent were government bills, 35 per cent were private member bills and 10 per cent were jointly sponsored by ministers and independent members, 'Irish MPs', 49. For the sake of comparison, I have taken the liberty of dividing the jointly sponsored number between ministers and independent members.

29 These summary conclusions are drawn from Jupp, *Reform*, 155–64, 176–9, 187–8; Crowe, 'Irish MPs', chs 2 and 3.

30 Jupp, *Reform*, 159–60, 163.

31 Crowe, 'Irish MPs', 57–61 (23 bills was 9 per cent of the total of Irish bills, 1833–41).

32 Crowe, 'Irish MPs', ch. 3, and p. 105 for the quotation.

33 They were: C. Browlow, M. Fitzgerald, J. Grattan, D. Jephson, H. Maxwell, Lord Oxmantown and T. Spring Rice. E. G. Stanley presented three bills on Church of Ireland leases but he was an English MP.

34 Crowe, 'Irish MPs', 50–1, 61.

35 Brownlow and Grattan and with 5, T. Spring Rice.

36 Crowe, 'Irish MPs', 61.

37 Throughout this period select committees were ad hoc bodies created to investigate different issues. Some were routine such as those appointed annually to examine expiring laws, some considered specific bills, and others investigated a particular subject. Only some issued reports. My own calculations have been based on the indexes of the *Commons Journals* which record all the different types of select committees. H. M. Clokie and J. W. Robinson, *Royal Commissions of inquiry: the significance of investigations in British politics* (Stanford, Ca., 1937), 61–3, 197 base their calculations on the number of *reporting* committees and state that their number increased in the early nineteenth century, giving an average of sixteen per annum, 1801–34, and double that by 1860. My calculations for all select committees, 1828–30, are eighteen sitting in the Lords and sixty-six in the Commons – an average of twenty-eight per annum, Jupp, *Reform*, 211.

38 Calculated from *CJ*, lxxxiii, 156, 204, 361; and lxxxv, 166, 469.

39 Crowe, 'Irish MPs', 107–14.

40 1828 bills to regulate the office of Registrar and to regulate the offices of sheriff and undersheriff; and the 1830 bill to amend the Sub-Letting Act.

41 Crowe, 'Irish MPs', 128.

42 See for references to circulation, *Mirror of Parliament* 1828, i, 510, iii, 1945, 2402, 2441; 1829, ii, 983.

43 On petitioning in general, see Jupp, *Reform*, 216–25.

44 Jupp, *Reform*, 162.

45 Crowe, 'Irish MPs', 66–7.

46 Crowe, 'Irish MPs', 67–8.

47 Calculated from *Acts passed 1800–1833*, 281 and *Number of acts of parliament . . . 1834–42*, 151.

48 B. Inglis, *The freedom of the press in Ireland, 1784–1841* (1954), 244; the numbers of newspapers in 1830 and 1836 are calculated from *Stamps issued to each newspaper in Ireland 1826–30* (PP 1829, XXII), 273 and (PP 1830, XXV), 349; *Number of stamps issued to each newspaper in the UK, Apr. to June 1830* (PP 1839, XXX), 483.

49 Inglis, *Freedom of the press*, ch. 4 and 244.

50 With regard to the readership of newspapers, the 1841 census provides statistics showing that of males born 1811–20 a lower proportion (38 per cent) were unable to read and write than hitherto, *ex. info.*, Professor S. J. Connolly.

51 P. Jupp, ' Urban politics in Ireland, 1801–31' in D. W. Harkness and M. O'Dowd (eds) *The town in Ireland* (Belfast, 1981), 111.

52 I am indebted to Martin McElroy for the information relating to the Munster towns and cities. I would also like to thank Dr Allan Blackstock for information relating to the Armagh Mechanics' Institute and an article on it by S. S. Duffy, 'The Armagh Mechanics' Institute (1825–1831)', *Seanchas Ard Mhacha* (*Journal of the Armagh Diocesan Historical Society*), xiii (1988), 122–72.

53 Belfast Central Library, Local History section, Alexander Riddell Papers, vols H7, J1-3, S6, vol. 8; *Belfast Directory for 1831–32* (Belfast, 1832); I am again indebted to Dr Allan Blackstock for alerting me to the Riddell Papers and for information about the Belfast Pitt Club.

54 Jupp, 'Urban politics', 103–23. Ridden, ' "Making good citizens" ' charts the growth of such an interest group in Limerick City.

55 This is a theme that is developed in P. Jupp and E. Magennis (eds), *Crowds in Ireland c. 1720–1920* (2000), 20–5. I am indebted to Professor Connolly for the point about a new generation of Catholic priests.

56 I am indebted to Martin McElroy for this point.

57 For the background see Jupp, *Reform*, 163.

58 *Hints for Hardinge, being a series of political essays published originally in the Dublin Morning Register . . . with an appendix containing observations on the report of Mr. Spring Rice's Committee on the state of the poor in Ireland* (Dublin, 1830).

59 H. MacCormac, *A plan for the relief of the unemployed poor* (Belfast, 1830); G. Grierson, *The circumstances of Ireland considered with reference to the question of poor laws* (Dublin, 1830); J. Bligh, *A letter to the . . . Earl of Darnley, on the introduction of a labour rate, for the employment of the poor in Ireland* (Dublin, 1831); J. Doyle, R.C. Bishop of Kildare and Leighlin, *Letter to T. S. Rice, on the establishment of a legal provision for the Irish poor . . .* (Dublin, 1831); P. E. H., *The desideratum; or Ireland's only remedy, 'poor laws and education'* (Dublin, 1831); H. Flood, *Poor laws: argument against a provision for paupers* (Dublin, 1830); R. J. MacGhee and R. Daly, Bishop of Cashel, *On the proposed system of non-scriptural education of the poor in Ireland* (Dublin, 1831); R. Ryan, *A letter to the Rt. Hon. E. G. Stanley . . . on the subject of the poor laws* (Dublin, 1831); Anon., *Thoughts on the poor of Ireland* (Dublin, 1831); J. Connery, *The reformer; or, an infallible remedy to prevent pauperism . . .* (Cork, 1831).

60 For the changes 1810–40, see P. Fraser, 'Public petitioning and parliament before 1832', *History*, xlvi (1961), 195–211; *Report of the select committee on public petitions* (PP 1831–2, V), 333. The estimate for 1839 is calculated from *The British Almanac and Companion . . . for . . . 1840*, 219–22.

61 I owe this point to Professor Connolly.

62 The figures for petitioning presented in this section are drawn from several sources. For 1818 and 1828, the calculations have been made by identifying the subjects of petitions in the indexes of the *Commons Journals* and then counting the number of petitions presented on specific days as recorded in the same source. They exaggerate the rate of increase because 1818 had fewer than normal as it was an election year and 1828 had more due to the prominence of the Catholic question, but they are indicative of the trend. For 1833–40, I have relied upon two sources. The principal one is the *British Almanac and Companion*, the organ for the Society for the Diffusion of Useful Knowledge, which from 1835 provides calculations of the number of public petitions presented to parliament on various issues and the number of signatures to them. The second is Crowe's 'Irish MPs', 65–8, where he provides figures for the number of petitions presented on Irish issues which he calculated from the *Commons Journals*. Crowe's figures for the number of petitions are invariably higher than those provided by the *British Almanac* and are probably more accurate. I have therefore used his figures for the number of petitions and those of the *British Almanac* for the number of issues and signatures but indicated that their real number must have been greater. The page references for the *British Almanac* are: 1835, 224–6; 1837, 226–8; 1838, 215–18; 1839, 216–18; 1840, 219–22.

63 For example, between 9 Feb. and 13 Apr. 1829, 2,624 petitions were sent to the Lords on the Catholic question but only 702 to the Commons, *Mirror of Parliament* 1829, iii, 2226.

64 National Library of Ireland, Brunswick Constitutional Club Papers, MS. 5017, fos. 38–61. I am indebted once more to Dr Allan Blackstock for this information.

9

Parliament and international law in the eighteenth century[1]

David Armitage

The study of parliament and international law in the eighteenth century illuminates crucial distinctions among nation, state and empire. For example, after 1603 but before 1707, the Scottish parliament in Edinburgh represented a nation but aroused English opposition whenever it tried to legislate as if Scotland were an independent state. Before 1801, the Irish parliament in Dublin represented only a very narrowly defined Irish nation and, prior to the repeal of Poynings' law in 1782, made no pretence of legislating as if Ireland were a state rather than a dependent kingdom. Only the Westminster parliament could claim that national representation authorised its legislating for the English (later, British) state and for the British Empire. Across the course of the century, war and revolution tested the limits of that parliament's sovereignty, especially in the decades succeeding the Seven Years War. These developments occurred within European, imperial and global contexts. As scholars of nineteenth-century British history have shown, most strikingly in relation to the Reform Acts of 1832 and 1867, domestic settings alone cannot explain the course of parliamentary history.[2]

The defining moments of British parliamentary history in the 'long' eighteenth century have often be associated with a single date: for example, 1688, 1707, 1765, 1776, 1801, 1832. At each of these points, the powers, the capacities or the scope of parliamentary authority changed. In 1688 and 1832 – the conventional boundaries of a long century of revolution and reform – the Glorious Revolution and the Great Reform Act shifted first the balance of power between crown and parliament and then between parliament and people (however narrowly defined). In 1765 and 1776, the crises following the passage of the Stamp Act and the American Declaration of Independence heralded years of arguments across the Atlantic and British bloodshed before the nature and extent of parliament's imperial sovereignty could be settled. In 1707, that sovereignty had been extended to encompass Scotland by incorporation; in 1801, it was further expanded to include Ireland, thereby to reach its greatest territorial extent. The process of incorporating the three kingdoms into the embrace of the

Westminster parliament extinguished the competing and parallel legislatures in Edinburgh and Dublin just as it also formally abolished the English Parliament in 1707. By 1801, parliamentary sovereignty had apparently been settled exclusively at Westminster in a pan-British and imperial legislature, albeit one with greatly reduced fiscal powers over its dependent territories in the Caribbean and British North America.[3]

The calendar of British parliamentary history does not entirely correspond to the canonical moments in British international history in the eighteenth century. Within that chronology, 1688 and 1776 certainly have a place, but 1713, 1748, 1757, 1763, 1802 and 1815, for example, are the more salient dates. These were all moments in the contested history of the British state's positive engagement with other European states or of the involvement of quasi-state agencies like the East India Company with extra-European actors like the Nawab of Bengal.[4] Each date marked a moment of formal cessation of hostilities, cession of territory or the extension of British authority, and each became enshrined within British historical memory. These were events in the international history of the British state: not 'mere parliamentary wrangle', as J. R. Seeley invidiously put it, but rather 'the history of England [sic] . . . in America and Asia'.[5]

The Glorious Revolution changed England's foreign policy and determined its confessional orientation. Louis XIV confirmed that orientation in the eyes of Europe by his recognition of the Protestant succession in the Treaty of Utrecht. The succession itself became a matter of international dispute between Scotland and England in 1703, when the Scottish parliament expressed its independent ability to determine the succession. The Union of 1707 solved that difficulty (among others) by creating a new political entity – the United Kingdom of Great Britain – and in the process abolished two previously existing states, the kingdoms of England and Scotland. The Anglo-Irish Union did not add to or subtract from the sum of states because Ireland had had no separate or distinct international standing except for a brief period in the 1640s.[6] After 1801, a multinational, multi-denominational British state assumed an expanded territorial presence on the international stage.[7]

The relationship between these competing chronologies of parliamentary and international history and the history of 'identities' is conceptually fraught. This is largely because the term 'identity' is an ambiguous one for any period before the closing decades of the eighteenth century. 'Identity' in the sense of individuality (or 'identicality') first appeared in the early seventeenth century, but it did not gain more general acceptance until its philosophical application by John Locke and David Hume. Its meaning of 'identification' – and, more precisely, of 'self-identification' – does not antedate Rousseau and seems to have had little circulation in English before the 1780s, when Edmund Burke employed it in a recognisably modern (though still, for its time, suspiciously avant-garde) sense.[8] Even then, it would have to wait almost a century before it would be qualified by the adjective 'national'. When the term 'national identity' did first appear, in 1872, it was used tentatively, and was immediately trumped by considerations of 'race': 'as personal identity has been affirmed to consist in the consciousness of personal identity, so it might be argued . . . that national identity consisted merely in the consciousness of national identity. Nevertheless, blood does usually assert itself in greater or lesser degree, and questions of race and descent are therefore well worthy of the attention of political students.'[9]

National 'character' or national 'interest', rather than national identity, would be a more aptly idiomatic term for the eighteenth century. Even then, 'loyalty, station, degree, honour, connection, orthodoxy and conformity' – whether applied to individuals or social groups – possessed more imaginative appeal and explanatory power for contemporary Britons than 'identity'.[10] It was indeed possible, at least by the early nineteenth century, to conceive that '[e]very nation, as an organized being, must have a principle of individuality' because '[s]uch a nation is a political person',[11] but this was more comparable to earlier Hobbesian conceptions of the personality of the state than to later transferred metaphors of psychological identity.[12] Any deployment of 'national identity' to apply to periods before the late nineteenth century is, therefore, strictly anachronistic and beset by competing conceptions of ethnic or political community.

Likewise, to apply the adjective 'national' to the identity or sovereignty of parliament at any point after the Reformation is also inherently ambiguous. A strict conception could define the nation as that body of people represented in – and hence subject to – parliament, as Lord Shelburne did in 1775: 'No man can be at a loss to know, that a majority of both Houses, however constituted, are the nation.'[13] However, that did not correspond to the English realm nor, with the expansion of that realm, did it map closely onto the British Empire. Beginning with the Anglo-Welsh Union of the 1530s, the English parliament legislated for more than one nation; with the incorporation of Scotland and Ireland, and later the conquest of territory and subjugation of non-British, non-white, and non-Protestant peoples from Québec to Bengal, it included a greater wealth of nations than could be defined by, or identified with, the ambit of parliamentary sovereignty alone. According to Burke's theory of representation, 'Parliament is not a congress of ambassadors from different and hostile interests . . . but parliament is a *deliberative* assembly of *one* nation, with *one* interest, that of the whole.'[14] He therefore distinguished between a homogeneous nation, identifiable with a single interest, and a heterogeneous 'empire . . . the aggregate of many states under a common head; whether this head be a monarch, or a presiding republic'.[15]

Parliament could neither legislate nationhood into being nor expunge conceptions of nationhood that competed with the Anglo-British version propagated from Westminster with increasing force after 1707. It could only determine the internal boundaries of the state by virtue of its capacity for legislation and taxation.[16] As events in British America after the Seven Years War showed, that capacity (and the resulting determination of boundaries) was essentially contestable. The American Revolution temporarily settled the contest, but only at the expense of confirming the multi-national nature of the British Empire and the limits on parliament's authority to legislate beyond the Three Kingdoms.[17] The English – later, British; still later, imperial – parliament had been multi-national since the 1530s, but it took a crisis of sovereignty to show that nation and state were concentric but still distinct. The American colonists may have claimed membership in a pan-Atlantic British nation but their attempt to capitalise on that nationhood ultimately drove them to declare separate statehood for each of the thirteen former colonies.[18] Intra-imperial relations, mediated through parliament, thereafter became international relations, conducted between the United Kingdom and the United States, the one determinedly unitary (by virtue of common allegiance to the king), the other avowedly plural (at least until 1865, when 'the United States' became a singular entity for all but diehard Confederates and defenders of states' rights).[19]

Parliament's capacity to define and expound the national interest, particularly in an international context, was institutionally and constitutionally limited. 'Parliament could serve as both an institution in which political groups could define their identity and express their views, and one in which ministerial schemes could be expounded and presented as national interests to both domestic and international audiences.'[20] However, that did not mean that it was the only arena for such acts of definition and exposition, which could take place informally in the public prints or formally among lawyers and diplomats, for instance. For as long as foreign affairs remained a matter of royal prerogative and only came before parliament at the discretion of monarchs and ministries, parliament's role in sustaining Britain's international standing would necessarily be circumscribed and episodic.[21]

The conception of parliament's omnipotence in municipal matters contrasted with its relative impotence in foreign affairs. As Sir William Blackstone argued, in an account of parliamentary authority almost Diceyan in its scope:

> It hath sovereign and uncontrollable authority in making, confirming, enlarging, restraining, abrogating, repealing, reviving, and expounding of laws, concerning matters of all possible denominations, ecclesiastical, or temporal, civil, military, maritime, or criminal; this being the place where that absolute despotic power, which must in all governments reside somewhere, is entrusted by the constitution of these kingdoms. . . . It can regulate or new model the succession to the crown; . . . It can alter the established religion of the land; . . . It can change and create afresh even the constitution of the kingdom and of parliaments themselves; as was done by the act of union, and the several statutes for triennial and septennial elections. It can, in short, do every thing that is not naturally impossible; and therefore some have not scrupled to call it's power, by a figure rather too bold, the omnipotence of parliament.[22]

Over domestic matters, parliament was thus absolute, despotic, even omnipotent; over foreign affairs, its authority depended on the prerogatives of the crown. These, Blackstone argued, 'respect either this nation's intercourse with foreign nations, or it's own domestic government and civil polity'. 'With regard to foreign concerns', he continued:

the king is the delegate or representative of his people. It is impossible that the individuals of a state, in their collective capacity, can transact the affairs of that state with another community equally numerous as themselves. Unanimity must be wanting to their measures, and strength to the execution of their counsels. In the king therefore, as in a center, all the rays of his people are united, and form by that union a consistency, splendor, and power, that make him feared and respected by foreign potentates; who would scruple to enter into any engagements, that must afterwards be revised and ratified by a popular assembly. What is done by the royal authority, with regard to foreign powers, is the act of the whole nation: what is done without the king's concurrence is that act only of private men.[23]

The royal prerogative included – indeed, still includes – sending and receiving ambassadors; entering into treaties, leagues, and alliances; and making war and peace.[24] The Act of Settlement had demanded parliamentary consent for any war fought to defend non-British interests, though 'not once was this parliamentary control driven home' during the eighteenth century.[25] As Lord Strange warned during the 1754 debate on the East India Mutiny bill, 'Supposing it should become necessary to declare war against some neighbouring potentate: do we not know, that our sovereign may do so by virtue of his prerogative, and without the authority of an act of parliament?'[26] One major theoretical constraint on the prerogative thus proved unenforceable in practice. Yet, if that prerogative encompassed all collective dealings with foreign powers, it did not have exclusive authority over transactions with individual foreigners or with their vessels at sea: 'our laws have in some respect armed the subject with powers to impel the prerogative; by directing the ministers of the crown to issue letters of marque and reprisal upon due demand' and to grant safe-conducts to distressed foreigners and to 'strangers who come spontaneously'.[27] Parliament also limited the prerogative power by preventing foreign enlistment and regulating foreign loans and, after 1783, commerce with the United States. The division of labour between crown and parliament was therefore not absolute but relative, though in foreign affairs the balance always tipped decisively in the crown's favour.

Municipal affairs took place within the ambit of national law while foreign affairs were transacted under the law of nations. On these grounds, Blackstone (in one of his rare speeches in the House of Commons) heartily supported parliament's authority to tax the American colonies during the Stamp Act crisis: 'If the colonies reject a law of taxation, they may oppose any other, and they will become a more distinct separate dominion under one head. All the dominions of this country have been subject to parliament', even if only Calais had ever sent representatives to Westminster.[28] Parliament could legislate municipally but could only apply the law of nations or incorporate it into national legislation. What then *was* the relationship between a sovereign, imperial parliament (as defined by the Henrician Act in Restraint of Appeals of 1533) and the law of nations, 'a system', according to Blackstone, 'of rules, deducible by natural reason, and established by universal consent among the civilised inhabitants of the world'? Blackstone's answer defined the conventional legal wisdom of the mid-eighteenth century:

since in England no royal power can introduce a new law, or suspend the execution of the old, therefore the law of nations (wherever any question arises which is properly the object of it's jurisdiction) is here adopted in it's full extent by the common law, and is held to be part of the law of the land. And those acts of parliament, which have from time to time been made to enforce this universal law, or to facilitate the execution of it's decisions, are not to be considered as introductive of any new rule, but merely as declaratory of the old fundamental constitutions of the kingdom; without which it must cease to be part of the civilized world.[29]

Blackstone's judgment affirmed the supremacy of statute and the integrity of the common law by encompassing the law of nations within them rather than erecting it as a higher law above them. It did not imply that the law of nations could be used to overturn English law, nor that explicit references to the law of nations in legislation could be deemed to graft alien principles onto English statutes. (Blackstone's view was, however, strictly English, and contrasted starkly with Scots lawyers' understandings before 1707 of the relationship between municipal and natural law: for them '[t]heories of sovereignty might stress statutes or customs; natural law had primacy over them'.)[30] If the principles of the law of nations were already enshrined in the common law, and if common law and statute law were necessarily harmonised with one another, then the law of nations must, logically, be in concert with, and intrinsic to, the law made by parliament itself.

Yet the relationship between the law of nations and municipal law was not quite as straightforward, or indeed as immemorial, as Blackstone would have liked his readers to believe. In 1754, Mansfield, speaking in the case of *Triquet* v. *Bath*, recalled that in the earlier case of *Buvot* v. *Barbuit* in 1737, 'LORD TALBOT declared clear Opinion – "That the *Law of Nations*, in its *full* Extent, was Part of the Law of England." . . . "That the *Law of Nations* was to be *collected* from the *Practice* of the different nations, and the Authority of *Writers*." Accordingly, He argued and determined from such Instances, and the Authority of *Grotius*, *Barbeyrac, Binkershoek, Wiquefort, &c.*, there being no *English* writer of Eminence, upon the Subject'.[31] Mansfield (when still plain Mr Murray) had acted as counsel in *Buvot* v. *Barbuit*; likewise, Blackstone acted as counsel in *Triquet* v. *Bath*.[32] A clear line of transmission can thus be traced for the doctrine that the law of nations was part of English law, running back from Blackstone through Lord Mansfield to Lord Talbot. However, Mansfield's account of Talbot's ruling was not published until 1771, and the standard report of *Buvot* v. *Barbuit* (first published in 1741) contained no statement to the effect that the law of nations was part of the law of England.[33] The doctrine therefore cannot be traced any earlier in print than Blackstone's *Commentaries*.

In both *Buvot* v. *Barbuit* and *Triquet* v. *Bath* the point at issue had been the immunity of diplomats from civil and criminal prosecution. In each case, diplomatic immunity was taken to be a recognised principle of the law of nations but not one that had therefore always been enshrined in English law. However, even during the Commonwealth and Interregnum, aggrieved ambassadors appealed to the Council of State or the Protector (as did the brother of the Portuguese ambassador Dom Pataleone de Sá in 1653–54) rather than parliament. Until the early eighteenth century, offenders against diplomatic immunity were punished by prerogative action rather than by the common-law courts.[34] This particular principle of the law of nations, at least, had therefore not been historically part of the common law of England.

Prior to 1709 there had been no formal recognition of the principle that the law of nations was part of the law of England. In that year, parliament passed the Act of 7 Anne *c.* 12 which guaranteed ambassadors and their servants immunity from arrest or prosecution, '[t]he deficiency of the laws, to punish insults, in the case of Foreign Ministers being apparent'.[35] Creditors of the heavily indebted Russian ambassador Andrei Artemonovich Matveev had him arrested after his final audience in 1708. In the process, the arresting sheriff and his men beat the ambassador, assaulted his footmen, bundled him into a carriage and briefly detained him. Seventeen men responsible for issuing and enforcing the writ against Matveev were tried and convicted on the facts, though their guilt in law was never determined. The English government admitted that the law of nations had been breached, but no criminal charges could be brought because neither statute nor the common law had been broken.[36] When Peter the Great demanded the culprits' execution, Queen Anne placed a bill before parliament declaring all writs against accredited diplomats or suits for the seizure of their property to be void because '[c]ontrary to the law of nations, and in prejudice of the rights and privileges, which ambassadors, and other public ministers . . . have at all times been thereby possessed of, and which ought to be kept sacred and inviolable'.[37]

The opinion that 7 Anne *c.* 12 'was not an *Alteration* of the Law from what it was before' seems to have originated with Blackstone, when he acted as counsel in *Triquet* v. *Bath*, in which proceedings it then had been approved and elaborated by Lord Mansfield himself.[38] Blackstone noted in 1765 that 'in consequence of this statute, thus enforcing the law of nations, these privileges are now usually allowed in the courts of common law'.[39] By the time the second edition of his *Commentaries* appeared in 1766, this passage had become even more emphatic: 'In consequence of this statute, thus declaring and enforcing the law of nations, these privileges are now held to be part of the law of the land, and are constantly allowed in the courts of common law.'[40] His first account acknowledged that this was a recent development in the courts ('*now* usually allowed'); his second, that the Act of 7 Anne *c.* 12 had applied a principle of the law of nations that had acquired increasing force and application ('now . . . *constantly* allowed in the courts of common law'). Thus, even Blackstone admitted that there had been historical change in the relationship between English law and the law of nations, both in its incorporation into statute and in its application in the courts. Indeed, when at the conclusion of the *Commentaries* he enumerated '[t]he chief alterations of the moment' in English law, the first he listed was 'the solemn recognition of the law of nations with respect to the rights of embassadors'.[41]

The Act of 7 Anne *c.* 12 was one of only two statutes during the long eighteenth century that expressly referred to the law of nations.[42] Its enactment had demonstrated that the principle of diplomatic immunity had not been enforceable in English law before 1709, while the almost complete dearth of statutory reference to the law of nations thereafter in the long eighteenth century revealed the distinction between the two species of law. The relationship between English law and the law of nations was evidently not one of explicit declaration or complete incorporation.[43] However, English legal doctrine (as Mansfield affirmed in *Heathfield* v. *Chilton* in 1764) did consistently hold the view that an act of parliament could not alter the law of nations.[44] This principle implied that natural law could not be affected by a merely human enactment: as Burke argued in 1781, '[t]he rights of war were not . . . limited by the learning of the schools, by the light of philosophy, by the disquisitions of councils, by the debates of legislatures, or by the sense of delegated assemblies'.[45] It also implied that parliament could make no laws that did not accord with natural reason, and hence with the law of nations that derived from the universal assent of rational creatures. Though English law and the law of nations remained distinct in their application, they could still be assimilated in principle, so that the law of nations presented no challenge to the supremacy of parliament and the absolute power of parliament posed no threat to the highest of all laws. The law of nations could thus be deployed in matters beyond national jurisdiction, as when it was applied in the Court of Admiralty or when the law-merchant was gradually taken up by common-law courts;[46] it could also be adopted selectively by statutory incorporation. Either way, each form of law remained independent, and was thereby no threat to the authority of the other within its own proper sphere.

In the light of the preceding discussion, the question of parliament's relationship to international law in the eighteenth century might seem utterly *mal posée*. After all, parliament had no formal role in conducting foreign policy and hence in directly negotiating matters subject to the law of nations. The moments at which it exercised its rights of review and debate over international agreements were relatively few and hence particularly notorious, as in the case of the argument over the Anglo-French Commercial Treaty of 1786.[47] The occasions on which parliamentary statute appealed to the law of nations were vanishingly small in number, nor (according to English legal doctrine) could legislation supersede that higher law.

However, even taking these important objections into account, there remain at least three areas in which the question of parliament's relationship to international law can be genuinely illuminating. The first lies in the reconsideration of parliamentary action within the acknowledged context of the law of nations, for example, during the Glorious Revolution, in the course of the Anglo-Scottish Union negotiations or the debate on the recognition of American independence in 1782–83. The second lies in the use of international law in parliamentary debate, where it was always more conspicuous than in legislation, and where it became more noticeable after the Seven Years War: that is, during the period when imperial and military matters progressively came to dominate deliberation and discussion at Westminster. The third area is the extra-parliamentary development of the law of nations itself, especially as it came to be reconceptualised in the closing decades of the eighteenth century (and not just in Britain). This was, in fact, just the point at which the term 'international law' entered English vocabulary, as part of Jeremy Bentham's far-reaching attempt to clarify the differences between municipal and international law. Out of these discussions on the scope and nature of international law emerged conventional and abiding distinctions between internal and external forms of law which in turn mirrored differences between domestic and international histories and rendered them mutually incomprehensible.

The relevance of the law of nations to English and, later, British definitions of parliamentary legitimacy and authority demonstrates the artificiality of such enduring distinctions and differences. This became especially clear in the period between the Glorious Revolution and the Anglo-Scottish Union of 1707. In contrast to later Whig interpretations of the Revolution, Tories and radical Whigs had understood the Revolution as an event within European history and hence within the categories of the law of nations. William's invasion, whether seen as motivated by the imperatives of his own foreign policy or as a generous response to English concern at dynastic instability, was nonetheless an external intervention into the affairs of a divided country. The presiding authority in international law at the time of the Glorious Revolution was Hugo Grotius. He had enumerated the extenuating conditions under which resistance or intervention might be justifiable, and provided authoritative support for those in England who wished to defend the Revolution on grounds other than that of *force majeure*. According to those who appropriated Grotius's arguments during the Revolution debate of 1689–93, William had defeated James in a just war and could thus claim title to the English throne as a legitimate conqueror.[48] Understood as an invasion of one sovereign by another, the Revolution was an event in the relations between states and hence covered by the law of nations rather than by English law alone. Such arguments found more purchase in pamphlets than they did within parliament, but even there – or, rather, in the Convention – it was argued that because the nation had been returned to state of nature by James's dereliction, the law of nature and of nations provided the only guide: a 'gentleman cries, where is the Law? When we cannot find it, we must have recourse to the law of nations'.[49]

The law of nations, and more specifically Grotius's account of it, also provided an explanatory framework for the Anglo-Scottish Union of 1707. In this context, it was invoked not to supply an absence of law (as in the Convention debates of 1688) but rather as the means to understand the legislative union of two sovereign powers. Proponents of union frequently referred to Grotius's account of the union between the Romans and the Sabines, in which the great jurist argued that the two peoples had not lost their separate rights but had instead communicated them to one another as they made up one new state (Grotius, *De Jure Belli ac Pacis*, II. ix. 9).[50] Because the Union of England and Scotland was negotiated between two separate states (albeit two states sharing a single monarch), the negotiations occurred within the terms set by the law of nations. However, the commissioners who negotiated the terms of the treaty of Union had been appointed by the English and Scottish parliaments and not by the royal prerogative, and thus the treaty of Union was not procedurally equivalent to a treaty as defined in public international law. Moreover, acceptance of the terms of the treaty by the two parliaments extinguished each of them, created a new British legislature at Westminster and introduced a wholly new state, the United Kingdom of Great Britain. The Treaty of 1707 could not subsequently be challenged or renegotiated under the terms of international law because the parties to it no longer existed as international entities: '[t]he reason . . . is that, paradoxically, the Law of Nations is concerned – not with nations [like England and Scotland] – but with states [like the United Kingdom]'.[51] Under the terms of the Treaty, the two nations remained separate in matters of private law, for example, but in the eyes of public law they had become one. With a single legislature to complement a single crown, there need no longer be collisions between two parliaments pursuing competing foreign and commercial policies (the dangers of which the Scots Darien venture had magnified in the 1690s), though the constitutional distinction between executive and legislative, and hence between prerogative and parliament, remained as it had been since 1688: treaties needed only to be laid before parliament if they necessitated either new fiscal exactions or an act of parliament to enforce their provisions.[52]

The prominence of Grotius in the Union debates stemmed, in part, from the centrality of the modern tradition of natural law to legal and ethical education in Scotland and, increasingly, in England.[53] However, prior to the Seven Years War, citations from continental authorities on the law of nature and of nations appeared mostly in the literature out of doors; only in the latter half of the eighteenth century do they seem to have become an essential part of the oratorical arsenal of the well-prepared parliamentary debater. It was therefore no surprise to see Grotius repeatedly cited in the Commons' debates at the opening of the Seven Years War, for example.[54] Such texts became even more prominent in parliament as they were more thoroughly assimilated into the literature of the English common law. In this regard, one of the more notable features of the later volumes of Blackstone's *Commentaries* is their reliance on continental legal thought: not just Beccaria's recently published *Essay on crimes and punishments* (1764; Eng. trans. 1767) but also such writers as Pufendorf, Bijnkershoek, Montesquieu and Vattel.[55] Likewise, Mansfield's reliance on '[t]he Roman code, the law of nations, and the opinion of foreign civilians' in his rulings on commercial law, and his much-admired 1753 memorial on Prussian neutrality (which earned him the plaudits of both Montesquieu and Vattel), may also have made such authorities more familiar to British lawyers and parliamentarians.[56]

The debate on the preliminary articles of peace after the American War provided a test-case for the utility of the law of nations by bringing to a head debate on the relative authority of parliament and the crown. Unlike the Seven Years War, the American War entailed the dismemberment, rather than the augmentation, of the British Empire and a fundamental reassessment of the authority of the British state, with consequent reconsideration of British nationhood in a world where fellow-Britons had become rebels and rebels then became independent actors within the extended European state-system.[57] Even though the King had declared the colonists to be in rebellion by the autumn of 1775, he had not thereby absolved them of allegiance to the British crown. According to the principle *nemo potest exuere patriam*, the colonists could not renounce their British citizenship by their own unilateral declaration of independence.[58] Recognition of American independence also demanded the cession of territory formerly part of the crown's dominions in North America. Because the crown could not divest itself of territory by prerogative alone, nor could it unilaterally dissolve the acts of parliament that had comprised the constitution of the empire, parliament had to intervene in the framing of the peace-treaty. Such an intervention was not, of course, unprecedented: similar questions had arisen with reference to the return of Dunkirk to France in 1662, in relation to Gibraltar in 1720 and with regard to the cessions of territory after the Seven Years War.[59] Under the terms of a 1782 Act, parliament had empowered the crown to cede the former territory of the British colonies to the Americans, 'any Law, Act or Acts of Parliament, Matter or Thing, to the contrary in anywise notwithstanding'.[60] This move was intended to circumvent disquiet regarding 'the right of the crown to dismember the empire without sanction of parliament; and, for the sake of making peace, to resign a territory not acquired during the war', raised by the Earl of Carlisle in the Lords' debate on the articles of peace in the following year.[61] Opponents of the peace-articles argued that the 1782 Act had only authorised the crown to recognise American independence, not to cede territory in North America to the United States or fishing rights in Newfoundland and the gulf of St Lawrence, for example. Though parliament ultimately ratified the terms of the treaty, the larger question remained unresolved until the cession by parliament of Heligoland in 1890, which seemed to settle the matter in favour of statute rather than prerogative.

The debate of 1782–83 on American independence, which Lord North called 'an object of the greatest magnitude that ever came under parliamentary discussion', was partly conducted in the language of the law of nations, and with the aid of the best modern authorities.[62] Those authorities did not agree with one another: Burlamaqui, for one, held that the ruler of a patrimonial kingdom might alienate any part of his territories at will; however, Vattel denied that England was such a kingdom, and argued instead that the Kings of England 'cannot alienate any part of their dominions without the consent of parliament'.[63] Lord Hawke cited Pufendorf to support the crown's right to cede East Florida; in response to speakers who 'gravely referred their lordships to Swiss authors for an explanation of the prerogatives of the British crown', the Lord Chancellor, Lord Thurlow, scoffed at the 'lucubrations and fancies of foreign writers' and denied the authority of 'Mr Vattel and Mr Puffendorf'.[64]

The standard European texts of international law became more readily available in English and French translations, which may partly explain or even excuse the notorious backwardness of British (meaning, mostly, English) lawyers in contributing to contemporary international jurisprudence. European observers, and later historians discerned only four lasting eighteenth-century British additions to the corpus of international thought: Mansfield's memorial of 1753; Jeremy Bentham's 'Pacification and emancipation' (better-known as his 'Essay for universal and perpetual peace') (c. 1789); Robert Ward's *Enquiry into the foundation and history of the law of nations in Europe, from the time of the Greeks and Romans, to the age of Grotius* (1795); and Sir James Mackintosh's *Discourse on the study of the law of nature and nations* (1799).[65] Bentham's plans arose most immediately from his critique of Pitt's foreign policy; Ward compiled his *Enquiry* at the suggestion of his patron, the Solicitor-General, Lord Eldon; and Mackintosh's *Discourse* was in part a recantation of his anti-Burkean *Vindiciæ Gallicæ* (1791).[66] Bentham's plans remained among his papers until their publication in the mid-nineteenth century, but Ward's *Enquiry* and Mackintosh's *Discourse* gained greater fame in their own time. Ward's *Enquiry* became a standard history of the law of nations for the positivist era. Its author was sceptical of the utility of deriving international norms from conceptions of natural law which were clearly not universal, and instead described the laws of a Christian civilisation clearly confined to Europe and its imperial outposts and successor-states, but also threatened by the atheistical French republican attempt to legislate its own conception of the law of nations.[67] Even more starkly counter-revolutionary was Mackintosh's *Discourse*, the preface to the enormously successful set of lectures, eclectically derived from German histories of philosophy, the jurisprudence of Montesquieu and the canon of international law from Grotius to Vattel, which he delivered in Lincoln's Inn hall in early 1799 to a distinguished audience including six peers and twelve members of parliament.[68] However, most prominent of all in bringing 'the elements and principles of the law of nations, the great ligament of mankind' to the attention of parliament was surely Edmund Burke, who drew upon them repeatedly in the Hastings trial and who, like Charles James Fox, argued over the relevance of Vattel to the justification of war with the French Directory.[69]

The prominence of these authorities on the law of nations was symptomatic of burgeoning interest in the definition of international law itself in the last two decades of the century. That interest was not confined to parliament, or to Britain; it was in the nature of the subject itself to be transnational in scope. The very term 'international law' entered English juridical discourse only in 1789, when it appeared in Bentham's *Introduction to the principles of morals and legislation* (first printed in 1780, but not published until 1789).[70] Bentham coined the term to denote the body of law dealing specifically with the relations between sovereign states, rather than between nations or peoples, whether individually or collectively: 'inter*state* law' might therefore have been a less ambiguous designation. His neologism did not catch on more generally in anglophone usage for a quarter of a century, though the need for the word 'international' was one sign that the law of nations (or, we might say, states) had now to distinguished from the law of nature (with which it had been traditionally held to be almost entirely homologous). It was therefore more closely identified with customary or positive law, the actions of states and the positive agreements between them. This, in turn, created greater demand for collections of treaties as evidence of international norms. As Charles Jenkinson put it, in the preface to his treaty-collection of 1785, 'The Utility of such a Work is sufficiently obvious to the Gentleman, and the Politician. To the Statesman it is a Code, or Body of Law; since a Collection of Treaties is to him of the same Use, that a Collection of Statutes is to a Lawyer.'[71]

The rise of interest in the decades following the Seven Years War in the theory and practice of the law of nations paralleled the expansion of imperial and extra-national legislation by the Westminster parliament. As Joanna Innes has shown, the ratio of legislative activity devoted to imperial and other (including international) legislation – rather than to local, national or 'British' legislation – declined across the course of the century. However, her calculations also show that the absolute volume of imperial and international legislation did increase dramatically after 1763.[72] Parliament's willingness to legislate extra-territorially was, of course, no novelty in the late eighteenth century: the Navigation Acts had ring-fenced global trade since the 1650s and laws against piracy had swept non-state actors from the seas in the half-century before 1720, for example.[73] The suppression of the slave-trade is, of course, the most spectacular evidence of parliament's desire to enforce norms of international law – by treating slave-traders as enemies of humankind (*hostes humani generis*), as pirates had traditionally been designated – but it was hardly unique.[74] From the early nineteenth century, parliament legislated not just for the nations of Britain and Ireland and for the territories comprising the realm, but even further abroad for territories under the protection of the crown, such as Honduras or Tahiti (Murders Abroad Act, 57 George III *c.* 53), the Pacific Islands (9 George IV *c.* 83 § 4), Hong Kong (3 & 4 William IV *c.* 93 §§ 5–16, 6 & 7 Victoria *c.* 80) or the Cape (6 & 7 William IV *c.* 57).[75] 'This was more obviously an "imperial parliament": a parliament superintending the affairs of several, interacting but distinct politico-cultural entities': but clearly not just within the ambit of Britain and Ireland alone.[76]

The causes of change across the eighteenth century were obvious to Edmund Burke: 'as Commerce, with its Advantages and its Necessities, opened a Communication more largely with other Countries; as the Law of Nature and Nations (always a Part of the Law of *England*) came to be cultivated; as an increasing Empire; as new Views and Combinations of Things were opened ... antique Rigour and over-done Severity gave Way to the Accommodation of Human concerns, for which Rules were made, and not Human Concerns to bend for them'.[77] The particular prominence of international law in parliamentary debate and the willingness of parliament to legislate extraterritorially may however have helped to harden distinctions between municipal and international law rather than to relax them. The pre-eminence of statute, and the evident impossibility of enforcing international norms without the force of legislation, encouraged theorists of positive law, most notably John Austin, in their denial that international 'law' was law in any recognisable sense, precisely because it lacked a sovereign legislator, could not be construed as a command and carried with it no enforceable sanctions.[78] This distinction between municipal and international law reinforced the abiding distinction between domestic and international history.

Parliamentary history has usually been understood as the history of municipal legislation and debate, and hence as part of domestic rather than international history. In part, such a description of parliament's capacities derived from the constitutional divisions between executive and legislative; however, in so far as law-making and discussion came ever more to encompass imperial issues and to be conducted in the language of the law of nations, parliamentary debate became more international and even transnational in scope while legislation increasingly regulated actions or events in ways that transcended national frontiers, whether within Britain and Ireland or far beyond them. Evidently, parliament had to pay increasing attention to the norms of international law in a century of imperial rivalry, global war and republican revolution. Equally evidently, historians of Britain, parliament and 'identities' in the eighteenth century can no longer ignore the *inter*national activities of a distinctly *multi*-national parliament.[79]

Notes

1 I am especially grateful to Joyce Chaplin, Julian Hoppit, David Lieberman, Peter Marshall and Robert Travers for their advice and comments. My thanks also to the Charles Warren Center for Studies in American History at Harvard University for fellowship support during the research and writing of this essay.

2 C. Hall, 'Rethinking imperial histories: the Reform Act of 1867', *New Left Review*, 208 (1994), 3–29; C. Hall, K. McClelland and J. Rendall, *Defining the Victorian nation: class, race, gender and the Reform Act of 1867* (Cambridge, 2000); M. Taylor, 'Empire and parliamentary reform: the 1832 Reform Act revisited' in A. Burns and J. Innes (eds), *Rethinking the age of reform: Britain and Ireland c. 1780–1850* (forthcoming); Taylor, 'Colonial Representation at Westminster, 1800–60', in this volume.

3 F. W. Maitland, *The constitutional history of England*, ed. H. A. L. Fisher (Cambridge, 1908), 339.

4 H. V. Bowen, *Revenue and reform: the Indian problem in British politics, 1757–1773* (Cambridge, 1991), 30–47; T. R. Travers, 'Contested notions of sovereignty in Bengal under British rule, 1765–1785' (University of Cambridge Ph.D. thesis, 2000).

5 J. R. Seeley, *The expansion of England* (1883), 9.

6 J. Ohlmeyer, 'Ireland independent: confederate foreign policy and international relations during the mid-seventeenth century' in Ohlmeyer (ed.), *Ireland from independence to occupation, 1641–1660* (Cambridge, 1995), 89–112.

7 W. Doyle, 'The [British-Irish] Union in a European context', *Transactions of the Royal Historical Society*, 6th series, x (2000), 167–80.

8 P. Force, 'Self-love, identification, and the origin of political economy', *Yale French Studies*, xcii, (1997), 45–64; D. Wootton, 'Unhappy Voltaire, or "I shall never get over it as long as I live"', *History Workshop Journal*, i (2000), 148, 152–3; and, more generally, C. Taylor, *Sources of the self: the making of the modern identity* (Cambridge, Mass., 1989).

9 J. Beddoe, 'Anniversary address', *Journal of the Anthropological Institute of Great Britain and Ireland*, i (1872), xxvi.

10 C. Kidd, *British identities before nationalism: ethnicity and nationhood in the Atlantic world, 1600–1800* (Cambridge, 1999), 291.

11 T. Pownall, *Memorial addressed to the sovereigns of Europe and the Atlantic* (1803), 32.

12 Q. Skinner, 'Hobbes and the purely artificial person of the state', *Journal of Political Philosophy*, vii (1999), 1–29.

13 Cobbett, *Parliamentary History*, xviii, col. 162.

14 E. Burke, 'Speech to the electors of Bristol' (3 Nov. 1774), quoted in L. S. Sutherland, 'Edmund Burke and the relations between members of parliament and their constituents', *Studies in Burke and His Time*, x (1968), 1005.

15 Cobbett, *Parliamentary History*, xviii, col. 503.

16 J. A. W. Gunn, 'Eighteenth-century Britain: in search of the state and finding the quarter sessions', in J. Brewer and E. Hellmuth (eds), *Rethinking Leviathan: the eighteenth-century state in Britain and Germany* (Oxford, 1999), 117.

17 E. H. Gould, 'American independence and Britain's counter-revolution', *Past and Present*, 154 (1997), 107–41 and 'A virtual nation: greater Britain and the imperial legacy of the American Revolution', *American Historical Review*, civ (1999), 476–89.

18 D. Armitage, 'The Declaration of Independence and international law', *William and Mary Quarterly*, 3rd series, lxix, (2002), 39–64.

19 J. G. A. Pocock, *La ricostruzione di un impero. Sovranità britannica e federalismo americano* (Manduria, 1996), 57–111.

20 J. Black, *A system of ambition? British foreign policy, 1660–1793* (2nd edn, Stroud, 2000), 47.

21 J. Black, 'A parliamentary foreign policy? The "Glorious Revolution" and the conduct of British foreign policy', *Parliaments, estates and representation*, xi (1991), 69–80, 'Parliament and foreign policy 1739–1763', *Parliaments, estates and representation*, xii (1992), 121–42 and 'Parliament and foreign policy 1763–1793', *Parliaments, estates and representation*, xiii (1993), 153–71.

22 W. Blackstone, *Commentaries on the laws of England*, 4 vols (1765–9), i, 156, 'Of the parliament' (all further references are to this edition unless otherwise noted); compare R. Chambers, *A course of lectures on the English law* (1767–73), ed. T. M. Curley, 2 vols (Madison, Wis., 1986), i, 140.

23 Blackstone, *Commentaries*, i, 245, 'Of the king's prerogative'; compare Chambers, *Lectures*, i, 158, and A. Hamilton, 'The Federalist no. 69' (14 Mar. 1788), in Hamilton J. Madison and J. Jay, *The Federalist papers*, ed. G. Wills (New York, 1982), 351–2.

24 *Halsbury's statutes of England and Wales* (4th edn, 1985–), xviii, 720–1, §§ 1406, 1407; P. G. Richards, *Parliament and foreign affairs* (1967); C. Carstairs and R. Ware (eds), *Parliament and international relations* (Buckingham, 1991).

25 Black, *A system of ambition?*, 14.

26 Cobbett, *Parliamentary History*, xv, col. 275.

27 Blackstone, *Commentaries*, i, 250, 251.

28 'Parliamentary diaries of Nathaniel Ryder, 1764–7', ed. P. D. G. Thomas, *Camden Miscellany*, xxiii, Camden Society 4th series, vii (1969), 268. Chambers concurred: 'It appears therefore reasonable to conclude that all colonies may be taxed by that state on which they depend for support, and to which they fly for protection, and that English colonies may . . . be taxed by an English legislature': Chambers, *Lectures*, i, 292.

29 Blackstone, *Commentaries*, iv, 66–7, 'Of offences against the law of nations'. Chambers was more circumspect: 'in England in particular the municipal law in this instance [regarding diplomatic immunity from arrest for debt or civil contract], *as in most if not all others*, perfectly conforms itself to the law of nations': Chambers, *Lectures*, i, 262 (my emphasis).

30 J. W. Cairns, 'Scottish law, Scottish lawyers and the status of the Union' in J. Robertson (ed.), *A union for empire: political thought and the British Union of 1707* (Cambridge, 1995), 254 (quoted), 268.

31 *Triquet and Others* v. *Bath* (1764), in *Reports of cases adjudged in the Court of King's Bench since the time of Lord Mansfield's coming to preside in it*, ed. J. Burrow, 5 vols (1771–80), iii, 1480; A. Nussbaum, *A concise history of the law of nations* (New York, 1947), 136–7; D. Lieberman, *The province of legislation determined: legal theory in eighteenth-century Britain* (Cambridge, 1989), 105–6. The writers named are Hugo Grotius (1583–1645); Jean Barbeyrac (1674–1744), Swiss editor of Grotius and Pufendorf; Cornelis van Bijnkershoek (1673–1743), Dutch author of *De foro legatorum in causa civili, quam criminali* (1721); and Abraham de Wicquefort (1606–82), Dutch author of *Mémoires touchant l'ambassadeur et les ministères publics* (1676).

32 H. Lauterpacht, 'Is international law a part of the law of England?', *Transactions of the Grotius Society*, xxv (1940), 53; E. R. Adair, 'The law of nations and the common law of England: a study of 7 Anne Cap. 12', *Cambridge Historical Journal*, ii (1928), 296.

33 *Buvot* v. *Barbuit* (1737), in *Cases in Equity during the time of the late Lord Chancellor Talbot* (1741), 281–3.

34 Adair, 'The law of nations', 292–4.

35 7 Anne *c.* 12, 'An Act for preserving the privileges of ambassadors, and other publick ministers of foreign princes and states'; Cobbett, *Parliamentary History*, vi, col. 792.

36 L. S. Frey and M. L. Frey, *The history of diplomatic immunity* (Columbus, Ohio, 1999), 227–9.

37 Cobbett, *Parliamentary History*, vi, col. 793.

38 *Reports of King's Bench*, iii, 1478–79, citing 31 Henry VI *c.* 4, Grotius, Bijnkershoek and various English court-cases.

39 Blackstone, *Commentaries*, i, 248.

40 W. Blackstone, *Commentaries on the laws of England*, 4 vols (2nd edn, Oxford, 1766–69), i, 256–7; compare Chambers, *Lectures*, i, 262.

41 Blackstone, *Commentaries*, iv, 434, 'Of the rise, progress, and gradual improvements, of the laws of England.'

42 The other was 55 George III *c.* 160, sec. 58, 'An Act for the encouragement of seamen'; T. E. Holland, 'International law and acts of parliament' in Holland, *Studies in international law* (Oxford, 1898), 193.

43 C. M. Picciotto, *The relation of international law to the law of England and of the United States* (London, 1915), 75–108.

44 W. Holdsworth, *A history of the English law*, ed. A. L. Goodhart and H. G. Hanbury, 17 vols (1937–72), x, 372.

45 Cobbett, *Parliamentary History*, xxii, col. 230.

46 H. J. Bourguignon, *Sir William Scott, Lord Stowell: judge of the High Court of Admiralty, 1798–1828* (Cambridge, 1987); J. H. Baker, 'The law merchant as a source of English law' in W. Swadling and G. Jones (eds), *The search for principle: essays in honour of Lord Goff of Chieveley* (Oxford, 1999), 79–96.

47 J. Black, *British foreign policy in an age of revolutions, 1783–1793* (Cambridge, 1994), 104–11, 491–2.

48 [C. Blount,] *The proceedings of the present parliament justified by the opinion of . . . Hugo Grotius* (London, 1689); Cobbett, *Parliamentary History*, v, col. 69; M. Goldie, 'Edmund Bohun and *jus gentium* in the Revolution debate, 1689–1693', *Historical Journal*, xx (1977), 569–86.

49 Cobbett, *Parliamentary History*, v, col. 128.

50 J. Robertson, 'Empire and union: two concepts of the early modern European political order' and Robertson, 'An elusive sovereignty: the union debate in Scotland, 1698–1707' in Robertson (ed.), *Union for empire*, 18–19, 221.

51 T. B. Smith, 'The Union of 1707 as fundamental law' in Smith, *Studies critical and comparative* (Edinburgh, 1962), 8.

52 G. C. Gibbs, 'Laying treaties before parliament in the eighteenth century' in R. Hatton and M. S. Anderson (eds), *Studies in diplomatic history: essays in memory of David Bayne Horn* (1970), 118–24.

53 J. Cairns, 'Scottish law, Scottish lawyers and the ltatus of the Union' in Robertson (ed.), *Union for Empire*, 258–9; Lieberman, *Province of legislation*, 38–9; Lieberman, 'Codification, consolidation, and parliamentary statute' in Brewer and Hellmuth (eds), *Rethinking Leviathan*, 363.

54 Cobbett, *Parliamentary History*, xv, cols. 554 (Gilbert Elliot), 556 (Welbore Ellis), 568 (Charles Townshend).

55 See, for example, Blackstone, *Commentaries*, i, 43; ii, 390; iii, 70, 401; iv, 16–17, 66, 185, 238; Lieberman, *Province of legislation*, 205–8.

56 [W. Murray, et al.,] *The Duke of Newcastle's letter, by His Majesty's order, to Monsieur Michell* (1753); 'Junius' (*sc.* Philip Francis), letter xli, to Lord Mansfield (14 Nov. 1770), in *The letters of Junius*, ed. J. Cannon (Oxford, 1978), 208; Lieberman, *Province of legislation*, 112.

57 S. Conway, 'From fellow-nationals to foreigners: British perceptions of the Americans, circa 1739–1783', *William and Mary Quarterly*, 3rd series, lix (2002), 65–100.

58 [F. Plowden,] *An investigation of the native rights of British subjects* (1784); [Plowden,] *A supplement to the investigation of the native rights of British subjects* (1785); J. H. Kettner, 'Subjects or citizens: a note on British views respecting the legal effects of American Independence', *Virginia Law Review*, xxii (1976), 945–67; T. S. Martin, '*Nemo potest exuere patriam*: indelibility of allegiance and the American Revolution', *American Journal of Legal History*, xxxv (1991), 205–18.

59 Gibbs, 'Laying treaties', 125–9 (on Dunkirk and Gibraltar); A. Smith, *Lectures on jurisprudence*, ed. R. L. Meek, D. D. Raphael and P. G. Stein (Oxford, 1978), 324–5 (report of 1762–3), citing Pufendorf, Cocceius and Hutcheson.

60 22 George III, *c.* 46, 'Act to enable His Majesty to conclude a peace, or truce, with the revolted colonies in North America.'

61 Cobbett, *Parliamentary History*, xxiii, col. 378; compare cols. 484, 514–15.

62 Cobbett, *Parliamentary History*, xxiii, col. 560.

63 Marquis of Carmarthen in Cobbett, *Parliamentary History*, xxiii, col. 379 (citing J. J. Burlamaqui, *The principles of natural and politic law*, English trans. (1763), ii, 215–16, and Vattel, *Droit des gens*, I. iii. 117); Gibbs, 'Laying treaties', 125, n. 40.

64 Cobbett, *Parliamentary History*, xxiii, cols. 390 (referring to Samuel Pufendorf, *De jure naturæ et gentium libri octo* (1688), VIII. v. 9), 431–2.

65 J. Bentham, 'Pacification and emancipation' (c. 1789), Bentham MSS. XXV, University College London, heavily edited in *The works of Jeremy Bentham*, ed. J. Bowring, 11 vols (1843), ii, 546–60; R. [P.] Ward, *An enquiry into the foundation and history of the law of nations in Europe, from the time of the Greeks and Romans, to the age of Grotius*, 2 vols (1795); Sir James Mackintosh, *A discourse on the study of the law of nature and nations, &c.* (1799).

66 S. Conway, 'Bentham versus Pitt: Jeremy Bentham and British foreign policy 1789', *Historical Journal*, xxx (1987), 803–9; E. Phipps, *Memoirs of the political and literary life of Robert Plumer Ward, esq.*, 2 vols (1850), i, 15; K. Haakonssen, *Natural law and moral philosophy: from Grotius to the Scottish Enlightenment* (Cambridge, 1996), 278–80 (on Mackintosh).

67 Ward, *Enquiry*, ii, 338.

68 J. Mackintosh, 'Extracts for lectures on the law of nat: and nations begun Cambridge Augt 7th 1799', BL, Mackintosh MSS. My thanks to Edmund Garrett and Christopher Wright for facilitating access to these manuscripts.

69 E. Burke, *First letter on a regicide peace* (20 Oct. 1796), in *The writings and speeches of Edmund Burke, IX: the Revolutionary War, 1794–1797 [and] Ireland*, ed. R. B. McDowell (Oxford, 1991), 240; C. J. Fox, 'Address on the King's speech at the opening of the session' (21 Jan. 1794), in *The speeches of the Right Honourable Charles James Fox in the House of Commons*, 6 vols (1815), v, 156; P. J. Stanlis, 'Edmund Burke and the law of nations', *American Journal of International Law*, lxvii (1953), 397–413; F. G. Whelan, *Edmund Burke and India: political morality and empire* (Pittsburgh, 1996), 287–91; D. Armitage, 'Edmund Burke and reason of state', *Journal of the History of Ideas*, lxi (2000), 617–34.

70 J. Bentham, *An introduction to the principles of morals and legislation*, ed. J. H. Burns and H. L. A. Hart, introduction F. Rosen (Oxford, 1996), 6, 296; M. W. Janis, 'Jeremy Bentham and the fashioning of "international Law"', *American Journal of International Law*, lxxviii (1984), 408–10.

71 C. Jenkinson, *A collection of all the treaties of peace, alliance, and commerce between Great-Britain and other powers, from the treaty signed at Munster in 1649, to the treaties signed at Paris in 1783*, 3 vols (1785), i, iii–iv.

72 J. Innes, above, 19, Figure 2.1.

73 A. Pérotin-Dumont, 'The pirate and the emperor: power and law on the seas, 1450–1850', in J. D. Tracy (ed.), *The political economy of merchant empires: state power and world trade, 1350–1750* (Cambridge, 1991), 214–18; R. C. Ritchie, *Captain Kidd and the war against the pirates* (Cambridge, Mass., 1986).

74 D. B. Davis, *The problem of slavery in the age of revolution, 1770–1823* (rev. edn, New York, 1998), 113–19.

75 Holdsworth, *History of the English law*, xiv, 81–6.

76 Innes, above, 38.

77 'Report on the Lords Journals' (30 Apr. 1794), in *The writings and speeches of Edmund Burke, VII: India: the Hastings trial, 1789–1794*, ed. P. J. Marshall (Oxford, 1998), 163.

78 J. Austin, *The province of legislation determined* (1832), ed. W. E. Rumble (Cambridge, 1995), 123, 160, 171, 175–6.

79 Compare J. Innes, 'The local acts of a national parliament: parliament's role in sanctioning local action in eighteenth-century Britain', *Parliamentary History*, xvii (1998), 23–47.

10

Slaves, sati and sugar: constructing imperial identity through Liverpool petition struggles

Joshua Civin

In 1833, the *Liverpool Times* reported: 'The most illustrious of the Dicky Sams, the Magnates of the Town Hall and of the 'Change, have been dancing attendance on still greater men from the opening of the Session.' Lobbying was not restricted to 'Liverpool grandees'. In addition, 'a host of tar jackets and freemen' testified before parliamentary committees.[1] This intensive lobbying shows the lengths to which Liverpool townsfolk were increasingly prepared to go to ensure that parliament addressed their concerns. The 825 petitions that Liverpool groups presented to the House of Commons between 1775 and 1835 do not account for all the instances in which residents put pressure on parliament.[2] But as the most publicly visible of the tools in lobbyists' arsenals, they provide a unique vantage point from which to evaluate the range of identities deployed to mobilise collective action by inhabitants of a specific place. Moreover, Liverpool petitions allow us to explore the intersection between policy debate and imperial identity during a pivotal era in the evolution of the British empire. Elsewhere in England, people may not have reflected deeply about what it meant to live at the centre of a global empire, but relations with the broader world were often implicated when inhabitants mobilised in the nation's largest provincial port.[3]

At first glance, Liverpool might not seem an appropriate focus for an exploration of the phenomenal rise of extra-parliamentary agitation in the late eighteenth and early nineteenth centuries. In these years, MPs not only had to adjust to massive volumes of mass petitions; they also had to respond to entirely new categories of petitioners and qualitatively different subject matter. These developments have usually been explained by well-worn narratives of transition: from mercantilism to laissez-faire; from competition among vested interests to popular agitation for social reform; from empire as a commercial and strategic endeavour to empire as a civilising and evangelising mission. Industrialists, radicals, and London cosmopolitans are typically depicted as the inventors of new forms of extra-parliamentary agitation.[4] In contrast, Liverpool has been caricatured as a conservative bastion of resistance.[5] Analysis of Liverpool petitioning reveals, however, that even the 'gentlemanly capitalists' who dominated the port's economic and social life were willing to innovate in parliamentary claim-making. Nor was the port unified in opposition to the rise of humanitarianism, social and political reform, or free trade. Nevertheless, embracing innovations in the rituals, rhetoric, and tactics of mobilisation proved risky for Liverpool petitioners. Often in spite of themselves, they helped make petitioning a more competitive endeavour. It became increasingly difficult for any one group to support the claim that its particular vision of how the empire should work deserved parliamentary promotion.

The reason why Liverpool petitioners were amenable to these innovations was because they could be used as weapons in the port's intense power struggles. In all civic conflicts, there were two fundamental approaches to mobilising support. Organisers could appeal either to an affiliational interest (to those who shared occupational, status, religious, or institutional bonds) or to a community (those who lived and worked in a particular place). Competition among interests and among communities was channelled and exacerbated by parliament's decision-making processes.

Consider the two most popular topics addressed by Liverpool petitions during this period: economic regulation and civic improvement (see Figure 10.1). Both kinds of petition advocated state support for economic development, but one sought incentives to promote the profitability of certain business interests while the other concentrated on improving municipal services (e.g. street-paving, water-works) and the infrastructure (e.g. docks, canals, turnpikes) of particular locales.[6] Economic regulation and civic improvement petitions loomed so large because successful enterprise was never solely the product of individual skill, market factors, or chance. As importantly, state policies structured incentives. Policy outcomes characteristically reflected a search for compromise solutions, pursued in part by a process of individuating policies, so that they could be adjusted to take account of the specific array of interests bearing on each case. Thus, parliament rarely assessed taxes by a uniform index across the entire economy; instead, tariffs, duties, and other regulatory policies discriminated among occupations, goods, and crops. This approach encouraged interests to lobby vigorously for preferential treatment.[7]

Similarly, parliament's preferred approach to civic improvement was to address the needs of particular communities rather than either to delegate broad discretionary powers to local officials or to pass general legislation enabling a uniform approach nationwide. In consequence, a fresh round of petitioning was required whenever a community desired a new street or sewer. Eager to protect their relative standing, localities were quick to emulate successful improvements initiated elsewhere or alternatively to organise counter-petitions to prevent other locales from luring away residents.[8]

As often as petitions were provoked by rivalries among communities and among interests, they were spawned by factionalism *within* communities and *within* interests. Place-based loyalties were a major factor undermining unity within particular interests. In 1818, for instance, Liverpool watchmakers attacked a bill that would 'render them subject' to London artisans.[9] Conversely, rivalries

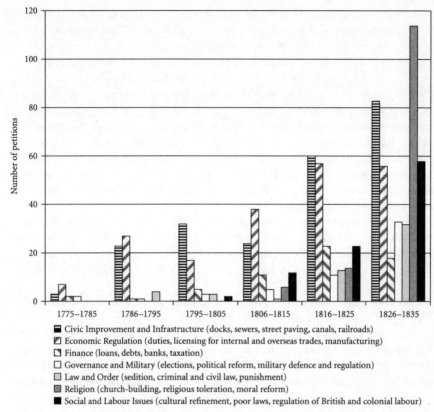

Figure 10.1 Petitions to the House of Commons, 1775–1835
Source: *CJ*, xxxv–xc (1775–1835). Due to the occasional short session,
each ten-year time span includes eleven sessions with one exception (1786–1795).
For details on my categorisation scheme, see footnote 6.

among different interests could impede community solidarity. For instance, in 1811, a Liverpool Common Council petition for authority to raise funds for dock improvements caused substantial divisions. While the West Indies, American, and Ship-Owners Associations mobilised in support, counter-petitions came from local pilots, salt-shippers, Irish traders, the parish vestry, householders, and two groups of Lancashire gentry.[10] Friction was even more marked when certain interests gained control over civic institutions and used their power to exclude competitors.

Not all instances of multiple petitioning on a single issue reflected conflict. Given the possibilities for polarisation among and within communities and interests, MPs always suspected that petitions did not embody the wishes of the entire group that they supposedly represented, but rather were the crafty manipulations of a self-interested few. Evaluating the inclusiveness of petitioning campaigns was not a great problem when they were orchestrated by institutions with defined memberships. Otherwise, it was difficult. MPs often knew only a handful of individuals even in their own constituencies. One way to suggest wide support was by recruiting hundreds of signers, but numbers alone did not necessarily represent broad-based backing. For a community, a good way to convey the sense that diverse segments of the population were on board was for several different interests to send up petitions. Likewise, interests could impress parliament by co-ordinating petitions from a variety of places. This tactic had particular appeal when one object was to marginalise a small group of hold-outs who had petitioned against an initiative that had broad-based support. As the threshold for demonstrating both conflict and consensus rose, the number of petitions submitted per issue increased much faster than the number of issues on which Liverpool townsfolk lobbied.

Identities rooted in community and interest were in any case less durable than petitioners – or historians – admitted. Individuals were increasingly on the move from place to place in search of opportunity. Similarly, they switched occupations, parties, and even religions in pursuit of profit, status, or spiritual or ideological epiphany.

Differing interests associated with the diverse geography of overseas commerce provided a major source of friction among interests within the Liverpool community. By the 1820s, there were associations for traders to the West Indies, East Indies, United States, Baltic, Mediterranean, Ireland, British North America, Brazil and South America, and Mexico. To Liverpool inhabitants, these had quasi-official status. Thomas Fletcher had no doubt that he owed his invitation to a dinner for the Prince of Wales in 1805 to his chairmanship of the West India Association: 'I should have had no chance of such a distinction in my private capacity.'[11]

Organising by geographic specialty within the town made sense for at least two reasons. First, parliament was receptive to such approaches because it regulated imports according to the country or region whence they came.[12] Second, Liverpool merchants did not trust competitors in other towns to look out for their interests in nationwide economic mobilisations. They were especially eager to contest the leadership of London merchants, who had a history of manoeuvring to exclude provincial outports from lucrative trades.

Friction within Liverpool's merchant elite made it difficult to present a community consensus in support of civic improvement. Careful behind-the-scenes negotiation among commercial associations, however, could forge a united front. For instance, the Liverpool and Manchester Railroad overcame the impact of the Common Council's opposition by rallying endorsements from all geographic specialties. But just as often commercial polarisations were impediments. The American Chamber of Commerce (composed of merchants trading with the United States) initially opposed the establishment of a London office to co-ordinate Liverpool lobbying. Moreover, customs officials, harbour pilots, and even the Common Council wrested concessions from commercial associations by playing them off against each other. Nevertheless economic interests were not always clear-cut. Many merchants joined more than one geographic specialty association and found it challenging to prioritise allegiances.[13]

Competition among commercial interests did not intensify until the late eighteenth century when the War of American Independence, and then the Revolutionary and Napoleonic Wars, reoriented the British imperial system. These disruptions provided opportunities to challenge the terms on which particular trades were conducted. The stances which Liverpool groups took when parliament debated regulating trade in slaves, sugar, or cotton can only be understood in terms of their evolving relationships with each other and with other merchants elsewhere. The main task of this chapter will be to unravel the logic of these developments. One consequence of the furore of petitioning provoked by these disruptions was that townsfolk repeatedly had to conjure up visions of their own place within the empire. Thus, in their interactions with parliament, Liverpool petitioners had to ponder the nature of imperial identity.

Although historians debate what fuelled Liverpool's meteoric rise, few eighteenth-century inhabitants doubted that the African slave trade was the key to the prosperity of the port. When the slave trade came under attack, there was little tension between community and interest. The surge in economic regulatory petitioning from 1788 through 1807 was largely a result of Liverpool's orchestrated campaign to convey civic consensus against the abolitionists. In addition to numerous merchant petitions, the Council weighed in during each session that the slave trade was debated, stressing the impact that any regulation would have on the entire town. Further emphasising the widespread devastation that abolition would cause, Liverpool metal trades, bakers, gunsmiths, and six ship-building trades sent petitions in 1789.[14]

Though Liverpool interests were publicly united in defence of the slave trade, they found it harder to form a common front with merchants in other ports to co-ordinate an attack on abolitionism. Liverpool slavers could not forget the struggle that their predecessors had waged over the past century, first to break the monopoly of the Royal African Company and then to sweep away the remaining regulations favouring metropolitans. Still distrustful of London commercial institutions, Liverpool merchants spearheaded their own lobbying and were reluctant to collaborate with pro-slave-trade forces elsewhere.[15]

Aggressive lobbying staved off abolition for over two decades, but Liverpool's unrivalled status as the slaving capital of the world worked to its disadvantage in parliamentary claim-making. Abolitionists were able to marginalise the slave trade as a special interest whose importance was confined to Liverpool and the colonies. Challenging the abolitionists' geography of interest, Liverpool petitioners tried to redirect attention to another issue on which their sentiments were more in sync with those of the nation at large. Their target was the East India Company. The Company was controlled by London merchants who jealously guarded their exclusive monopoly over trade with India and China. Each time the Company's charter was up for renewal (1793, 1813, 1833), Liverpool's anti-monopoly committee became the central co-ordinating body for a provincial assault on the metropolis.[16]

Despite Liverpool's leadership of provincial anti-monopoly campaigns, enthusiasm for the cause within the town was hindered by rivalries that heated up after the abolition of the slave trade in 1807. Various commercial interests struggled to persuade fellow citizens that their speciality was as essential to the future of the port as the slave trade had been. In the first decade of the nineteenth century, competition for precedence between the West India Association and the American Chamber of Commerce was exacerbated by wartime policies. The Orders in Council of 1807, demanding that all neutral trade to the Continent first pass through Britain or be subject to seizure, advantaged Liverpool's West Indies merchants, by excluding US competitors from Caribbean-Continental trading routes. By contrast, Liverpool American merchants suffered when the United States retaliated by embargoing British goods.[17]

This commercial friction complicated efforts to rally the entire port against the East India Company's monopoly. Liverpool anti-monopoly mobilisations were only partly about current trade practices; they also propounded idealised visions of how the empire should work. Liverpool merchant philosophers turned out numerous tracts projecting elegantly functioning global systems. India was the linchpin for Liverpool commercial visionaries. Anti-monopolists promised: '[W]e do hold in our hands the power of an unlimited extension of commerce, and of thereby giving employment and prosperity to every class in the community.'[18] Yet there were disagreements about what India could most profitably produce.

Envisioning India as a supplier of cotton for Lancashire's booming textile industries was appealing because of the instability of British relations with the United States, which had become the leading source of cotton imports. Each time the East India Company's charter came up for renewal, as it happened, US–British relations were at a low point. In 1792–93, animosity still lingered from the American Revolution. Twenty years later, the countries were openly at war. Twenty years after that, British resentment was stirred by high US tariffs.[19]

Anti-US jingoism, however, presented difficulties for Liverpool's American Chamber of Commerce. Members were eager to open new markets for provincial traders, but they were suspicious of West Indians' sudden eagerness in 1812 to mobilise against the East India Company. Five years earlier, American merchants had tried to rally opposition to a government loan to the Company. The West Indians had resisted for fear of embarrassing the ministers whose war policies they supported and the Americans opposed. By 1812, however, the situation had changed. Britain's decision to wage war against the United States was increasingly unpopular in Liverpool due to the economic depression that had ensued. Liverpool's American merchants blamed the depression on the war and organised a nationwide campaign for peace. West Indians tried to undercut their rivals' mobilisation by exploiting anti-monopoly sentiment and redirecting the blame for economic distress towards the East India Company.[20]

The West Indians also had other motives for endorsing an anti-monopoly campaign in 1812. In the midst of the war with the United States, the West Indians petitioned for a wholesale ban on American cotton imports. Private letters confirm that the true goal of Liverpool West Indies merchants was to promote Caribbean cotton.[21]

Despite these varying hopes, neither the East nor West Indies successfully challenged US cotton production. After 1813, when parliament lifted most of the restrictions that had excluded non-Company merchants from trading with India, Liverpool traders discovered that sugar was a more profitable import than cotton. But the emergence of an alternative source for sugar threatened a West Indian staple. In 1821, Liverpool's West India Association petitioned for additional discriminatory duties on top of the already substantial protection that their sugar imports enjoyed.[22]

The recently founded Liverpool East India Association – composed of merchants newly able to trade with India – was reluctant to get dragged into this sugar controversy. It undermined the Association's efforts to abolish the East India Company's remaining privileges. At first, members consented only to defend the existing differential. But when parliament caved in to the West Indians' demands, the Association petitioned for across-the-board equalisation. Even though the interests of the Liverpool East India Association may have been temporarily aligned with those of the Company, it did not moderate its agitation against its chief foe. Behind the scenes, the Association tried to reorient the debate back to the monopoly question.[23] Liverpool West Indies merchants were also more willing to compromise on sugar duties than their London counterparts. One reason was the substantial overlap between the memberships of the Liverpool East and West India Associations – far more than in the metropolis where the two trades were more differentiated and entrenched, far more even than had been the case a decade earlier with Liverpool's West Indies and American merchants.[24]

Due to the very different agendas of London and Liverpool interests, equalisation remained a tricky issue for local anti-monopolists. When the anti-monopoly campaign was revived in 1828, Liverpool activists tried to avoid polarisation over equalisation. To ensure West Indian support, public meetings again emphasised Asia's potential as a source for cotton rather than sugar. Between 1828 and 1830, these efforts paid off. As in the 1790s and 1810s, this mobilisation was so broad-based that the Common Council underwrote it.[25]

Late in 1830, however, local East Indies merchants again faced a quandary. The Liverpool West India Association joined a national campaign for even more preferential duties in favour of Caribbean sugar. A petition from the East India Association's president urged moderation, but a renegade group of merchants sent a strident pro-equalisation memorial.[26] Temporarily, the East and West India Associations found common ground. They jointly attacked the privileges enjoyed by British sugar refineries.[27] By 1831, however, energetic activism by London interests precluded any possibility of avoiding local polarisation over sugar duties. The Liverpool anti-monopoly campaign suffered as a result.

Because policies tended to confer favours or powers on particular groups, parliamentary claim-making was typically a comparative enterprise. Petitioners had to make a case for why they should be privileged over others. In seeking to win parliament's favour, however, Liverpool overseas traders were not always as candid about their self-interests as the preceding discussion has been. Whether their petitions were designed to promote communities or interests, they touted the worthiness of their claims as measured on a scale of either public welfare or equity; or, if they were creative, in terms of both metrics.

The most effective lobbies were those that convincingly asserted their significance for the public welfare. Liverpool soap manufacturers were particularly imaginative in 1831. Reducing duties, they claimed, would promote the 'comfort and cleanliness of the people'.[28] Not all public welfare claims were trade-related. By continuing to impose the death penalty for forgery, one 1818 Liverpool public meeting proclaimed, 'our national character suffers in the estimation of other countries'.[29] Appeals to equity tended to be more defensive, often being employed when public welfare claims failed. Like the Liverpool retailers who mobilised in 1786 against an additional duty imposed on their shops, affected groups expressed their willingness to pay their 'fair share' but protested when what they claimed were excessive burdens impeded their ability to compete on an equal footing with others. As Rosemary Sweet shows in her chapter, equity claims could be reinforced by appeals to precedent – by reciting a long history of preferences on which an interest or community had traditionally depended.[30]

The existence of two metrics for evaluating claims made it difficult for any interest or community to maintain a consistent justification for their pursuits. When free trade, humanitarianism, and other new imperial ideologies came on stream, lobbyists did not abandon older forms of appeal; rather, these developments presented new opportunities and obstacles as Liverpool economic interests tried either to argue that their specialty contributed more to the public welfare than others did or, at the very least, that they should have the freedom to pursue their own enterprises without discrimination.

Within the Liverpool community during this period, laissez-faire remained a selectively deployed rhetoric, used to condemn benefits conferred upon rivals. Some of the same townsfolk who lobbied for 'unrestricted trade in corn and in every article constituting the Food of Man' supported ship-owners and Canadian timber importers in their defence of the Navigation Laws.[31] Even within specific interests, there was little consistency. Liverpool anti-abolitionism was not uniformly protectionist, for instance. In their attacks on the Royal Africa Company early in the eighteenth century, Liverpool slavers mounted one of the first assaults on an entrenched commercial interest. And when it became apparent that monetary compensation would not be forthcoming for abolition, Liverpool leaders employed what sounded like free-trade rhetoric when they demanded that they should be allowed to redirect their efforts into the East Indies trade, previously restricted to Londoners.

Even these arguments against the East India Company, however, embodied something less than pure free-trade principles. Liverpool merchants' real concern was their right, as provincial traders, to equitable treatment. At an anti-monopoly meeting in 1829, a leading merchant proclaimed:

> Though Liverpool has a leg tied up, she is now running a race with the metropolis; they are neck and neck, and let but that leg be untied . . . and we may venture to anticipate that the same enterprise which has carried Liverpool so far, will soon lead her beyond the port of London itself.[32]

Anti-monopoly advocacy also appealed to economic nationalism. Ending the monopoly would not significantly weaken the Company, it was argued. Liverpool and the other out-ports would merely squeeze out the US merchants who had sneaked in and exploited opportunities that the Company had not vigorously pursued. In essence, the campaign against the East India Company entailed the recasting of a traditional component of country patriotism. The Company's failure to pursue a sufficiently expansionist strategy overseas arguably showed that it was morally as well as economically corrupt. While abolitionists cast Liverpool slavers as villains, anti-monopolists evoked the equally hated image of the 'nabob' to discredit the Company.[33]

Nor was the struggle between the Liverpool West India and East India Associations over sugar duties a clear battle between mercantilists and free traders. The majority of both organisations embraced the moderate economic liberalisation policies of Canning and Huskisson, successively the town's MPs. Moreover, even as the West Indians pushed for increased protection against East Indies sugar, they also urged parliament to support negotiations with the United States for bilateral tariff reduction. The Liverpool East India Association was quick to point out that this was inconsistent from the perspective of political economy. But Liverpool East Indies merchants were not opposed to all tariffs – on the contrary, they favoured any policy that discriminated against foreign cotton.[34]

Humanitarian claims were equally tactical. In contrast to what some historians argue, Liverpool anti-abolitionists did not concede the humanitarian argument to their opponents.[35] Appealing to the public welfare, Liverpool traders argued that abolition would devastate imperial prosperity without effectively decreasing global slave-trading. Other states would eagerly fill the gap left by the British. This would only increase African suffering, for the English traded 'with a greater degree of humanity than by any other Nation and with as strict attention to the health and lives of the Natives of Africa as it is possible to pay'.[36]

Appealing to equity, Liverpool anti-abolitionists also insisted that their long-standing property rights were as sacred as the individual autonomy that was at the core of the abolitionists' humanitarian appeal. Equity was folded together with appeals to precedent. Merchants had entered the slave trade in the expectation that it would continue to enjoy legislative sanction. Regulation might be necessary, but it should be compensated, as any other government taking of property would be. Abolitionists also had to compete on both metrics. Equity was easily invoked. But they overcame parliamentary opposition only when they argued that prohibiting British ships from carrying slaves to colonies of belligerents was sound wartime policy.[37]

Liverpool anti-monopolists embraced humanitarianism just as eagerly as the anti-abolitionists had. They fomented agitation against the East India Company's charter restrictions that denied non-Anglican missionaries the right to preach on the sub-continent. In 1813, Liverpool supporters of the Baptist and the Church Missionary Societies petitioned along with 900 other groups nationwide. However, this religious activism was not wholly beneficial to the Liverpool-led provincial coalition. Most missionary associations thought the Company would be a more effective moral reformer than provincial merchants.[38]

Not all in Liverpool were prepared to debate about sugar duties on 'purely mercantile grounds'.[39] In 1823, a bold amendment to the East India Association's pro-equalisation memorial was proposed by James Cropper, the most prominent East Indian and US trader in Liverpool: 'That your petitioners are not blind to the distress of the West India Planters, but they contend that it is to the forced cultivation of Sugar by Slaves, that those distresses are mainly to be ascribed . . .' The amendment represented a new way of combining public welfare and equity claims. According to Cropper, slavery was not only immoral, it was also harmful to consumers and a drain upon public revenues.[40]

When the majority in the Liverpool East India Association rejected this amendment, Cropper searched for a more receptive audience. He organised a local anti-slavery society and helped revive the national movement. Much ink has been spilled over whether anti-slavery activists were motivated by economic self-interest. Surely Cropper was sincere in his claim that abolishing duties that protected West Indian colonial sugar would undermine slavery in the Caribbean. Yet the timing of his involvement was also deeply connected with the sugar trade. Cropper confided that it might not be bad if anti-slavery activists were defeated initially because this would force them to embrace the case for commercial equalisation more fervently. Moreover, he was not above speculative investments based on the premise that emancipation would affect cotton and sugar prices worldwide.[41]

Whatever Cropper's motivations, his success in reviving the anti-slavery movement created as many problems as opportunities for East Indies interests. Liverpool East India merchants may have been reluctant to embrace anti-slavery, but the East India Company had no such encumbered allegiances. It pushed hard to link the campaign against preferential sugar duties with emancipation. Meanwhile, the Liverpool West India Association eagerly invoked humanitarianism to tar its opponents. It derided East Indians for sensationalising 'the *imaginary* cruelties committed upon the negro labourers in the colonies' while ignoring the even more 'wretched' conditions endured by Indian workers.[42] West Indians did not deny that humanitarianism should be paramount in the Caribbean colonies; they only contested what qualified as a responsible balance among political stability, imperial welfare, and equity for slaves *and* planters. To undercut further the Anti-Slavery Society, they sponsored a gradual emancipation resolution in 1823. To be fair, this was not simply a delaying tactic. John Gladstone and other Liverpool West Indies activists professed an evangelical commitment to improve plantation conditions.[43]

Cropper's innovative attempt to infuse humanitarian values into the sugar controversy also caused trouble when he, Gladstone, and other Liverpool activists re-launched anti-monopoly agitation in the late 1820s. The East India Company insinuated that this renewed agitation was an anti-humanitarian conspiracy:

> We do not inquire whether any of the individuals composing the deputation in support of the slave trade now rank among the partizans . . . . We ask only that the Legislature and the people of England will not hastily conclude that all which is alleged by the Liverpool partizans is true: they may, in the present case, as in the former, be – MISTAKEN . . .[44]

To inoculate themselves against attacks from both the West Indian merchants and the Company, Liverpool East Indies stalwarts needed additional humanitarian arguments on their side. As in 1813, they piggybacked on the popularity of evangelisation in Asia. More forthrightly than the missionaries, Liverpool anti-monopolists blamed the Company for perpetuating Hindu idolatry. It derived revenue from the taxation of pilgrimages and had failed to eradicate either infanticide or the sati, the burning of widows on the pyres of their deceased husbands.[45] In 1830, more than half of the petitions against these 'barbaric' Hindu rituals came from Liverpool and nearby Lancashire towns.[46] Yet as hard as anti-monopoly activists worked to sustain a humanitarian gloss on their campaign, the potency of the movement against Hindu 'idolatry' was defused once the Company began to address what English people perceived as the most offensive of Indian customs. By mid-1830, the sati had been banned throughout British India.[47]

If the anti-sati campaign helped legitimate the anti-monopoly mobilisation, it was not wholly beneficial to the anti-slavery cause in Liverpool. For anti-sati petitions proved far more popular. In 1829–31, Liverpool submitted twenty anti-sati petitions compared to fifteen against slavery. Moreover, humanitarian interests engaged in comparative imperial analysis just as commercial associations did. One anti-sati activist claimed that India should be more of a priority than the Caribbean colonies: 'It is said that we have a long accumulating debt to pay off with regard to the natives of Africa, but that is nothing compared to the debt the Company owe to India . . .' Such arguments had the unfortunate by-product of bolstering the West Indians' position.[48]

The initial impetus for both the local anti-sati and the revived anti-slavery campaigns came from Liverpool's East India merchants, but activists found that the best way to organise on these issues was through the town's Dissenting congregations. Yet a purely commercial appeal was not well designed to rouse Dissenting support. Only one Dissenting petition explicitly linked government intervention to end the sati with the abolition of the East India Company's monopoly.[49]

The reason why Dissenters gravitated to the anti-sati and anti-slavery campaigns had to do with the politics of religious toleration. These movements allowed Dissenters to strengthen their own claim to equitable treatment. Besides arguing against the sati, congregations sought state intervention to ensure that non-Anglican missionaries throughout the empire enjoyed 'the same unrestricted Freedom and secure Protection, as far as British Law and Authority extend, as is happily enjoyed in this favoured Kingdom'.[50] The anti-slavery crusade likewise gained momentum because of concern over equitable treatment of missionaries. In Demerara in 1824 and in Jamaica in 1831, Dissenting missionaries were blamed for inciting slave uprisings. English sympathy for persecuted colonial missionaries outstripped enthusiasm for emancipation.

Dissenting involvement in the anti-sati and anti-slavery campaigns accelerated in Liverpool only after the religious toleration mobilisations of 1827–8. Strategically, these imperial campaigns sustained Dissenter mobilisation in the brief interlude after the abolition of the Test and Corporation Acts. Beginning in 1831, Dissenters re-focused on removing all remnants of Anglican preference and on sabbatarianism until the apprenticeship issue revived the anti-slavery movement in the late 1830s.[51]

The increase in the number of anti-slavery and anti-sati petitions had as much to do with mobilising tactics as it did with the intrinsic popularity of these issues. The earliest toleration petitions represented their signers as a coalition of different Dissenting sects, or more broadly as Liverpool inhabitants who supported religious freedom. However, opponents suspected that these petitions were orchestrated largely by particular congregations – and indeed, this was often the case.[52] Petitioning separately by congregation was the perfect way to articulate diverse religious support. Once again, parliamentary petitioning encouraged the segmentation of communities, only now the fault-lines were based on congregational affiliation rather than economic interest. If we chart the number of issues petitioned about each session rather than the number of petitions per session, the 1826–35 surge in the religious and labour categories becomes much less marked.

Even when considering congregational petitioners, it would be a mistake to see humanitarian rhetoric as marking the triumph of an ideal of universal equity. Increasingly, humanitarian arguments synthesised welfare and equity claims by distinguishing the particular concerns of those within the empire from those elsewhere. The ideal was 'to extend the blessings of the British Constitution to all its subjects, without distinction of colour, caste or degree', as one Liverpool anti-slavery petition insisted.[53] Women petitioners were crucial to re-imagining the boundary of imperial subjecthood. In the anti-sati campaign, for instance, the women of Cockspur Street Chapel petitioned separately from male congregants, legitimating their own civic activism as well-placed to focus attention on the suffering of Indian sisters.[54]

Ironically, enshrining petitioning as a right of all British imperial subjects actually constrained other forms of claim-making. For it was not a far stretch to conclude that petitioning was all that was necessary for grievances to be addressed, given the constitution's safeguards. Outside the British empire, subjects who rebelled against tyranny were lionised as freedom-fighters. Liverpool public meetings supported Greek struggles against the Ottoman Empire and urged the government to recognise the independence of South American nations. Liverpool activists saw more than commerce at stake in these cases: 'As citizens of a free state, whose ancestors fought and bled for the rights of Englishmen, we came forward to join our sympathies with nations who had themselves fought and bled in the same glorious cause.'[55]

Within the empire, however, rebellion was sedition. Opprobrium was heaped both upon the uprisings of Caribbean slaves and upon the vigilante methods used by West Indies colonists to restore order. At home as well as abroad, workers were expected to appeal to parliament to resolve their problems rather than resort to direct collective action. In 1827, Liverpool journeymen shipwrights went on strike. Appealing to equity, they complained that they had to shoulder the brunt of the general depression. Liverpool's merchants believed that this was the wrong approach. They lobbied parliament to re-instate high levels of protection on ship-building and urged artisans to support them. Meanwhile, the commercial associations joined ranks and decisively crushed the strike.[56]

Implicitly, merchants expected that artisans and others would defer to the decisions of those of higher status as to the best petitioning agenda to pursue. After the outpouring of artisan petitions against abolition in 1789, however, they could not always count on loyalty from skilled labourers. In 1813 and 1815, shipwrights were the one group in Liverpool that struck a cautionary note about opening trade with India. They petitioned for protection against competition from ships built in Asia. The largest petitioning campaign by artisans, the 1825 mobilisation in defence of the right to organise, clashed with local merchants who urged parliament to reinstate the Combination Laws.[57] The only non-commercial, non-religious group to support the anti-monopoly campaign was the First Co-operative Society. Since this mutual aid project deliberately rejected the deference that the commercial associations demanded, their petition was at once a boon and a challenge to Liverpool anti-monopolists.[58]

By the 1820s, the backing of congregations seemed more appealing than that of trades associations as a way of manifesting diversity of support. Merchants were congregational trustees and could manipulate support through contributions. But congregations also proved cantankerous. In 1827, Dissenters attempted to divert a pro-commercial reform meeting in Liverpool by insisting on presenting a petition advocating religious toleration. And in 1830, ministers condemned the Liverpool and Manchester Railroad for operating on Sundays.[59] Merchants once had clear control over the mechanisms for mobilising collective action, but by the late 1820s, commercial associations increasingly had to devote effort to maintaining control over the levers of civic power in order to represent themselves as enjoying broad-based support.

Nor was it only Liverpool elites who worried about controlling the tide of petitions. In the mid-1830s, a bipartisan effort streamlined parliamentary procedures. Petitions were sidelined to committees rather than being received on the floor. Petitioning continued to be trumpeted as the only legitimate tool for redress, but these procedural changes insured that Chartists, anti-Corn law agitators, and workers would be far less effective than they had been in previous campaigns. Thus, despite the Reform Act's pronouncements, parliament was more insulated from direct civic activism by the late 1830s than it had been previously. Moreover, a general trend toward rationalising policy-making discouraged the recognition of particularised identities. Interests and communities continued to seek assistance for economic development, but they had to figure out more creative approaches.[60]

Attempts to reconcile free trade and humanitarianism meanwhile demonstrated the continuing tension between equity and public welfare standards. Petitions for political reform, religious toleration, and commercial liberalisation all alleged that it was an insult to 'British character' not to provide equal rights to all subjects, but this rhetoric could also exonerate merchants who traded with areas outside the empire from any liability for the forms of production pursued there. Liverpool merchants who traded with the United States argued wildly that American slavery was less severe than in the British Caribbean, but ultimately they admitted that the primary difference was that they had less influence on US slave policy than West Indian merchants had in the colonies.[61] Liverpool Brazilian traders also extended the logic of commercial equity beyond the boundaries of the empire. The Brazil Association was the only local commercial body that ever petitioned against colonial slavery, although with less than pure motives. Its members salivated at the potential for non-colonial slave-grown sugar coming to market on the same terms that West Indians received.[62]

Within the empire, public welfare arguments impeded egalitarianism. The yearning to Christianise subjects played an important role in justifying increasing British authoritarianism in India. It helped confirm an asymmetry between coloniser and colonised which informed trading petitions regardless of which specialty they promoted. The Liverpool East India Association proposed nothing less than the reorientation of the entire logic of trade flows in Asia by dismantling a thriving Indian cotton industry and replacing it with sugar plantations:

> while we are thus interfering with the present applications of Native industry, it is due to our Indian subjects, and highly important to our Commercial Interests, that a new and profitable direction should be given to that portion of their labour which is thus displaced.[63]

Similarly, the British government consented to emancipation but required that freed Caribbean slaves endure a long period of apprenticeship to ensure that they would remain a reliable and subservient plantation workforce.

Unlike most studies of extra-parliamentary agitation, this chapter has analysed patterns of petitioning from a single place rather than focusing on a particular cause. Using Liverpool petitioning as a prism through which to inspect expressions of imperial identity emphasises the self-interest of agitators. This is not surprising since petitioning was conceived as a local and particularised activity. Andrew Porter has shown how wary nineteenth-century evangelicals were of linking commerce and Christianity. By contrast, Liverpool commercial interests saw new ideologies of humanitarianism and free trade as ways of broadening support by allowing them to frame their petitions as more than just parochial pleas.[64] Yet the problem with such strategic manipulations of language was that lobbyists operated in a world in which comparisons were always being drawn. In the stories they told about community and interests, petitioners struggled to identify consistent principles upon which the empire should work. Rivals however were often able to trap opponents by pointing out the logical implications of their rhetoric and tactics. Thus, competition for civic power within Liverpool, alongside struggles between provincial and metropolitan interests, encouraged the proliferation and expression of different strands of imperial identity. If there was a common denominator among the identities deployed by these shifting communities and interests, it was the insistence that the legitimacy of state action and the very essence of Britishness should be rooted in a commitment to equity and public welfare. Yet the tension between these two metrics ensured that parliamentary claim-making – and thus, identity construction – would always be contentious.

Notes

1 *Liverpool Times*, 19 Mar. 1833.
2 Inhabitants lobbied the House of Lords less frequently. When they did, they usually presented similarly worded petitions to both Houses at the same time, except when they sought to influence legislation that the two houses were considering on different schedules.
3 P. J. Marshall, 'Imperial Britain', *Journal of Imperial and Commonwealth History*, xxiii (1995), 379–94.
4 S. Drescher, *Capitalism and antislavery: British mobilization in comparative perspective* (1987). P. J. Cain and A. G. Hopkins, *British imperialism: innovation and expansion, 1688–1914* (1993). P. J. Marshall, 'The first British empire' and C. A. Bayly, 'The second British empire' in R. Winks (ed.), *Oxford history of the British empire, V: historiography* (Oxford, 1999), 43–72. C. Tilly, *Popular contention in Great Britain, 1758–1834* (Cambridge, MA, 1995).
5 J. Belchem and N. Hardy, 'Second metropolis: the middle class in early Victorian Liverpool' in A. Kidd and D. Nicholls (eds), *The making of the British middle class? Studies of regional and cultural diversity since the eighteenth century* (Stroud, 1998), 58–71.
6 Quantitative analysis is based on the indexes and journals of the House of Commons. I adapted the categorisation scheme in J. Hoppit (ed.), *Failed legislation, 1660–1800: extracted from the Commons and Lords Journals* (1997) with minor modifications so as better to incorporate nineteenth-century developments. First, I split his 'social issues' category in two. 'Health and community' petitions are lumped with his 'communications' category to create a more comprehensive portrait of 'civic improvement'. Petitions for and against the abolition of colonial slave labour – but not pro- and anti-slave

trade – are placed with the remainder of his 'social issues' to form my 'social issues and labour' grouping. For a detailed methodological discussion, see my 'Civic experiments: community building in Liverpool and Baltimore, 1785–1835 (University of Oxford D.Phil. thesis, forthcoming).

7 J. Brewer, *The sinews of power: war, money and the English state, 1688–1783* (1989). A. Olson, *Making the empire work: London and American interest groups, 1690–1790* (Cambridge, MA, 1992). P. O'Brien, 'Inseparable connections: trade, economy, fiscal state, and the expansion of empire, 1688–1815', in P. J. Marshall (ed.), *Oxford history of the British empire, II: eighteenth century* (Oxford, 1998), 53–77.

8 P. Langford, *Public life and the propertied Englishman, 1689–1798* (Oxford, 1991), 139–278. R. Sweet, *The English town, 1680–1840: government, society and culture* (Harlow, 1999); J. Innes, 'The local acts of a national parliament: parliament's role in sanctioning local action in eighteenth-century Britain', *Parliamentary History*, xvii (1998), 23–37.

9 *Mercury*, 29 May 1818. *CJ*, lxxiii, 392.

10 *CJ*, lxvi, 65, 186, 191, 195, 218, 224, 229, 316.

11 *Autobiographical memoirs* (Liverpool, 1893), 87.

12 P. Gauci, *The politics of trade: the overseas merchant in state and society, 1660–1720* (Oxford, 2001).

13 Liverpool Maritime Museum, D/LUA/1/1: Underwriters Association, Minutes, 1802–46. *CJ*, lxxx, 14, 130, 197, 215, 335, 346, 466; lxxxi, 14, 118, 122, 127, 164. Liverpool Record Office, 380 WES 1/2: West India Association, Minute Book, 1824–35; 380 AME 1: American Chamber of Commerce, Minutes, 1801–35. F. Neal, 'Liverpool shipping in the early nineteenth century', and D. M. Williams, 'Liverpool merchants and the cotton trade, 1820–1850' in J. R. Harris (ed.), *Liverpool and Merseyside* (1969), 147–211. F. E. Hyde, *Liverpool and the Mersey: an economic history of a port, 1700–1970* (Newton Abbot, 1971). S. Chapman, *Merchant enterprise in Britain: from the industrial revolution to World War I* (Cambridge, 1992).

14 *CJ*, xliii, 507, 515, 650–1; xliv, 380; xlv, 463; xlviii, 808; li, 504, 689; liii , 569, 596, 636; liv, 402, 419, 432; lix, 323; lx, 100; lxi, 211; lxii, 123–4.

15 D. Hall, *A brief history of the West India Committee* (Barbados, 1971). L. Penson, 'The London West India interest in the eighteenth century', *English Historical Review*, xxxvi (1921), 373–92. F. Sanderson, 'The Liverpool delegates and Sir William Dolben's bill', *Transactions of the Historic Society of Lancashire and Cheshire [THSLC]*, cxxiv (1972), 57–84. K. G. Davies, *The Royal African Company* (London, 1957).

16 *Mercury*, 3 Apr., 1 May, 26 June 1812; 24 Sept. 1813; 19 Mar. 1830; 4 Mar. 1831. *Liverpool Times*, 2 May, 9 June 1829; 5 Aug., 9 Nov. 1830. East India Association, *Statement . . . issued by the Liverpool Committee, as the Central Committee for the principal cities and towns of the kingdom* (Liverpool, 1828).

17 Liverpool University, Rathbone Papers, II/4/16, fos. 62–87: Broadsides and Newspaper Clippings, 1807–9. *CJ*, lxiii, 144, 149; lxvii, 320, 375. S. G. Checkland, 'American versus West Indian traders in Liverpool, 1793–1815', *Journal of Economic History*, xix (1958), 141–60; B. Tolley, 'The Liverpool campaign against the order in council and the war of 1812' in Harris (ed.), *Liverpool and Merseyside*, 98–146.

18 East India Association, *Report of a committee . . . appointed to take into consideration the restrictions on the East India trade* (Liverpool, 1822), 53. See also, West India Association, *The correspondence between John Gladstone, esq., MP and James Cropper, esq., on the present state of slavery in the British West Indies and in the United States of*

America; and on the importation of sugar from the British settlements in India . . . (Liverpool, 1824). E. Corrie, *Letters on the subject of the duties on coffee* (London, 1808). J. Cropper, *Present state of Ireland . . .* (Liverpool, 1825). S. Mintz, *Sweetness and power: the place of sugar in modern history* (New York, 1985).

19 East India Association, *Proceedings of the public meeting on the India and China trade . . .* (Liverpool, 1829), 25. British Library [BL] Add. MSS. 38746, fos. 76–95, 98–114: J. Gladstone and K. Finlay correspondence, 1822–23.

20 Liverpool University, Rathbone Papers, II/1/169 fos. 318–321: W. Rathbone to B. Tarleton, 6 Aug. 1807. Liverpool Record Office, 920 ROS (Roscoe Papers), no. 463, no. 484, no. 1752A, no. 1753, nos. 1778–82, no. 3060; *Mercury*, 20 Mar.–26 June 1812. K. Charlton, 'Liverpool and the East India trade', *Northern History*, vii (1972), 54–72. W. O. Henderson. 'The American Chamber of Commerce for the port of Liverpool, 1801–1908', *THSLC*, lxxxv (1935), 1–61.

21 *CJ*, lxviii, 407–8. BL, Add. MSS. 38746, fos. 115–126: Gladstone to Canning, 6 Jan. 1823.

22 T. Martin, 'Some international aspects of the anti-slavery movement, 1818–23', *Journal of Economic and Business History*, i (1928–29), 137–48. L. J. Ragatz, *The fall of the planter class in the British Caribbean, 1763–1833: a study in social and economic history* (New York, 1928), 333–64.

23 East India Association, *At a general meeting of the Association held 10 May 1822* (Liverpool, 1822) and *At a general meeting of the Association held 13 May 1822* (Liverpool, 1822). *CJ*, lxxvi, 312; lxxvii, 306; lxxviii, 331.

24 BL Add. MSS. 38744, fos. 149–50, 165–6, 172–4: Gladstone to Huskisson, 6, 11, 15 Mar., 1823; fos. 218–23: J. Hibberson- Huskisson correspondence, 17, 23 May 1823; fos. 157–60: Gladstone to C. Ellis, 18 Apr. 1812, 21 Feb. 1813; fos. 151–2: C. Ellis to Huskisson, 9 Mar. 1823. J. R. Ward, *British West Indian slavery, 1750–1834: the process of amelioration* (Oxford, 1988).

25 Liverpool Record Office, 352 MIN/COU I 2/8: East India Committee, Minutes, 1812–13, 1829–30, 1833. 328 PAR 3/81: J. Ewart to Huskisson, 23 Apr. 1828; 3/99: N. Robinson to Huskisson, 3 June 1829. East India Association, *Report . . . on the subject of the trade with India* (Liverpool, 1828). Weekly coverage can be followed in the *Liverpool Times, Billinge's Advertiser, Mercury,* and *Albion*, Feb. 1828–Mar. 1831.

26 *Liverpool Times*, 2 June 1829; 25 May, 22 June 1830. *Mercury*, 25 June 1830. *CJ*, lxxxv, 331, 501, 572.

27 *CJ*, lxxxvi, 758, 820.

28 *CJ*, lxxxvi, 372.

29 *Mercury*, 1 May 1818. *CJ*, lxxiii, 323.

30 *CJ*, xli, 156. See chapter 3 above.

31 The quotation is from *CJ*, lxxxix, 138. Other anti-corn law petitions include *CJ*: lxix, 327; lxx, 155; lxxv, 253, 402; lxxix, 404, 476; lxxx, 343; lxxxii, 292, 305. Petitions in defence of the Navigation laws include: *CJ*, lxxv, 269, 275; lxxxii, 208; lxxxvi, 395; xc, 381, 424. See also: S. Palmer, *Politics, shipping and the repeal of the Navigation Laws* (Manchester, 1990). B. Semmel, *The rise of free trade imperialism: classical political economy, the empire of free trade and imperialism, 1750–1850* (Cambridge, 1970).

32 East India Association, *Proceedings on India and China*. A. Webster, 'The political economy of trade liberalization: the East India Company Charter Act of 1813', *Economic History Review*, xliii (1990), 404–19.

33 K. Wilson, 'Empire of virtue: the imperial project and Hanoverian culture, *c.* 1720–1785' in L. Stone (ed.), *An imperial state at war: Britain from 1689 to 1815* (1994), 128–64.

34 *CJ*, lxxvii, 148. Liverpool East India Association, *At a General Meeting . . . 10 May 1822* (Liverpool, 1822). BL Add. MSS. 38758, fos. 72–5: W. Myers to Huskisson, 22 Dec. 1829. B. Hilton, *Corn, cash, commerce: the economic policies of the Tory government, 1815–1830* (Oxford, 1977).

35 Compare S. Drescher, 'The slaving capital of the world: Liverpool and national opinion in the age of abolition', *Slavery and Abolition*, ix (1988), 128–43.

36 *CJ*, xliii, 650.

37 *CJ*, xliii, 507. R. Anstey, *The Atlantic slave trade and British abolition, 1760–1810* (1975), 363–88.

38 *CJ*, lxviii, 430, 481, 513. E. Elbourne, 'The foundation of the Church Missionary Society: the Anglican missionary impulse' in J. Walsh, C. Haydon and S. Taylor (eds), *The Church of England, c. 1689–c. 1833: from toleration to Tractarianism* (Cambridge, 1993), 247–64. A. Porter, '"Commerce and christianity": the rise and fall of a nineteenth-century missionary slogan', *Historical Journal*, xxviii (1985), 527–621.

39 BL Add. MSS. 41267A, fos. 102–3: J. Cropper to Z. Macaulay, 2 May 1822.

40 *Hints suggested for consideration, in drawing up a petition to parliament on the subject of the East India trade* (Liverpool, 1822). The quotation comes from a manuscript draft attached to the University of London Archives copy.

41 *CJ*: lxxxi, 367; lxxxiii, 412; lxxxvi, 456; lxxxviii, 363. A. Cropper, *Extracts from letters of the late James Cropper . . .* (Liverpool, 1850), 21–2. Cropper, Benson and Co., *Circular on the cultivation of cotton* (Liverpool, 1822). V. Nolte, *Fifty years in both hemispheres* (1854), 288–320. D. B. Davis, 'James Cropper and the British anti-slavery movement, 1821–33', *Journal of Negro History*, xlv (1960), 241–58; xlvi (1961), 154–73. K. Charlton, 'James Cropper and Liverpool's contributions to the anti-slavery movement', *THSLC*, cxxiii (1971), 57–80.

42 *Billinge's*, 25 Nov. 1823.

43 Liverpool Record Office, 920 MD 140: J. Gladstone, Letterbook, 1823–26. S. G. Checkland, *The Gladstones: a family biography, 1764–1851* (Cambridge, 1971).

44 *Asiatic Journal*, Mar. 1829. See also July 1828; Feb., May, Oct. 1829.

45 W. Ward, 'Letter to the ladies of Liverpool, and of the United Kingdom', *Times*, 3 Jan. 1821. *CJ*, lxxxiii, 313, 5 May 1828. *Albion*, 31 Mar. 1828. L. Mani, *Contentious traditions: the debate on sati in colonial India* (Berkeley, 1998).

46 *Liverpool Times*, 24 Feb. 1829. *CJ*, lxxxv, 235, 242, 590.

47 C. Midgley, 'Female emancipation in an imperial frame: English women and the campaign against sati (widow burning) in India, 1813–30', *Women's History Review*, ix (2000), 95–122.

48 Liverpool East India Association, *Proceedings on India and China*, 42. *CJ*, lxxxv, 235, 242, 590; lxxxvi, 160, 167, 175, 444–5, 454–6.

49 *CJ*, lxxxv, 235: Murray Street (Methodist New Connexion) congregation petition.

50 *CJ*, lxxxv, 235: Cockspur Street (Baptist) congregation petition.

51 *CJ*, lxxxii, 472, 545, 548; lxxxiii, 95–6, 101; lxxxviii, 142, 284, 322, 393, 590; lxxxix, 21, 114, 137, 142, 145, 187, 287, 377, 539; xc, 200.

52 G. Ditchfield, 'The campaign in Lancashire for the repeal of the Test and Corporation Acts, 1787–1790', *THSLC*, cxxvi (1977), 109–38.

53 *CJ*, lxxxi, 367.
54 *CJ*, lxxxv, 235. See also *Billinge's*, 25 March 1829. *Liverpool Times*, 17, 24 Feb. 1829. C. Midgley, *Women against slavery: the British campaigns, 1780–1870* (1992).
55 *Times* (London), 7 June 1824. See also *Mercury*, 20 Feb.–12 Mar., 11 June 1824. *CJ*, lxxvii, 485.
56 *Billinge's*, 3 Apr.–17 July 1827. F. Neal, 'Bigots or patriots? The political and religious allegiances of the Liverpool ships' carpenters, 1815–1851' in L. Fischer (ed.) *From wheelhouse to counting house: essays in maritime history in honour of Professor Peter Davies* (St. Johns, 1992), 153–202.
57 *CJ*, lxviii, 249; lxx, 154; lxxx, 374.
58 *CJ*, lxxxv, 512. *Mercury*, 12 Mar.–17 Dec. 1830. R. B. Rose, 'John Finch, 1784–1857: a Liverpool disciple of Robert Owen' in H. Hikins (ed.), *Building the union: studies on the growth of the workers' movement: Merseyside, 1756–1967* (Liverpool, 1973), 31–52.
59 BL Add. MSS. 38749, fos. 175–6: Huskisson to T. Fletcher, Apr. 1827; fos. 244–9, 255–6, 260: Huskisson and W. Shepherd correspondence, 1–11 May 1827. *Mercury*, 12 Nov. 1830.
60 P. Fraser, 'Public petitioning and parliament before 1832', *History*, xlvi (1961), 195–211. B. Enright, 'Public petitions in the House of Commons', House of Lords Record Office typescript (1960). J. Prest, *Liberty and locality: parliament, permissive legislation and ratepayers' democracies in the nineteenth century* (Oxford, 1990).
61 *Albion*, 27 Aug. 1832; *Mercury*, 24 Aug. 1832.
62 Brazilian Association, *Some remarks and explanatory observations on a petition to parliament . . .* (Liverpool, 1833). *CJ*, lxxxviii, 610. H. Temperley, *British anti-slavery, 1833–70* (1972).
63 East India Association, *At a general meeting . . . 10 May 1822.* C. A. Bayly, *Imperial meridian: the British empire and the world, 1780–1830* (1989), 188.
64 Porter, '"Commerce and christianity"'.

11

Colonial representation at Westminster,
c. 1800–65

Miles Taylor

On 5 November 1800 George III issued a proclamation which did away with the parliament of the Kingdom of Great Britain.[1] In doing so, he not only succeeded where Guy Fawkes had failed on the same day 195 years earlier, but he also paved the way for the opening of the new 'imperial parliament' of Great Britain and Ireland, which duly opened its doors for its first session at the beginning of February 1801. The British was to remain an imperial parliament – legislating for and reflecting the interests of not only Ireland, but its far-flung dominions and settlements worldwide as well – in practice until the onset of colonial constitutional devolution in the 1850s and 1860s, and in name until the Statute of Westminster of 1931, when parliament became known more modestly as the parliament of the United Kingdom.[2] And yet the British parliament was never 'imperial' in any real representative sense. If anything, Westminster became more English and less imperial as the nineteenth century progressed. The Act of Union of 1801 did away with an Irish parliament in Dublin and imposed instead Protestant representation on a largely Catholic population. Even when that was remedied by Catholic Emancipation in 1829, the new Irish franchise discriminated heavily against rural Catholic voters.[3] Scotland fared only slightly better. The first two reform acts (of 1832 and 1867) greatly expanded the Scottish electorate, but at the same time barely increased the number of Scottish MPs.[4] A similar imbalance is detectable in the House of Lords. Although there was a considerable Scottish and Anglo-Irish peerage creation in the later Hanoverian years, by 1885 only 12 per cent of the upper house was comprised of Scottish or Irish peers.[5] But nowhere was this process of Anglicisation clearer than with respect to the colonies and dependencies. In 1820 approximately one-fifth of the House of Commons was made up of MPs in the West India or East Indies interest.[6] The 1832 Reform Act cut a swathe through that bloc. The disfranchisement of 152 small seats effectively closed off the route into parliament for men lacking English territorial connections. Within thirty years of its formation, the imperial parliament had become a resolutely English affair. This chapter is concerned with this paradox and its consequences – that is, by what means an expanding overseas empire was represented at home by an English parliament.

George III equivocated over his new imperial title. On New Year's Day, 1801, royal instructions were despatched to the principal cities of the empire, detailing the new style and mode of address to be used in all future communications with the imperial king. The title of 'Emperor of Britain and Hanover' was rejected, and 'King of Britain and Ireland' was opted for instead.[7] Parliament, however, was considerably more enamoured of its new imperial moniker. When the Palace of Westminster was redesigned, rebuilt and refurbished in the 1840s – based on the designs of Barry and Pugin – imperial iconography loomed large in the scenes and portraits chosen to line the walls and panelling of the new rooms and corridors. In a refit which, for the most part, deliberately emphasised the Anglo-Saxon and medieval traditions of parliament at the expense of anything after 1649, space was made for modern paintings commemorating Robert Clive at Plassey, the death of General Wolfe, the abolition of 'suttee' and of colonial slavery, and the colonisation of Australia.[8] Historians have been rather less impressed by such imperial pretensions. A series of historiographical traditions have combined to marginalise interest in the relationship between the history of metropolitan parliamentary institutions and overseas dominion in the nineteenth century. The first of these traditions is the benign interpretation of the evolution of the British Commonwealth, in which Parliament is seen to have given up its authority over settlement colonies as they moved towards self-government and sovereignty over all local legislation, and in which parliament appears to have conceded its authority over crown colonies to careful management by the Privy Council, the Colonial Office and the colonial governors.[9] The second tradition comes from the nationalist historiography of many of the former constituent countries of the British empire – a historiography which has tended to see the establishment of local legislative control as marking the foundation-moment of a separate national history, in which the imperial parliament played no major part, either as a sovereign authority to be obeyed or as a model to be copied.[10] Finally, and perhaps inevitably, post-colonial histories of the British empire have adopted a rather monolithic notion of imperial power, in which it has become difficult to see how the dynamics of the metropolitan parliament are to be distinguished from all the other practices of the imperial state.[11]

Yet looked at in its own terms, and without slipping into the grooves of these various historiographies, the scope and functions of the imperial parliament in the first two-thirds of the nineteenth century were as impressive as the historical tableaux in the new Palace of Westminster suggested. Contemporary constitutional commentators had no doubt as to the supreme authority that parliament enjoyed over all its colonial, dependent and conquered territories. Although it was recognised that the King and parliament had renounced their right to impose colonial taxation by the Declaratory Act of 1778, this only applied to North America and the West Indies, and if it was adhered to thereafter in the rest of the empire it was only because of a judicious reticence on the part of Britain, rather than any statute.[12] Mid-nineteenth-century constitutional writers also poured cold water on the idea that emigrating Britons took their freedoms with them, thereby enjoying in their new settlements, the same protection afforded by parliament to Britons at home. George Cornewall Lewis and Alpheus Todd, amongst others, pointed that out that English case law, as long ago as the 1780s, had settled that Englishmen only enjoyed those rights which existed at the time of their departure, and were they to settle in conquered territories, such as parts of the formerly French, Spanish and Dutch Caribbean, or the Cape, then they were subject to local laws, until if and when the British parliament chose to amend them.[13] The same writers also asserted the sovereignty of parliament over the actions of Governors in the Crown Colonies, arguing that although the Governor represented the Queen-in-Council, he was responsible for his actions to parliament, just as the Colonial Office was subject to parliamentary scrutiny as well.[14] Nor did the Privy Council displace the appellant functions of parliament. Indeed, it was argued after the Privy Council Act of 1833, that colonial appeals to the Privy Council became dominated by individual complainants remonstrating against colonial courts' decisions, and no longer became a process whereby colonial subjects might lobby the crown as corporate interests.[15] Chartered companies were also subject to parliamentary scrutiny and control. In 1833, the rule of the East India Company came under greater not less parliamentary accountability with the renewal of the Company's Charter, and the assumption by the crown of India's territorial revenues.[16] And all Victorian commentators on the constitution agreed that the granting of local legislative control to the settlement colonies in the 1850s actually meant an increased role for the imperial parliament in ensuring that individual colonial acts were compatible with empire-wide legislation, particularly in regard to trade, shipping and tariffs. Until the Colonial Laws Validity Act of 1865 there was considerable uncertainty over the doctrine of 'repugnancy' – that is, how much autonomy colonial legislatures had over their own statute, with legal opinion erring on the side of imperial prerogative and colonial subordination.[17] In other words, just as at home in Britain the 1830–60 period was celebrated as an era of 'parliamentary government', in which the Commons and the Lords monitored and controlled the executive at home, so too was it in the British empire.[18] Settler colonies may have been given more local 'municipal' control over their affairs, but parliament always retained the legislative upper-hand. As the Jamaican and Canadian legislatures were to find in the 1830s, the West Indian sugar economies and the Canadian fishery and timber interests in the 1840s and 1850s the imperial parliament had no aversion to stepping in to impose uniformity and compliance when necessary. Thomas Erskine May summed it up, in an early work in 1841. '[T]he authority of parliament', he wrote, 'extends over the United Kingdom and all its colonies and foreign possessions. There are no other limits to its power of making laws for the whole empire.' Similarly, Walter Bagehot described the members of the House of Commons as '[t]hese are the persons who rule the British empire, – who rule

England, – who rule Scotland, – who rule Ireland, – who rule a great deal of Asia, – who rule a great deal of Polynesia, – who rule a great deal of America, and scattered fragments everywhere'.[19] This was to change after 1860. A pattern emerged whereby across the empire greater colonial legal codification together with legislative devolution produced more of a light touch to the relationship between metropole and colony.[20]

That said the volume of imperial legislation passing through parliament was hardly burdensome. Until 1865 the Colonial Office reviewed all the separate legislation initiated in the individual colonies and turned over for Privy Council approval any colonial statute which appeared to be in conflict with imperial laws. Parliament remained responsible for all imperial legislation which did not specifically name an individual colony in its remit. It was calculated in 1871 that one-quarter of all public acts dealt with 'imperial statute', either directly, or indirectly – that is, where there were technical imperial implications in a bill which had to be considered,[21] but that was to define 'imperial' very elastically, stretching the term to include Wales, Scotland and Ireland as well as the overseas empire. As far as the empire beyond the British Isles was concerned the ratio of imperial to United Kingdom statute only ever reached 1:6 in the 1890s, as the Table 11.1 indicates.

But even as a steady drip, as opposed to a flood, imperial legislation could be complex. By the 1870s and 1880s, one of the overwhelming arguments for greater imperial federation was that a separate 'imperial' senate was required (alongside devolved chambers for Scotland and Ireland), not simply to keep up the appearance of a strong empire, but more practically, to off-load imperial business from Westminster.[22] Clearly, parliament was thought of as an imperial assembly, even if representation of the empire was at best indirect. In 1776 the American

Table 11.1 Imperial statutes, 1801–1900

	Of general application	Of special application	Total imperial	All statutes
1801–10	4	3	7	1,322
1811–20	6	8	14	1,487
1821–30	10	17	27	1,013
1831–40	26	8	34	1,011
1841–50	23	17	40	1,129
1851–60	38	51	89	1,123
1861–70	49	41	90	1,248
1871–80	48	55	103	853
1881–90	59	37	96	725
1891–1900	66	34	100	629

Sources: Compiled from F. T. Piggott, *The imperial statutes applicable to the colonies*, 2 vols (1902); *Chronological table of and index to the statutes* (1870–1947).

colonies may have severed formal constitutional links with the metropole, but elsewhere in the empire it remained business as usual for much of the following century. Such was the jumbled collection of dependencies and different and often ambiguous forms of jurisdiction and justice that comprised the second British empire, it is not surprising that Westminster remained a focal point for the representation of interests and for conflict resolution in the colonies, as it had been for much of the eighteenth century.[23] How was this achieved?

Before 1832 the British colonies and dependencies enjoyed, if that is the right word, a system of virtual representation, whereby MPs at Westminster with commercial or proprietorial interests overseas could be relied on to advocate or defend the needs of colonists, subjects and to a lesser extent native peoples. Small parliamentary boroughs in England allowed men lacking local connections to enter parliament and tend to the commercial and corporate needs of far-flung dependencies. 'Virtual' representation has been expertly explored in the case of English constituencies, but, if anything it was a function of the Commons that was even more appropriate to the overseas empire.[24] The best documented examples of this 'virtual representation' of empire were lobby groups such as the West India Committee, and those East India Company directors and proprietors who had seats in parliament. These were well-tuned and efficient organisations who primed and prepared sympathetic MPs on the eve of important parliamentary divisions, such as the renewal of the East India Company Charter (in 1813 and again in 1833), and the debates on ending slavery in the British empire in 1832–33. In 1813 the East India interest secured an extension of the Company's Charter and enjoyment of the monopoly of the China trade, seeing off both the rival attempts of Birmingham free-traders to open up Asian commerce, and the protests of evangelical MPs led by William Wilberforce. And in 1833 last-minute West India Committee pressure secured a massive compensatory grant to Caribbean slave-owners.[25] But this was ultimately an imperfect system of advocacy. Colonial MPs were often simply spokesmen for British merchants and fund-holders whose business lay overseas, rather than representatives who hailed from the colony itself. Moreover, colonial MPs often turned the Commons into something of a vipers' nest, especially over issues such as duties on imperial goods, with West India MPs dividing against East Indies MPs who sought sugar cultivation in the 'free-labour' conditions of British India. And 'newer' colonies, such as the Caribbean islands annexed from France in 1815 – whose interests were not the same as those of Jamaica – or Lower Canada, were less impressed with the haphazard system of representation that the old plantation colonies and India merchants. Rejecting the idea of separate colonial representation in 1831, the *Quebec Gazette* declared that 'Lower Canada has never condescended to buy a seat in the House of Commons.'[26]

Besides the great colonial commercial groups within the House of Commons, there were other MPs who took it upon themselves to look after overseas interests in a more routine and less spectacular way before 1832. For example,

Sir Francis Burdett, MP for Westminster, proved a diligent advocate of Irish Catholic interests in the years leading up to 1829, as did Henry Parnell. Sir James Mackintosh, MP for Knaresborough and Professor at the East India Company College at Haileybury, usually presented the petitions reaching the Commons from Bengal and Madras, both from British settlers there, and from native Hindus.[27] Perhaps the busiest colonial representative of all in the 1820s was the radical, Joseph Hume, MP for Aberdeen, of whom the Secretary of State for the colonies jibed in 1826, that he was the MP for New South Wales and the Cape.[28] In fact, Hume, like Mackintosh, was more of a virtual representative of India, and became a one-man clearing house for petitions, claims, and protests emanating from disgruntled East India Company servants and army officers, as well as Calcutta-based Hindu reform groups such as those led by Rammohun Roy.[29] Colonial petitioners made full use of the availability of such MPs to air their grievances. One of the largest petitions (i.e. containing the most signatures) ever presented to the pre-1832 House of Commons, came in May, 1828, where Mackintosh brought up a petition signed by 87,000 Canadians calling for representative institutions.[30] Repeal of the Test and Corporation Acts in Britain the following year stimulated petitions for the lifting of civil disabilities elsewhere in the empire: – for example, the 'free coloureds' in the West Indies, the Roman Catholics of Grenada, the ex-convicts of New South Wales and the Hindu and mixed-race residents of Calcutta – all these groups petitioned parliament in 1828–30. In other words, indirect representation of the empire, albeit imperfect, was an established mode of politics in the 'unreformed' House of Commons, conducted by radicals, Whigs and Tories alike.

By disfranchising so many small boroughs the 1832 Reform Act undermined this system of indirect colonial representation, and the concern over the fate of the empire within the new electoral map of Britain and Ireland became a central part of the Ultra-Tory case against the Whig measure.[31] In many ways, parliamentary reform completed the process of emasculation of colonial MPs already begun by the collapsing prosperity of the old empire in India and the Caribbean. The numbers of East India and West Indies MPs plummeted: from a combined total of ninety-eight after the 1830 election to sixty-four after 1832, with the bulk of the decrease affecting the West Indies interest. However, for the next thirty years or so the call for colonial representation was made frequently, attempting effectively to undo what the 1832 reform act had done. Most proposals followed Joseph Hume's amendment to the reform bill, made in August 1831, and sought to provide for a limited number of additional colonial MPs, but the supporting cases made differed. Some wanted selfishly to use colonial representation as a means of distributing the tax burden more equally between metropole and colony.[32] Others wanted to use colonial representatives to demarcate the interests of minority white settlers from native majorities,[33] although in 1861 E. B. Eastwick suggested in a paper delivered to the National Association for the Promotion of Social Science that the three Presidential cities of India should send two MPs each, elected by a constituency in each city of 12,000 Indians and 8,000

Europeans.[34] Intriguingly, when Lord John Russell returned to considering a moderate programme of parliamentary reform in 1848, colonial seats were part of his deliberations, and other leading politicians at mid-century as well as several mainstream reviews gave the idea some support.[35] However, the bulk of mid-Victorian writers had little time for colonial representation. Most followed John Stuart Mill in arguing that the system would be rendered unworkable by the problems of distance, whilst Herman Merivale pointed out that colonial representation would relocate sovereignty away from colonial legislatures and back to Westminster, which was perhaps the last thing that overseas settlers wanted: '[i]f the union is to be complete, provincial legislatures must be abolished. There can be no more a separate parliament for Canada than a separate parliament for Yorkshire.' George Cornewall Lewis neatly disposed of the classic argument for colonial representation put forward by Adam Smith, but recognised that 'it seems desirable that a dependency should have a representative agent in the dominant country to watch over the interests of his constituents, and serve as an organ or communication between them'.[36] By the 1870s the refrain was wholly different. The imperial federation movement wanted a separate imperial chamber, rather than simply the inclusion of colonial representatives in the existing House of Commons.[37] And by the 1880s the theme of colonial representation had become centred on the Lords, with reformers of the Upper House such as Rosebery and Curzon suggesting that amongst a recomposed working peerage should be included nominees from the colonies (but not India).[38] Such proposals as these from the 1870s and 1880s are usually viewed by historians as signs of the flowering of imperial sentiment in late Victorian Britain, but it perhaps makes more sense to see them as an indication of the vacuum left by the erosion of indirect representation of colonial interests.

What happened in practice to colonial representation after the 1832 Reform Act? The Whigs responded to the outcry against the disfranchisement of 'virtual' colonial constituencies by placing the whole business of colonial agency on a new footing. In 1833 a new system of joint colonial agency was established, whereby two Colonial Office clerks were given official responsibility for looking after the interests of most of the crown colonies.[39] But this was only a partial solution to the problem. Colonial agents had never been the same thing as colonial representatives. Colonial agents had traditionally been charged with negotiating loans and procuring salaries and supplies on behalf of the Governors of each crown colony. They were financial agents, but not advocates or representatives in any proper sense of the term. Moreover, before 1833, if they were MPs, as in the case of William Huskisson, the agent for Ceylon, this was coincidence rather than contrivance, and proved controversial as colonial agency was said to be an office of profit from the crown, and therefore incompatible with the independence of MPs.[40] After 1833, the new joint crown agents were never MPs, and although some of the Caribbean colonies retained as their own crown agents men who were still in the Commons, they were a depleted force.

Colonial agency in parliament did however continue, although on a more sporadic and less organised footing. A few examples will suffice. John Crawfurd, MP for Kilmarnock, acted, on occasion, as the advocate of the merchants of Calcutta. George Thompson, MP for Tower Hamlets in the late 1840s served as the agent of the Rajah of Sattara – the deposed Indian prince. Ross Mangles, MP for Guildford looked after the interests of the New Zealand Company in the 1840s.[41] Virtually all these of men were paid a retainer for their services, and all were instrumental in presenting petitions, stirring up support in the division lobbies, working behind the scenes with ministers and even drafting legislation on behalf of their colonial constituents. The two best documented examples of colonial representation in the post-reform act period came from the colonies of New South Wales and Lower Canada. Both, in their own way, point to the difficulties which arose for any MP advocating the views and desires of a vested interest in the atmosphere of the reformed Commons after 1832. Between 1834 and 1838 two MPs – Edward Lytton Bulwer and Charles Buller – acted as parliamentary agents for New South Wales, or rather for the self-styled Australian Patriotic Association. Lytton Bulwer did it for free, although the expenses of a secretary and an office seem to have been covered by the Association. Buller, on the other hand, demanded a salary of £500. The relationship between the two English MPs and their Australian 'constituents' brings out neatly the inherent problems in colonial representation after 1832. Neither man had a vested financial or family interest in New South Wales, and they struggled to know how best to do the job. Lytton Bulwer said in 1837 that his 'own notion of a person managing Colonial interests, is – that he should be the conciliator between two parties – by rendering proper explanations to each', and he spoke disparagingly of J. A. Roebuck's far more aggressive stance on behalf of Lower Canada. Lytton Bulwer did not believe that the colonial representative could simply be an advocate: effectively, he had to be a professional lobbyist. As he explained in 1835: 'They [the Association] confound the duties of a parliamentary agent with those of a member of parliament, although their duties are as distinct as the offices of attorney and judge.'[42] Buller, on the other hand, saw his role as beyond that of a mere intermediary, and, much to the Association's displeasure in the late 1830s and early 1840s, spent a great deal of time putting his own plans for Australian jury reform, representative government, control of crown lands and transportation, before the Commons, irrespective of the often quite contrary requests he was receiving from Sydney.[43]

Fellow radical MP, John Arthur Roebuck, had a similar relationship to Buller with his colonial constituency of Lower Canada, although 'old Tear'em' proved a far more pugilistic advocate than either Buller or Lytton Bulwer. In 1835 Roebuck was appointed agent of the Assembly of Lower Canada on a salary of £500 per annum, and began to take instructions from its Speaker, Louis Papineau, with a view to pressing the claims of the colony at Westminster.[44] Like Buller, Roebuck found himself in a quandary. He objected to being merely 'the organ of official communications' and insisted on using his discretion to represent their 'feelings and sentiments'. Privately, however, he confessed to not being 'a voluntary agent', but being bound to serve his 'clients' whether they were right or wrong.[45] The Colonial Office shut the door in his face, with Lord Glenelg refusing to meet with him, and a year into his tenure, Roebuck was made the subject of a debate in the Commons on the propriety of paid agency. It was objected that he not only drew a salary from the colony, but that he was 'identified . . . with a particular party in Canada, and could not take a general view of the whole interests of the country'. Roebuck explained that he was the agent for the Assembly, just as Henry Labouchere was the agent for the Legislative Council of Lower Canada, and if the House of Commons did away with such forms of agency, 'it would sweep from the House half of its Members'. Roebuck compared his role to that of East India and Bank of England directors, and cited the precedents of agents such as Huskisson. But the sense of parliament had clearly changed, with Tory MPs such as John Hanmer leading the charge against the idea of paid colonial agency.[46] It was one thing for MPs to have a casual or fortuitous harmony of interest with a colony, but it was unacceptable for there to be a contractual relationship. A similar verdict was returned by the Colonial Office on the activities of Francis Scott, the MP for Roxburghshire who also doubled up as paid agent for the Legislative Council of New South Wales between 1842 and 1848, but found himself rebuffed by successive Secretaries of State.[47]

After the failed experiments of the mid-1830s direct representation of colonial interests died away, and, as with domestic forms of pressure from without, professional lobby groups, deputations to the Colonial Office, and the newspaper press became the main means of representing and advocating imperial interests. Periodicals such as *Simmonds' Colonial Magazine*, *Alexander's East India Magazine* and the *Colonial Gazette* took over the role of opinion-forming which one-off monitoring publications such as Roebuck's *Canadian Portfolio* had attempted a few years earlier. Extra-parliamentary organisations emerged. In 1851 the Cape parliament instructed a team of its politicians to travel to London to air the grievances of the colony over defence costs and the composition of the new electoral franchise.[48] In 1852 the Bombay Association employed an agent in London to lobby MPs and peers with a view to bringing petitions relating to the renewal of the East India Company's Charter.[49] In 1857 the Australian Colonies Association assembled in London to press the Colonial Office for further constitutional devolution.[50] In all these cases the British government proved more amenable to dealing with voluntary pressure groups, than with paid parliamentary agents, whose status had not only undermined the authority of the crown in the shape of the Governor in the colony, but also was at variance with the wider ideals of parliamentary representation in Britain in the age of reform.

One significant new feature of colonial representation in the decades after 1832 was the increasingly prominent role played by the House of Lords. It is a topic worthy of further research and can only be touched upon here. But a preliminary survey of the journals of the Commons and the Lords reveals that

Table 11.2   Colonial petitions to parliament, 1821–50

	Lords	Commons	Total
1821–30	16	94	110
1831–40	166	59	225
1841–50	112	65	177

Sources: *CJ*, xliii–liv, 1821–32, *LJ*, liii–lxxxii, 1821–50; *General index to the reports of public petitions* (PP 1854–55, LIV).

the upper house had become the chosen destination of colonial petitioners of parliament by mid-century.

Three of the most intense petitioning campaigns involving the Lords were the controversy over the Clergy Reserves in Upper Canada in the early 1840s, the opposition to the renewal of the East India Company Charter in 1853, and the reaction to the Indian 'mutiny' of 1857. It is not entirely clear why the Lords became targeted by colonial petitioners in these instances. These were campaigns undertaken by largely religious bodies – Anglicans and non-Conformists in the case of the Clergy Reserves, missionary groups in the case of India – and the Lords, with its Episcopal members and ecclesiastical responsibilities, was seen as an obvious forum for appeal.[51] But the explanation may also lie with the fact that the House of Commons was now deemed to be a predominantly insular chamber: penny-pinching, anti-imperial and lacking MPs with colonial expertise.

Colonial representation was thus more than just an incidental footnote to the history of parliamentary reform in the nineteenth century. In the half century or so which spanned the opening of the imperial parliament of Great Britain and Ireland and the wave of colonial constitutional devolution of the 1850s and 1860s, Westminster remained an important presence in the political landscape of both white settlement colonies overseas and the empire of conquest. Imperial-wide legislation remained a part of the parliamentary agenda, and the Commons was also seen as a forum for expressing dissatisfaction with colonial authority, be it rival settler communities, chartered companies, or crown authority itself. In a remote empire of multiple and often confused forms of sovereignty, parliament was an obvious means of redress. Hence, the desire for colonial representation remained alive and well throughout the period. But increasingly after 1832 colonial representation raised more questions than it answered. Burke's famous declaration that MPs were not agents, and that parliament was not a congress of ambassadors or delegates advocating conflicting interests, but rather a deliberative inquest on the affairs of the whole nation – his classic definition of the role of MPs – sat awkwardly with the task of articulating and pursuing the claims of far-flung subjects. Burke, after all, *had* been an agent (for New York) as well as being MP for Bristol.[52] Before 1832, when MPs with proprietorial interests overseas could find a way into parliament through the backdoor of the small boroughs, a system of colonial representation worked, although not very systematically. After 1832, virtual representation, though it survived in many different ways, became associated in the colonial context with nabobs and planters, the very demons of 'old Corruption'. Ironically, it was left to the most vehement critics of 'old Corruption' – men such as Buller and Roebuck – to discover for themselves just how unfashionable colonial MPs had become. And, equally ironically, the much-maligned House of Lords found a new role in the age of reform as the imperial chamber of choice.

Notes

1 *Times*, 8 Nov. 1800, 8.
2 For a recent overview, see P. Burroughs, 'Imperial institutions and the government of empire' in A. Porter (ed.), *The Oxford history of the British empire, III: The nineteenth century* (Oxford, 1999), 170–97. For specific changes in nomenclature and sovereignty, see D. Swinfen, 'The genesis of the Colonial Laws Validity Act', *Juridical Review*, xii (1967), 29–61; A. B. Keith, *The constitutional law of the British dominions* (1933), ch. 2.
3 P. J. Jupp, 'Irish MPs at Westminster in the early nineteenth century', *Historical Studies*, vii (1969), 65–80; K. T. Hoppen, *Elections, politics and society in Ireland, 1832–1914* (Oxford, 1984), 1–11.
4 M. Dyer, '"Mere detail and machinery": the Great Reform Act and the effects of redistribution on Scottish representation, 1832–68', *Scottish Historical Review*, lxii (1983), 17–34; I. G. C. Hutchison, *A political history of Scotland, 1832–1924: parties, elections and issues* (Edinburgh, 1986), 1–2.
5 M. W. McCahill, 'Peerage creations and the changing character of the British nobility, 1750–1850', *English Historical Review*, xcvi (1981), 259–84; A. Adonis, *Making aristocracy work: the peerage and the political system, 1884–1914* (Oxford, 1993), 18.
6 G. P. Judd, *Members of parliament, 1734–1832* (New Haven, Ct., 1955), 63–9, 92–4; C. H. Philips, *The East India Company, 1784–1834* (Manchester, 1940), 307–35; B. W. Higman, 'The West India interest in parliament', *Historical Studies (Australia and New Zealand)*, xiii (1967), 1–19.
7 *A proclamation, declaring His Majesty's pleasure concerning the royal stile and titles, appertaining to the imperial crown of the United Kingdom of Great Britain and Ireland, and its dependencies, etc* (1801); Duke of Portland to the King, 31 Oct. 1800, Archbishop of Canterbury to the King, 26 Dec. 1800 in *The later correspondence of George III*, ed. A. Aspinall, 5 vols (Cambridge, 1967), iii, 435n, 458.
8 T. S. R. Boase, 'The decoration of the new Palace of Westminster, 1841–63', *Journal of the Warburg and Courtauld Institute*, xvii (1954), 319–58. On the fusion of Gothic style and monarchical symbolism in the new Palace, see R. Quinault, 'Westminster and the Victorian constitution', *Transactions of the Royal Historical Society*, 6th series, ii (1992), 79–104.
9 W. P. Morrell, *British colonial policy in the age of Peel and Russell* (1930); P. Knaplund, *Sir James Stephen and the British colonial system* (1953); D. M. Young, *The Colonial Office in the early nineteenth century* (1961); J. M. Ward, *Colonial self-government: the British experience, 1759–1856* (1976).

10 This is particularly well-documented in the case of Australia: F. Farrell, *Themes in Australian history: questions, issues and interpretations in an evolving historiography* (Kensington, NSW, 1990), ch. 4; L. Trainor, *British imperialism and Australian Nationalism: manipulation, conflict and compromise in the late nineteenth century* (Cambridge, 1994), 166–71; S. McIntyre, 'Australia and the empire', in R. Winks (ed.), *The Oxford history of the British empire, V: historiography* (Oxford, 1999), 166–72 and also in the same volume D. R. Owram, 'Canada and the empire', 149–51.

11 A fairly typical notion of colonial governmentality – the 'logic of rule' – as hegemonic, is expressed by C. Hall in her 'Introduction' to Hall (ed.), *Cultures of empire: colonisers in Britain and the empire in the nineteenth and twentieth centuries* (Manchester, 2000), 7.

12 F. Madden (with D. Fieldhouse) (eds), *Imperial reconstruction, 1763–1840: the evolution of alternative systems of colonial government. Select documents on the constitutional history of the British empire and commonwealth*, 3 vols (1992), iii, 18; C. Clark, *A summary of colonial law, the practice of plantations, and of the laws and their administration in all the colonies* (1834), 10–16.

13 G. C. Lewis, *Essay on the government of dependencies* [1841] (2nd edn, 1891), 187–201; A. Todd, *Parliamentary government in the British colonies* [1880] (2nd edn, 1894), ch. 7; compare W. Burge, *Commentaries on colonial and foreign laws generally and in their conflict with each other and with the law of England*, 4 vols (1838).

14 Lewis, *Government of dependencies*, 155–8; Todd, *Parliamentary government*, ch. 4.

15 S. Bannister, *On the right to be heard, on petitions to the crown; and the control of the Privy Council (by appeal) over Indian, colonial and home affairs, etc* (1844), 8–9. On the Privy Council, see: P. A. Howell, *The judicial committee of the Privy Council, 1833–76* (1979); D. Swinfen, *Imperial appeal: the debate on the appeal to the Privy Council* (1987).

16 C. Ilbert, *The government of India: a brief historical survey of parliamentary legislation relating to India* (Oxford, 1922), 85–6.

17 Clark, *Summary of colonial law*, 68–81. On repugnancy, see D. Swinfen, *Imperial control of colonial legislation, 1813–65: a study of British policy towards colonial legislative powers* (Oxford, 1970), ch. 5.

18 A. Hawkins, '"Parliamentary government" and Victorian political parties, 1830–80', *English Historical Review*, civ (1989), 638–69; J. Parry, *The rise and fall of Liberal government in Victorian Britain* (1993), 7–10.

19 T. E. May, 'The imperial parliament' in *Knight's store of knowledge for all readers* (1841), 101; W. Bagehot, *The English constitution* [1867] (Oxford, 2001), 104. On the imperial parliament over-ruling colonial legislatures, see: R. L. Schuyler, *Parliament and the British empire: some constitutional controversies concerning imperial legislative jurisdiction* (Columbia, NY, 1929), ch. 4 and *The fall of the old colonial system: a study in British free trade, 1770–1870* (1945), chs 4–5.

20 The position by the close of the century is well-described in C. Ilbert, *Legislative methods and forms* (Oxford, 1901), ch. 9.

21 [E. Jenkins], 'Imperial federalism', *Contemporary Review*, xvi (Jan. 1871), 181.

22 F. P. de Labilliere, *Federal Britain; or unity and federation of the empire* (1894), 196. On the movement for imperial federation in late nineteenth-century Britain, see M. Burgess, 'Imperial federation: continuity and change in British imperial ideas, 1869–71', *New Zealand Journal of History*, xvii (1983), 60–80; A. S. Thompson, *Imperial Britain: the empire in British politics, c. 1880–1932* (Harlow, 2000), 26.

23 A. G. Olson, 'Parliament, empire and the parliamentary law' in J. G. A. Pocock (ed.), *Three British revolutions: 1640, 1688, 1776* (Princeton, 1980), 289–322; P. Miller, *Defining the common good: empire, religion and philosophy in eighteenth century Britain* (Cambridge, 1994), ch. 4; D. Armitage, *The ideological origins of the British empire* (Cambridge, 2000), 7–8.

24 P. Langford, 'Property and virtual representation in eighteenth-century England', *Historical Journal*, xxxi (1988), 83–115.

25 D. J. Moss, 'Birmingham and the campaigns against the orders-in-council and East India Company charter, 1812–13', *Canadian Journal of History*, xi (1976), 173–88; I. Gross, 'The abolition of negro slavery and British parliamentary politics, 1832–3', *Historical Journal*, xxiii (1980), 63–85; D. G. H. Hall, *A brief history of the West India Committee* (Kingston, 1971); Higman, 'West India interest'; Philips, *East India Company*, ch. 7.

26 *Quebec Gazette*, 5 Oct. 1831, 2; compare *The Times'* attack on the 'mercenary corps' mentality of colonial MPs: 19 Dec. 1832, 3.

27 P. O'Leary, *Sir James Mackintosh: the Whig Cicero* (Aberdeen, 1989), 174.

28 *Hansard*, 2nd series, xiv, col. 1125, (6 March 1826).

29 See my 'Joseph Hume and the reformation of India, 1819–33', in G. Burgess and M. Festenstein (eds), *English radicalism, 1550–1850* (Cambridge, forthcoming).

30 Mackintosh stated that although he was not an agent of the Canadian people, he was their advocate: 'Speech on the civil government of Canada' (2 May 1828), in J. Mackintosh, *Miscellaneous works*, 3 vols (1846), iii, 480.

31 For a fuller discussion, see my 'Empire and parliamentary reform: the 1832 Reform Act revisited' in A. Burns and J. Innes (eds), *Rethinking the age of reform: Britain and Ireland, c. 1780–1850* (Cambridge, forthcoming).

32 Anon., *How to do without customs* (1853); H. Clinton, *Suggestions towards the organisation of the British empire, by realising the parliamentary representation of all home and colonial interests* (1856). For a general survey of nineteenth-century arguments for colonial representation, see: L. G. Redmond-Howerd, *The case for colonial representation in parliament* (1923), 13–18 and G. Martin, 'Empire federalism and imperial parliamentary union, 1820–70', *Historical Journal*, xvi (1971), 65–92.

33 T. Banister, 'Britain and her colonial dependencies; and their right to be represented in parliament', *Asiatic Colonial Quarterly*, iv (Dec. 1848), 239, 247; W. Bousfield, *The government of empire: consideration of the means of representation of the colonies* (1877).

34 E. B. Eastwick, *The representation of India in the imperial parliament* (1861), 17–18.

35 For a full and extensive survey, see: Martin, 'Empire federalism', *passim*. For Russell's scheme, P. Scherer, *Lord John Russell: a biography* (1999), 189. Around the same time similar proposals were made for deputies to represent French plantations in the West Indies in the National Assembly: *Times*, 31 May 1847, 4.

36 J. S. Mill, *Considerations on representative government* [1861] in *Collected works of John Stuart Mill*, ed. J. M. Robson, (1977), vol. xix, 564–5; H. Merivale, *Lectures on colonisation and colonies* [1841–2] (3rd edn, 1928), 631–2; Lewis, *Government of dependencies*, 289–95.

37 [E Jenkins], 'An imperial confederation' *Contemporary Review*, xvii (April 1871), 78–9; de Balliere, *Federal Britain*, 196; G. F. Bowen, *Federation and the British empire* (1893), 13.

38 G. N. Curzon, 'The reconstruction of the House of Lords', *National Review*, xi (April 1888), 170; (Dunraven), *Hansard*, 3rd series, cccxxv, col. 530 (26 April 1888).

39 L. M. Penson, *Colonial agents of the British West Indies* (1924), ch. 12; A. W. Abbott, *A short history of the crown agents and their office* (1959).

40 For a full list of these agents, see *Return of the names of agents for colonies acting in Great Britain and recognized by the Colonial Office* (PP 1845, XXI). And for their later role in colonial commercial development, see V. Ponko, 'Economic management in a free trade empire: the work of the crown agents for the colonies in the nineteenth and twentieth centuries', *Journal of Economic History*, xxv (1965), 363–77; R. M. Kesner, 'Builders of empire: the role of the crown agents in imperial development, 1880–1914', *Journal of Imperial and Commonwealth History*, v (1977), 310–30.

41 J. Crawfurd, *Notes on the settlement or colonization of British subjects in India: with an appendix of proofs and illustrations* (1833); R. Bapuji, *The Rajah of Sattara. A letter to the Right Hon. J. C. Herries MP, President of the Board of Control. With the treaties, notes and authorities* (1852); [R. D. Mangles], *New Zealand and the New Zealand Company: being a consideration of how far their interests are similar. In answer to a pamphlet entitled how to colonize: the interest of the country, and the duty of government* (1842).

42 Lytton Bulwer to Sir John Jamieson, [undated but *c.* 1837], Bulwer Lytton papers, Norfolk Record Office, Norwich, BUL 1/8/33.

43 Australian Patriotic Association, *Letters to Charles Buller* (Sydney, 1838–49); D. A. Haury, *The origins of Liberal imperialism: the political career of Charles Buller* (1988), 125–31.

44 For the background, see R. E. Leader (ed.), *The life and letters of J. A. Roebuck with chapters of autobiography* (1897); P. Buckner, *The transition to responsible government: British policy in British North America, 1815–50* (1985), 29.

45 Roebuck to Papineau, 22 June 1835, J. A. Roebuck papers, University of Liverpool, D584/18/3/2; Roebuck to Francis Place, 29 Jan. 1838, BL Add. MS. 35, 151, f. 72.

46 *Hansard*, 3rd series, xiv, cols. 1107–19 (30 June 1836).

47 A. C. V. Melbourne, *Early constitutional developments in Australia, 1788–1856* (1934), ch. 7.

48 *Copies of correspondence with Lord John Russell, Sir A. Stockenstrom, and J. Fairbairn on representative government at the Cape of Good Hope* (1851); *The autobiography of the late Sir Andries Stockenstrom, bart.*, ed. G. W. Hutton, 2 vols (Cape Town, 1887), ii, 337.

49 *Minutes and Proceedings of the Bombay Association* (1852–53).

50 *Report of proceedings of a meeting of the General Association for the Australian Colonies held . . . 15 July 1857* (1857).

51 J. Moir, 'The settlement of the clergy reserves, 1840–55', *Canadian Historical Review*, xxxvii (1956), 46–62; A. Wilson, *The clergy reserves of Upper Canada: a Canadian mortmain* (Toronto, 1968), 156–61; B. Stanley, 'Christian responses to the Indian Mutiny of 1857', *Studies in Church History*, xx (1983), 277–89.

52 D. Eastwood, 'Parliament and locality: representation and responsibility in late Hanoverian England', *Parliamentary History*, xvii (1998), 68–81; L. S. Sutherland, 'Edmund Burke and the relations between members of parliament and their constituents', *Studies in Burke and his Time*, x (1968), 105–21.

Index

Note: 'n.' after a page reference indicates the number of a note on that page.